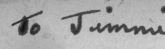

to Jimmie

PELICAN B

A 247

JAZZ

REX HARRIS

REX HARRIS

Jazz

My people laugh and sing,
And dance to death –
None imagining
The heartbreak under breath.

CHARLES BERTRAM JOHNSON

PENGUIN BOOKS

HARMONDSWORTH · MIDDLESEX

First Published 1952

Dedicated to

MY WIFE · MY PARENTS

and the Memory of

RALPH HILL

Made and printed in Great Britain
for Penguin Books Ltd
by Hunt, Barnard and Co, Ltd

Contents

Acknowledgements

I SHOULD like to take this opportunity to express my whole-hearted thanks and indebtedness to Ron Davies for his loyal help in launching this book.

For many months he devoted all his spare time to give criticisms and suggestions, and, in addition, helped me to mould the finished work by assisting me with the writing of many chapters.

I should have been at a loss without his technical skill in the preparation and drawing of the Chart and the maps which appear in the text. His help has been invaluable.

I must record, too, the enthusiasm and energy which his wife Marjorie put into the project, and her untiring assistance in searching through masses of files for data.

*

To the memory of the late Ralph Hill I must extend thanks and acknowledgements. Thanks to him as a friend of long standing who helped my appreciation of 'serious' music, and acknowledgements to him in his capacity as editor of *Penguin Music Magazine* for giving me permission to use much of the material from my article 'The Influence of Jazz on English Composers' which appeared in No. 2 of that publication. It is a great sorrow to me that he did not live to see the completion of the MS, since he often expressed a wish to see a really comprehensive book on the subject of jazz available in England, and many times during our eight years' partnership in lecturing, writing, and broadcasting he urged me to settle down to the project.

Max Jones, as editor of *Jazz Music*, has inadvertently helped me, as he has helped so many other jazz enthusiasts, by producing a magazine of consistently high standard during the eight years of its life. It is impossible to gauge the amount of knowledge and understanding of jazz which he has disseminated, and the three years which we spent in collaboration for the weekly jazz feature 'Collectors' Corner' in the *Melody Maker* gave me an insight into his sincerity of purpose. It would be churlish not to recognize the influence which he has exerted on jazz appreciation generally.

The editor of *Sound and Vision*, K. Chester Sherburne, also kindly allowed me to make use of some of the material from my serialized 'Story of Jazz', which appeared at monthly intervals in that periodical from January 1943 until June 1947.

I received the utmost co-operation from the Recording Companies, but would like to mention especially Mr J. K. R. Whittle of E.M.I. and Mr F. E. Attwood of Decca, both of whom afforded me every opportunity to hear records which were not otherwise available to me.

Finally, these acknowledgements would not be complete without a grateful mention of the hospitable way in which Percy Pring gave me free access to his enormous gramophone record library of old and rare discs. The assistance which these gave me in clearing up obscure points was most helpful.

R. H.

Foreword

This will not be a lengthy preamble, for I have said what I want to say in the body of the book.

I have endeavoured to trace the influences which produced jazz music, and at the same time give a picture of its many ramifications.

The omission of a chapter dealing with the great Blues singers is intentional. Ma Rainey, Bessie Smith and all the others were influenced *by* jazz, but *they* did not influence the course of jazz. Blues singing ran (and runs) a parallel course, and is dealt with in Chapter Three.

Some of the conclusions I have reached after many years of interest in jazz will no doubt cause lifted eyebrows among some of my friends in the dance-band world, but I would hasten to assure them that I have no wish to denigrate their valuable and excellent work *in that sphere*: it is only in the use of the word 'jazz' to label their music that I have any difference of opinion. Many of them hold the same opinion on the subject as I do, and some few have sturdily tried to live up to their principles.

Extravagant claims have been made for jazz, and equally extravagant diatribes have been directed against it. Dean Inge might well have had these extremists in mind when he wrote: 'There are two kinds of fools: those who say, "This is old and therefore good," and others who say, "This is new and therefore better." '

This book is an attempt to vindicate the integrity of those who have kept jazz alive during the long years of its eclipse behind the meretricious blaze of artificially exploited swing.

Whether jazz musicians are able to read music or not is immaterial. Whether they gain financially by playing jazz is beside the point. The vital and essential crux of the whole question is whether they express themselves in their music because they have something which they must express.

In other words it must be an art rather than a craft.

CHAPTER ONE

The Roots of Jazz

So much has been written about jazz having stemmed from the primitive music of the West African Negro via the slave ships to the New World that it would be as well to present a clear picture of the geography and history of West Africa in order that the story of jazz music and its progenitors may be traced as accurately as possible from the dim mists of antiquity through its varying vicissitudes up to the present time.

Geographically, the term 'West Africa' covers an area of about three million square miles, extending as it does to include the coastal lands from Senegal through Gambia, Sierra Leone, Liberia, the Ivory Coast, Ashanti, Dahomey, and Nigeria to the Cameroons – in fact the basins of the Niger, the Senegal, and all the rivers which flow into the Gulf of Guinea. But this is only the southerly regions, for to the east the limit is fixed by Lake Chad at the north-easterly tip of Nigeria, and to the north it continues to the Sahara Desert. An enormous area representing many types of physical structure and vegetation: coastal plains with their dense forests and mangrove swamps, some volcanic mountain ranges and low plateaux, and, in a wide belt to the north, the Savannah grasslands which lead eventually to the barren Sahara Desert.

In the interior, the climate is hot and dry, but in the coastal regions (with which, for reasons which will be specified later, we are more concerned), heat linked with humidity is the general rule, with a rainy season lasting for nine months or even more: malaria and dysentery being prevalent to such an extent among the non-acclimatized white occupiers that it has never been suitable for any kind of permanent occupation.

That such a vast area should have bred many different peoples each with its own language, customs, and religious observances is only natural. Certain it is that there were prehistoric inhabitants of West Africa, for stone implements have been unearthed in Nigeria, Gold Coast, Ivory Coast, and Senegal. Ethnology is dangerous ground to tread, but the probability is that the original Pygmies were gradually forced southwards from Central Africa by the ever-encroaching Negroes, who in their turn had been harried by the Mediterranean races and Eastern Hamitic people. It is generally assumed (and there seems to be no adequate reason for doubting the assumption) that the original stock of these spread outwards from that cradle of historic and prehistoric culture, Egypt, and that the varying clans and their successive waves of migration were responsible for the diversity of tribes scattered throughout the north, east and western areas of Western Africa. Linked as they were, albeit hazardously, with the Mediterranean world, they all, to some extent at any rate, shared and were influenced by its civilization.

As early as the third century A.D. there was a well-developed State in the northern area known as Ghana, and later arose the Empires of Melle and Songhoi west of the Niger. The Hausa people on the east bank of that river founded several states out of which grew the formidable empire of Bornu.

But it must be emphasized that this applies to the north-west and eastern areas only. To the south, however, the inhabitants of the Guinea Coast, protected as they were by dense forests to the north, and by the Atlantic Ocean to the south and west, had not been affected by the contact with the outer world for hundreds – perhaps thousands – of years until discovered by the Portuguese in the fifteenth century, at which time the Ashanti, Dahomey and the Benin had well-organized and often theocratically-run kingdoms whose respective kings ruled jointly with a local Archbishop, and also, surprisingly enough, under the control of a democratic local Westminster.

The reason for our preoccupation with the coastal regions of West Africa can now be explained. When the first Portuguese ship touched in on the Guinea Coast in the first half of the fifteenth century, the inhabitants must have felt that their long and trusted ally, the sea, had betrayed them, for by 1482 the first fort and trading station had been built, the first of many thorns which were to goad and bleed this rich coast. The very names of the commodities which were raided are perpetuated to this day, for any school atlas will reveal the Ivory Coast, the Gold Coast, and, what we are greatly concerned with, the Slave Coast.

This, perhaps, would be a suitable point to justify the stress laid on the slave trade and its attendant miseries in this chapter, and, to a certain extent, throughout the book. Man's inhumanity to man is such a feature of the human race, and, anthropomorphically speaking, of the whole animal kingdom, that critics may be tempted to carp at this singling out of the West African Negro for pity and indignation. 'Why,' they may ask, 'this obsession with the bondage of a relatively small proportion of human beings when there is such a vast field of religious and racial persecutions upon which to draw?'

The answer is simple. The horrors of (say) the Spanish Inquisition were perpetrated by men who were acting, rightly or wrongly, for an ideal, and they honestly believed that their victims' welfare was at stake. The idealists who plotted the French and Russian Revolutions were activated by Utopian conceptions. Even Hitler, in his frenzied anti-Semitic blood purge, had the grace to justify it on the grounds of a racial purity theory, ethnologically ignorant though he was. But the slave trade was the lowest degradation of mankind. Here were people who could be bought cheaply at the cost of fitting a ship and transporting them, and sold dearly in a sellers' market. In other words it was commercialization of human beings – the lowest and basest trade known to Man.

Finally, to conclude this *apologia*, the transportation of slaves to the New World was a link in the chain between the two Continents: a musical chain we shall test link by link in order to trace the many stresses and strains which have affected it; a full grasp of the implications of slavery is not only necessary, but vital, to a clear understanding of jazz.

Enough of this digression: let us return to the Guinea Coast and the establishment of the first fort, that of Sao Jorge da Mina (Elmina) in 1482. Prior to this date slavery had already flourished, but was confined mainly to Mohammedan Africa, and followed an overland route. It is a significant fact that America was discovered within ten years of the founding of that first fort, a circumstance which not only caused slavery to flourish exceedingly, but finally drew the attention of other European nations to a most profitable venture. Spain held back for a time, her hands tied by the papal bull of Alexander VI of 1493, but the Protestant Powers saw good business to be done. That great adventurer – pirate – admiral, call him what you will, Sir John Hawkins, kept up the Elizabethan maritime tradition by raiding the Guinea Coast, robbing the Portuguese ships of their slaves, and then trading them in the Spanish possessions in the New World in 1562–3.

For this episode, and similar ones which followed, he gained the approval of the Queen, having the doubtful honour of a coat of arms being granted which featured a chained Negro as his crest.

That there were some isolated humanitarians at that time is proved by the fact that the Bishop Bartolomé de las Casas visited Haiti, and was so distressed by the sufferings of the Indians there that he suggested to Charles of Spain that each Spanish resident in Haiti should be licensed to import twelve Negro slaves! Doubtless he meant well, probably thinking that Negroes could bear working in the mines more easily than the poor Indians, but the harm was done, nevertheless, for a patent was granted by Charles to one of his favourites for the exclusive right of supplying 4000 Negroes annually to Haiti, Cuba, Jamaica, and Puerto Rico. Thus arose the slave trade to the West Indies.

It fell to the Dutch to introduce the traffic into British America, for in 1618 twenty African slaves – 'twenty negars' – were landed at Jamestown in Virginia by a Dutch man-o-war. A small beginning, which grew slowly at first, but by 1790 had been augmented to the incredible number of 200,000 in Virginia alone! Bryan Edwards has estimated that in the course of just over a century – from 1680 to 1786 to be precise – the total import of African slaves into the British colonies of America and the West Indies reached the staggering figure of 2,130,000.

One might be pardoned for terming this figure 'astronomical', but even so, it represents only approximately *half* the number who were uprooted from their homeland, for it has been estimated by reliable historians that only about 50 per cent of the slaves exported lived to become effective workers. In our present-day language, they were expendable.

The gigantic demands of the various European nations who were involved caused even the native chiefs to become debauched with the sense of easy money, for they engaged upon a policy of setting fire to neighbouring villages and capturing the inhabitants as they tried to escape, selling them to the white man for gin, beads, tools, and all the native equivalents of a fat bank balance.

Having arrived at a point where we have recapitulated the general broad outlines of the geography of West Africa and the history of its inhabitants at the time of their involuntary exodus to the New World, what of the state of their musical progress? It is naturally impossible to give any accurate information since those who were engaged in the slave traffic were not interested enough in their cargoes to keep any permanent record of their habits and state of mental development. Nevertheless, there is evidence to show that they had melody and, to paraphrase a well-known tune, 'they had rhythm', but (and this is a significant point) they had no experience or knowledge of harmony. We can compare present-day West African music when it has remained uninfluenced by foreign impact: when three or more melodies are used, they pursue their own course independently.

Their drum language was not, as is generally believed, a kind of primitive Morse code, but was a mechanical reproduction of their own vocal language, achieved by different pressures on the drum head, whilst the more subtle vibrato of 'shaking' effects were produced by knee vibration against the drum. In this way it was, and still is, a method of talking phonetically on drums, and the term 'Speaking Drums' is an exact description.

Another fact which must be borne in mind with regard to their music is that it was essentially functional. Music to them was not a relaxation and luxury as it is to us to-day: it had a strictly utilitarian purpose. For education there were lullabies and game songs; initiation songs for the young men in adolescence. For mating there were the love songs – but since to our present-day minds the phrase 'love songs' brings an unpleasant association in the form of Tin Pan Alley 'slush', perhaps it would be better to des-scribe them as songs of courtship. For war they had battle songs which were designed with a twofold purpose: to stimulate the warriors and to frighten the enemy. Religion held its power by songs to bring rain, to cast spells, to inspire submissiveness, and, linked as it was with medicine, to heal and to hurt. Work Songs for work, Play Songs for play, and all the ceremonial songs and dances for births, weddings, and deaths which are common to mankind.

'Songs and dances.' That is the key to West African music and its Afro-American descendant Jazz. The song and dance were inseparable even as their language and their music were insepar-able, and it is in this way that, as we shall see later, African melody filtered through the early Work Songs via the Blues, and by an instrumental synthesis with the human voice, which made use of the language vibrati and glissandi, moulded one facet of the classic jazz of New Orleans. African rhythm, quiescent to a large degree during the musical void of American slavery, moulded another.

This, however, is anticipation. Let us follow the course of a

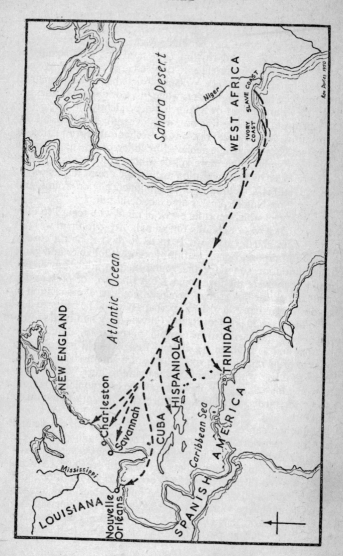

typical slave ship from the West Coast to the New World according to C. L. R. James in *The Black Jacobins*. . . .

Packed in the holds of the galleys, one above the other, the slaves were given no more than four or five feet in length and two or three feet in height so that they could neither lie at full length nor sit upright. They were chained, right hand to left leg, and attached in rows to long iron bars. In this position they spent the months of their foetid voyage, coming up once for less than a minute to empty their pails of vomit and excrement. The close proximity of so many naked human beings, their bruised and festering flesh, the prevailing dysentery and the general accumulation of filth made it impossible for any European to stay in the holds for more than a few minutes without fainting. The Africans fainted and recovered, or fainted and died. During the storms, the hatches were battened down and the heaving vessel hurled the slaves against their chains.

These were the people who brought their music and their dances to the Latin settlements of the New World Islands, where they eventually intermarried with the original Indians. Spanish folk songs, already affected by African music from the time of the Moorish invasion of Spain, played their part, too, in fusing with the West African songs, and long before the early slave ships had reached the North American mainland, new types of Afro-American dances had become established in the West Indies and the mainland of South America, each island developing its own distinctive type. The Rumba, so named after a West African dance step, arose in Cuba from the Habanera, which also gave birth to the Tango, the Son, Bolero, Bembé, and Danzon. Other regions of the New World produced the Calypso, the Beguine, and the Conga. Most of these preceded jazz by roughly a hundred years. They are not relevant to the development of the main stem of jazz, but have been mentioned at this point in order to give some idea of their chronological position in relation to its history. They certainly had a later influence, as may be seen from the chart (Appendix One), which also shows that Creole songs contributed to early Blues, and Ragtime absorbed a certain proportion of Spanish and French popular music.

Before dealing with the early stirrings of jazz in the latter part of the nineteenth century around the delta of the Mississippi, let us consider the conditions under which the slaves worked and lived before the Abolition of 1865, since we shall find that the Slave Code had a direct influence on the formation and location of jazz to a much greater extent than is generally realized.

CHAPTER TWO

The Slave Code

IT is a basic fact that the American Negro is descended from imported slaves and their descendants; it is also a basic fact that jazz is the music of the American Negro. It is seldom realized, however, how closely linked the classic jazz form is with the unwritten law of the American Slave Code. For it was the harshness of the Code which produced the environment and conditions which combined to form the very cradle of jazz. This is not a claim of direct cause and effect – that because there was slavery, therefore jazz followed; but this is a claim of something very near it. The abominable degradation of a section of the human race – the West African Negro slaves – which took place in the Southern States of the U.S.A. until 1865 struck the fundamental spark of incentive which gave birth to the first faint glimmerings of a new Folk Music; the impetus which created an original musical form. Original it had to be, in the narrowest and strictest sense of the word; because jazz developed in the space of a generation out of nothing.

The influence of American slavery upon jazz may be compared with the influence of a concrete slab laid upon an acorn. For a time, growth is completely stifled; to all intents and purposes there is no development whatever. Then a sledge-hammer smashes the slab and the first small tendril appears through a crack in the concrete. The seed is alive; it is able to make use of nourishment drawn from its surrounding element and to grow lustily into a young oak, virile, strong, and independent. So with slavery: the callous slave-owners of the South held their Negro vassals in a vice-like grip as effective as any concrete encasement – until the 1860's when Lincoln swung the sledgehammer at the diehard Southern slave slab, and, after a few mighty blows, gave, in 1865, freedom to the seed of Negro musical inspiration hitherto buried beneath the oppressive stone weight.

A glance at the constitution of this oppressive weight would not be inappropriate at this juncture. For it is an all-important factor which explains many things which may be condensed into four fundamental aspects of jazz:

(a) why it should have arisen in the Southern States of the U.S.A. – *and there alone;*

(b) why it should have been born just when it was – towards the end of the nineteenth century;

(c) why it should build its main structure upon a foundation of inspired improvisation, and

(d) why so many sources of inspiration whose influence could have been expected to be slight should have had an unusually intense effect upon the early hot music.

The workings of the American Slave Code – the so-called 'legal relationship between master and slave' – were based simply on custom and tradition. Nevertheless, the most fiendish of laws were enacted, enforced by legal statutes, giving solemn sanction to nothing less than atrocities. Laws of every Southern State were framed so as to make provisions for this 'legal relationship' which was inherently fallacious in that it defied the very essence of Christianity (the accepted religion of those States), accepting as it did the fact that there were two types of human being – the master type and the slave type. The slave owners who relied on the forced cheap labour in their cotton and rice fields and sugar plantations in the broad fertile area stretching from Louisiana to Virginia (even as far north as Maryland), knew that there was only one way to keep their slaves in continual serfdom and that was by a strict denial of every opportunity of social and mental advancement. The suppression of all education followed logically from this axiom, but what did not follow was the utter cruelty of a presumption which went much further – to acknowledge as inevitable that slaves should never be anything *but* slaves, and that their status should be reduced to that of animals. Indeed it is difficult to justify a claim that American Negro slaves were ever treated as well as animals. Sir John Hawkins himself could hardly have foreseen the extremes of barbarity to which the victims of the movement which he founded were subjected.

The slaves of the Greek and Roman Empires and of the ancient Germans were treated badly enough; but certain rights were accorded them, rights which went as far as granting the slave a 'peculium' – a certain maximum of small personal possessions which were his own. Not even the master could lay claim to them and this right, with other small privileges, was protected by law. Throughout the centuries which followed Roman domination, a period in which slavery was practised in many lands, the custom of giving the slaves some small rights was an accepted fact – and it was probably recognized that if it were not done on moral grounds, then it was justified on economic grounds – a slave would work better if contented; and if a small incentive would encourage greater effort, so much the better.

After the massed enforced migration of Negro slaves to the New World these assumptions still held good; and the slaves of the British, Dutch, French, and Spanish West Indies were permitted a life which was at least tolerable, and even allowed a degree of emancipation and manumission. But not so the Southern States of the U.S.A.

In the Civil Code of Louisiana:

A slave is one who is in the power of a master to whom he belongs. The master may sell him, dispose of his person, his industry and his labour. He can do nothing, possess nothing, nor acquire anything, but what must belong to his master.

And of South Carolina:

Slaves shall be deemed, sold, taken, reputed and adjudged in law to be chattels personal, in the hands of their owners and possessors, and their executors, administrators and assigns, to all intents, constructions, and purposes whatsoever.

Slaves were chattels; they were denied even the sensibilities of a brute animal. And this had become so much an accepted fact that Henry Clay, in an anti-abolitionist speech in the U.S. Senate, in 1839, based his argument on the fact that abolition would annihilate 1200 million dollars worth of slave *property*. Two hundred years of legislation, he said, had sanctified and sanctioned Negro slaves as property.

And property they indeed were. Like domestic animals they were referred to as 'stock' or as being 'sound'; a mature female slave was termed a 'breeder'; there were 'slave-consuming' States and 'slave-producing' States. The issue of female slaves was considered the property of the owner just like the foal of the owner's mare. At slave sales Negro women were advertised for sale 'with children or separately, as desired'. An advertisement in the papers of Charleston, S.C., on 28 September 1838, concerning a 'lot' of '120 likely young Negroes of both sexes' mentions 'several small boys without their mothers'. The slave could be mortgaged; he could be seized to pay off debts; he could even be pawned.

He had no family rights. *The Journal of the Life of John Woolman*, a philanthropist and minister, mentions that 'they óften part men from their wives by selling them far asunder, which is common when estates are sold by executors at vendue'. Marriage was forbidden, for the slave could not make a contract. The concept of marriage vows was incompatible with the rigid theory of slave ownership. Stroud's *Sketch of the Slave Laws* states, 'A slave cannot even contract matrimony, the association which takes place among slaves, and is called marriage, being properly designated by the word "contubernium" – a relation which has no sanctity, a nd to which no civil rights are attached.' They had no relief in the case of adultery. They had no right to petition on any grounds whatever . . . because they were property.

From the *Vicksburg (Miss.) Register*, 27 December 1838:

ARDOUR IN BETTING. Two gentlemen at a tavern having summoned the waiter, the poor fellow had scarcely entered when he fell down in a fit of apoplexy. 'He's dead!' exclaimed one. 'He'll come to!' replied the other. 'Dead for five hundred!' 'Done!' retorted the second. The noise of the fall, and the confusion which followed, brought up the landlord, who called out to fetch a doctor. 'No, no! we must have no interference; there's a bet depending!' 'But, Sir, I shall lose a valuable servant!' 'Never mind, you can put him down in the bill!'

The Act of 1740 of South Carolina:

In case any person shall wilfully cut out the tongue, put out the eye, castrate, or cruelly scald, burn, or deprive any slave of any limb or member, or shall inflict any other cruel punishment, *other than* by whipping or beating with a horsewhip, cowskin, switch, or small stick, or by putting irons on, or confining or imprisoning such slave, every such person shall, for every such offence, forfeit the sum of one hundred pounds, current money.

A light punishment in the days when a man could be hanged for stealing a sheep and the unconscious irony of the words 'other than' is expressive, to say the least.

There are instances of forced concubinage, the forced use of Negro slaves as human guinea pigs; 25 per cent deaths through exposure and acclimatization; day and night during the sugar boiling season.

A glorious licence was given by loop-holes in the phrases like 'moderate correction' as in the following excerpt from the Constitution of Georgia (Art. 4, Sect. 12):

Any person who shall maliciously dismember or deprive a slave of life, shall suffer such punishment as would be inflicted in case the like offence had been committed upon a free white person and *on like proof*, except in case of insurrection of said slave, and *unless such death should happen by accident in giving such slave moderate correction.*

Resistance or even preparation for self-defence made slaughter lawful; many cases can be quoted of murders justified purely because the victim resisted attack. Weld's *Slavery As It Is* quoted instances of floggings resulting in death; of a woman shot 'in consequence of some difficulty in his dealings with her as a concubine'; of a physician who whipped his slave to death, was tried and acquitted, and the next year *elected to the Legislature.* [1]

That learning and any sort of education should be ruthlessly suppressed was obligatory in such a system. No further comment need be made on this aspect of the oppression than the following quotation from Mr Berry, in the House of Delegates of Virginia, in 1832:

We have, as far as possible, closed every avenue by which light might enter their (the slaves') minds. If we could extinguish the capacity to see the light, our work would be completed; they would then be on the level with the beast of the field, and we should be safe! I am not certain that we would not do it, if we could find out the process, and that in the plea of Necessity.

The foregoing may have seemed an unnecessarily long catalogue in a book not concerned primarily with slavery; but it is most essential to bring into correct perspective the degree of ruthless suppression which existed over the Negro slaves before Abolition. For it is against this background of the denial of every form of culture, and the refusal of the most elementary education, that the Southern States of the U.S.A. became the breeding ground for the music we have come to call jazz.

Let us explore the reasons why this Slave Code should have determined the location of the origin of jazz. To realize the absolute negation of Negro culture, the utter annihilation of anything resembling an art form in the area between the Mason-Dixon Line and the Gulf of Mexico, is to realize how and why a *new* Folk Music, jazz, was born in the Southern States of America and nowhere else. For jazz was essentially the result of a search for a completely new musical territory and a completely new original form, a desire which was, at the same time a necessity. The desire was not a necessity, for example, in the islands of the Caribbean, where a more humane attitude to slavery prevailed; the slave there was granted his peculium; his little privileges provided for a

1. My italics.

basis of musical expression; he was not forced to delve so deeply into the innermost depths of his own intellect, nor to call so fully upon his reserves of inspiration; but was able, in varying degree, to rely upon precedents of structure and technique. Musical development in Cuba, Trinidad and Haiti proceeded along comparatively orthodox (to use the word in its broad sense) lines; a procedure which was impossible in the U.S.A., where, as far as the Negro was concerned, orthodoxy was non-existent, because all culture, including music itself, was non-existent.

Secondly, to summarize the deduction that the abolition of the Slave Code determined the date of the birth of jazz: The final emancipation of slaves took place in 1865, when the victorious North put an end to the basic causes of countless years of Negro misery and suffering under the lash of the white whip. *It cannot be coincidental that jazz was in its embryo stage just one generation after this date.* Consider the natural progression of the Negro onwards from the closing years of the social system in which they had become almost a separate species of the human race. Considered by their masters (who had complete power over them, including that of life and death) to be lower than animals, to their eternal credit, they contrived to remain in some miraculous way, a grade above the animal, but they were, nevertheless, psychologically so completely cowed and helpless as to lose all sense of human dignity.

Restoration of this dignity had to be the first goal. Equality in an immeasurable length of time . . . perhaps; but certainly not within a life's span. A reflexion on the conditions at the time when this book is being written, almost a century later, when a lynching in Georgia hardly hits the front page of the national press (and when the lyncher usually gets an acquittal) emphasizes the sober truth of this bald statement. Before equality had to come the difficult and slow process of rehabilitation. Overcoming subconscious fear and suspicion, forgetting accustomed subservience, acquiring a standard of morals and ethics, a realization of the right of possession and a sense of values, a basis of learning— even the very elements of the three R's, all these factors and the thousand other essentials necessary to civilized man could not come in the matter of a few short years.

The poor slave, of course, in his ignorance, was hardly better off after 1865. Reaction set in to such an extent that the Negroes refused to work for their former masters and with no organized labour the whole South was in danger of becoming impoverished. Gradually, however, the wheels of some sort of system began to turn creakingly. And it was against this background that jazz found its first inspirations, though it was several decades before the new musical form assumed a recognizable and determined shape. For perhaps twenty years the Negro's music was mostly vocal, for the simple reason he could not afford to buy an instrument. No doubt imagination and nimble fingers provided him with home-made banjos and percussive instruments; but little else, and even these were used purely for accompaniment purposes. The main vehicle for musical expression was still the voice.

Twenty years after the Abolition the Negro's musical aspirations had developed to a stage when he could beg, borrow, perhaps steal, even possibly *buy* a secondhand manufactured instrument, and with this cheap equipment at his disposal untold possibilities offered themselves and jazz suddenly flowered into being. Musical performance was now, for the first time among American Negroes, in the hands of men who had some sort of flimsy education; who had travelled a little of their own free will; who had had opportunities for absorbing fragments of other cultures and arts; who had been able to sing songs for pleasure, play simple instruments for pleasure, men in fact who had never known slavery.

The three hundred years of cultural hiatus which followed Sir John Hawkins' first voyage resulted in a musical void in the mind of the American Negro of 1865. Through this circumstance he was compelled to begin his musical education completely from scratch. The result of his self-teaching became evident in a definitive form at the earliest time when maturity was possible, approximately a generation after his mental emancipation, and produced at the turn of the century the music we now know as jazz.

The third point about the importance of the Abolition upon jazz is that it determined the degree of improvisation which was to become the foundation of jazz. Had the Negro, before 1865, always been given (short of freedom) reasonable opportunities for education, however elementary, and opportunities for musical expression, religious or otherwise, it is highly probable that development would have proceeded along more conventional lines; he would have fallen more in line with orthodoxy; his contribution to the field of music, whilst retaining, no doubt, elements of his own instinctive and time-honoured cultures, would have been no further divorced from Bach and Beethoven, for example, than is the music of Bartók or Stravinsky in the field of European classical music to-day.

An analogy might be helpful at this stage in assessing the situation:

Given the tools and the advantage of mechanization a boat-builder in England will manufacture a machine of which the demands for efficiency produces a stereotyped design. Improvisation is completely lacking because it is completely unnecessary. Similarly, a South Sea Islander, with primitive tools, is compelled to use a certain degree of imagination both in design and decoration; but improvisation is once again lacking – the outrigger canoe of 1950 bears a striking similarity to the canoe of 1000 years ago, being custom-built through centuries of tradition. Picture, however, the problem of a Berber, inhabitant of a waterless desert, suddenly faced with the urge to cross a newly discovered river or lake: with no tools, and no equipment, his powers of improvisation are going to be stretched to the fullest extent. In fact, improvisation will be the operative theme of his enterprise; it will be his God. The shape of his water-crossing vehicle will be determined entirely according to his natural resources available. But it would not necessarily bear any resemblance to foreign preconceived notions of a boat, though in the course of evolution certain similarities would no doubt become evident.

So, too, with the evolution of jazz and the emphasis upon improvisation. Like the Berber in his boat-building enterprise, the American Negro slave, faced in 1865 with an instinctive urge to create music and forced, in the absence of any previous knowledge, to start from rock-bottom, he was compelled to draw primarily upon the inspiration of his own mind. There being, as yet, neither the opportunity nor the equipment for providing a written musical language, it was completely natural that the Negro musician should base his art upon improvisation.

Finally, the fact that development of the musical form was beginning completely from nothing in 1865 meant that every available source of influence would have a much more marked effect. To continue the simile of the boats, the Berber's raft was constructed only of the material immediately to hand; in like fashion, the progenitors of jazz were forced to draw upon the only resources which were immediately available to them. First of all were their own simple Work Songs, which had in the past helped them to pass the long hours of labour; there was the religious music of the churches now freely open to all Negroes; the rhythms and structure of the Spanish and French music of the Gulf of Mexico; the march music of the brass bands; and underlying it all their instinctive aptitude and hereditary knowledge of rhythm.

Like the starving man who eats ravenously and indiscriminately the first food offered him, the Negro clutched at every accessible source. At his stage of educational progress he had no academic resources to draw upon, no knowledge of European classical form. Little wonder then that the local material played such a preponderant part in influencing the erection of a new musical structure, now known as jazz.

CHAPTER THREE

Formation of Classic Jazz

WE have seen in Chapter Two the status of the American Negro in the Southern States during the period from his importation to his emancipation, but what of his development; the slow but sure ripening of the seed of his own culture he had brought with him?

Work Songs played an integral part in fashioning a folk music which was later to become jazz. These, which were already part of the West African's musical experience at home, were transported to a new environment, where they were found to be of no little importance to the slaves' output of work.

One is tempted here to draw a parallel with the modern use of 'Music While You Work' in factories. Such an analogy on the face of it appears delightfully straightforward, but it must be borne in mind that the Work Songs were examples of self-expressionism and came from within: they were creative in the sense that although they were in many cases traditional, the worker himself used them as an incentive and lubricant for his task. In the case of 'Music While You Work' an external influence is directed towards the workers to relieve the monotony and to act as a productive agent. There is no creative instinct on the part of the worker-listener. It would be instructive for statisticians to experiment and compare the output by factory hands who sing for themselves, and contrast it with that of those who are radio spoon-fed. But we digress. . . .

The function of Work Songs both in West Africa and in the new surroundings was to ease the monotony of a regular task and to synchronize a word or exclamation with a regularly repeated action, whether swinging a hammer, 'toting a barge or lifting a bale' – although Jerome Kern's semi-humorous, semi-quizzical Negro in *Ol' Man River* is the character as the white man likes to picture him rather than the character as he actually was.

These songs were chanted or moaned as a man or group of men worked, and the stress was laid on a syllable at the moment of greatest strain, much in the same way that Sea Chanties developed along functional lines. Indeed, the Mississippi *was Ol' Man River* in the sense that it dominated the lives of many thousands of workers, [1] and produced its own river chanties which have been absorbed into the body of jazz. There is, for instance, *Heavin' the Lead Line* which must have been related, at any rate, to the one which gave Samuel Clemens the idea for his pen-name – Mark Twain.

> Tell me there's a buoy, a buoy right on the bar
> The light is twisted and you can see just how.
> Pull a little over to the larboard side.
> Lawd, Lawd.
> Quarter less twain,
> Quarter less twain,
> Lawd, Lawd, now send me quarter less twain.
> Throw the lead line a little higher out.

This, of course, is a relatively modern example; the recurrent beat which marked the Work Songs of earlier generations was typified by a graphic 'huh' as the hammer blow was made, the pick brought down on to the road, or the axe blade sunk into the tree.

Recorded examples of early Work Songs are, of course, non-existent, but many have been handed down from father to son during successive generations, and it is to the credit of one or two Recording Companies that they have made efforts to rescue some for posterity before they die the natural death of all folk music. Excellent reconstructions were made a few years ago in America by that fine folk singer and guitarist Josh White, and issued in 'The Chain Gang' album. [2] This contains such expressive titles as *Nine Foot Shovel*, *Chain Gang Boun'*, *Lord*, *Dis Timber Got to Roll*, and *Told my Cap'n*. The last song contains the revealing couplet:

> Raised my hand, wiped de sweat off my head:
> Cap'n got mad, shot my buddy dead.

Other Work Songs were recorded in England during his visit in 1950, and will be found listed below. [3]

The late Huddy Ledbetter or, to give him his more picturesque title, 'Lead Belly', has also recorded some of the traditional Work

1. Cf. the importance of the Nile to Egypt.
2. Chain Gang Album. American Columbia C–22.
3. *Like a Natural Man.* London. 810 (Others also).

Songs of his youth, but here again they are not generally available in England at the time of writing. Two, however, may be cited in which he is accompanied by the Golden Gate Quartet. The first[1] shows the chant and response theme beautifully evident. Lead Belly chants a phrase, and the quartet chimes in with a recurrent 'Huh'; gradually working up to a climax.[2]

The second[3] is an epic ballad which at times also did service as a Work Song. In it, the Golden Gate singers can be heard responding with the repetitive phrase: 'Lawd, Lawd, Lawd', following each of Lead Belly's lines, which are given below:

> It was one Sunday mornin'
>   Lawd, Lawd, Lawd! (Repeat after each line)
> The Preacher went a-huntin'
> He carried 'long his shot gun.
> Well, 'long come a grey goose.
> The gun went off boo-boo
> And down come a grey goose.
> He was six weeks a-fallin'
> And my wife an' yo' wife
> They gave him a feather pickin'
> They was six weeks a-pickin'
> An' they put him on to parboil.
> He was six weeks a-boilin'
> An' they put him on the table,
> An' the knife wouldn't cut him
> An' the fork wouldn't stick him
> An' they throwed him in the hog-pen
> An' the hog couldn't eat him
> Aw – he broke the hog's teeth out.
> They taken him to the saw-mill
> An' the saw wouldn't cut him
> Ah, he broke the saw's teeth out.
> An' the las' time I seed him
> He was flyin' cross de ocean
> With a long string o' goslin's,
> An' they all goin' 'Quack, Quack'.

It is impossible to convey the charm and intricacy of the responses in this folk song by the mere use of the printed word. In the first place, the words look trite and, to a certain degree, nonsensical. As Percy A. Scholes says:[4]

1. *Ham'n Eggs.* Amer. Victor. 27266.
2. This is also evident in *Like a Natural Man*, by Josh White.
3. *Grey Goose.* Amer. Victor 27267.
4. *The Oxford Companion to Music*. Folk Song. 4.

. . . although many lovely and sensitive folk poems exist, yet as a body the tunes are finer than their words, education being more of a factor in the production of a poem than of a tune. Frequently the words of a folk song have become so corrupted by successive singers as to contain lines that make strange sense or no longer make any sense at all. Obsolete expressions are preserved in some songs, as, for instance, old numerals in some children's singing games. The poems of some folk songs have a religious significance that is now lost, except to the archaeologist and anthropologist, and the motions of many folk dances point to pagan rites. The words of folk songs undergo much mutation, and the same tune can be found in different parts of the country set to different words. *A proportion of songs in every country has to do with particular occupations, to which they form an accompaniment.* [1]

Again, he says:

There are many instances where generations unable to read or write have lost the sense of particular words, retaining merely an approximation to the sounds, so that the meaning of certain lines can now no longer be even guessed. Many stanzas consist merely of several repetitions of a single line plus a line of refrain which occurs in every stanza and thus binds the song together. There is a frequent lack of continuity of thought from stanza to stanza. A great deal of song is half or wholly extemporized. Often one singer, serving as a kind of precentor, will give out a line or two in every stanza, the rest being added by the participating audience as a recurring refrain. (This is a typically African practice.)

Secondly, the bald statement that the phrase 'Lawd, Lawd, Lawd' is repeated after each line needs amplification. There are inherent rhythms and cross rhythms in the way those three words are repeated, sometimes sharply dividing the singer's lines, and sometimes encroaching on their margins. Perhaps W. E. Allen expresses the idea more clearly in *Slave Songs of the United States.* [2]

There is no singing in *parts*, as we understand it, and yet no two appear to be singing the same thing; the leader singer starts the word of each verse, often improvising, and the others, who 'base' him, as it is called, strike in with the refrain, or even join in the solo when the words are familiar. When the 'base' begins the leader often stops, leaving the rest of the words to be guessed at, or it may be that they are taken up by one of the other singers. And the 'basers' themselves seem to follow their own whims, beginning when they please and leaving off when they please, striking an octave above or below (in case they have pitched the tune too high), or hitting some other note that chords, so as to produce the effect of a marvellous complication and variety and

1. My italics.   2. Published in 1867.

yet with the most perfect time and rarely with any discord. And what makes it all the harder to unravel a thread of melody out of this strange network is that, like birds, they seem not infrequently to strike sounds that cannot be precisely represented by the gamut and abound in slides from one note to another and turns and cadences not in articulated notes.

The gradation between Work Songs and Blues is indefinite. For a music which developed in the circumstances it did, there are no absolutely watertight compartments: no neat pigeon-holes so dear to the tidy mind – but that criticism may be levelled, of course, at all art forms. Changes took place so gradually; various influences made themselves felt, at first slightly and then with an ever-increasing pressure, that the historian can never present positive and clear-cut divisions.

It is certain, however, that tribal Work Songs which started life in West Africa and were carried into the new atmosphere of the Southern States of America were one of the stepping stones to the Blues – one of the mainstays of jazz.

It is difficult to deal with the early Blues without referring to its cousin the Spiritual, but, whereas the former accepted foreign vocal influences from Creole songs, the latter drew largely from the English hymnal; both deriving to a certain extent from the English ballad. [1]

Undoubtedly the Blues arose following the time of the emancipation; it was a flowering of the Work Song plant which had remained dormant for so many years in the cold atmosphere of slavery, and what is more natural than that it should express the natural feelings and day-by-day experiences of a race which had no education and external images upon which to draw? We have seen earlier that West African music was always functional, and just as the Work Songs expressed the act of work, so, naturally enough, the Blues expressed the act of living, sleeping, eating, making love and dying, flavoured with all the usual human nuances of jealousy, hatred, fear, lust, envy and loneliness, to name but a few of our emotions. It will be noticed that the happier ones, such as joy, happiness and tenderness are not mentioned, but these were luxuries long denied a people in exile and slavery. Scholes [2] comments:

There is a general flavour of sadness about the words and music of

1. See Chart, pp. 220-1.
2. *The Oxford Companion to Music*, art. United States. 6.

Negro song. A European coming fresh to the subject would expect to find amongst a race that had suffered a quarter of a thousand years of slavery a good many rude poems of revenge allied to vigorous music. But in Negro song, slavery is barely mentioned and vindictiveness is entirely absent, and instead of it is a spirit of gentle, patient melancholy. . . . Slavery has been at an end since 1865, yet the tinge of sadness, relieved by the belief in a future glory, continues – *either because of the disabilities that still remain*[1] or because these moods are racial and ineradicable.

Vindictiveness is absent, true, but the myth that the Blues is entirely composed of gentle patient melancholy must be denied. That Negro poetry should be subjective is a natural outcome of his environment – years of physical and mental fear is not productive of sonnets to a mistress's eyebrows. Lashings and brandings and the stark horror of lynch-law guided the Negro poet into more sombre fields of thought. 'Scent of magnolia, sweet and fresh' was dashed from his nostrils by the macabre 'smell of burnin' flesh'.[2]

The disabilities that still remain are brought home forcibly by Claude McKay's poem *The Lynching*.

> His Spirit in smoke ascended to high heaven.
>   His father, by the cruelest way of pain,
> Had bidden him to his bosom once again;
>   The awful sin remained still unforgiven.
> All night a bright and solitary star
>   (Perchance the one that ever guided him,
> Yet gave him up at last to Fate's wild whim)
>   Hung pitifully o'er the swinging char.
> Day dawned, and soon the mixed crowds came to view
>   The ghastly body swaying in the sun.
> The women thronged to look, but never a one
>   Showed sorrow in her eyes of steely blue;
> And little lads, lynchers that were to be,
>   Danced round the dreadful thing in fiendish glee.

That satire entered into the Blues, as it has done in much Negro poetry, is undeniable, and Langston Hughes has captured the spirit of gentle irony and wedded it to something like an exultation in the following poem.[3]

1. My italics.
2. Quotation from *Strange Fruit*. Josh White. Bruns. 03749.
3. Florida Road Workers.

I'm makin' a road
For the cars
To fly on.
Makin' a road
Through the palmetto thicket
For light and civilization
To travel on.

Makin' a road
For rich old men
To sweep over in their big cars
An' leave me standin' here.

Sure,
A road helps all of us!
White folks ride –
An' I gets to see 'em ride.
I ain't never seen nobody
Ride so fine before.

Hey, buddy!
Look at me!
I'm makin' a road . . .

This excursion into the realms of Negro poetry has not been a
wasted journey: it will help to appreciate the background of the
music which by easy stages became part and parcel of the Blues
which was a form handed down from mouth to mouth: there
being no evidence of the Blues being set down on paper until
about ten years before the turn of the century.

E. Simms Campbell in *Jazzmen*[1] cites an excellent example of
the way in which the Work Song was used as a secret code to pass
information in the plantations and thus laid the early foundation
of the form of the Blues.

He says:

They worked and sang together and many of these songs carried a
meaning only to Negroes. To the white mind, it was perfect peace and
contentment among the blacks, but to Negroes it was often a means of
communication. 'Ya bettah breeze on down dat road – son – bettah
breeze on down dat road. Mistuh Charlie from town ain't feelin' good –
ya better lighten dat heavy load' – from one to another the song was
taken up and passed along the field. It simply meant that there was a
white man from a different town who had arrived on the plantation and

1. *Jazzmen*, by Frederick Ramsay, Jr, and C. E. Smith. Harcourt, Brace
& Co, New York.

J—2

the young Negro who was working among them, guarded zealously from whites 'at de big house' had better leave town. Negroes frequently hid one of their own who had sought refuge among them, and they were telling him in code that he had better leave the plantation that night. Such lyrics interspersed among well-known songs carried a world of significance to black ears.

You will note the repetition of the phrase: 'Ya bettah breeze on down dat road.' It is important, because it set the style of Blues lyrics which has crystallized into a form as rigid as the sonnet, but with the sonnet's freedom of variation within its own bounds. This repeating of the first line may have been occasioned by the urgency of a message; the first statement drew the attention of the listener, the second gave him time to register it – much as radio communication between planes is repeated: 'Red Leader calling Squadron, Red Leader calling Squadron, etc.'

Another factor which must not be overlooked is the improvisational aspect. The third line of the Blues lyric, even if it does not rhyme, is usually assonant, and the repetition of the first line gave the singer time to feel for a phrase which would be expressive and, at the same time, 'round off' the song in a satisfactory manner. A parallel may be drawn with the Calypso singers of the West Indies, who specialize in extemporaneous singing. 'Gorilla', a well-known Calypso singer, once produced this:

> Calypso is a thing I'm telling you
> When you are singing you must learn to be impromptu.
> Never mind your English but mind your rhymes
> When you get the gist of it just sing in time
> For veteran Calypsonians are known to be
> Men who can sing on anything instantaneously.

If the scansion seems unorthodox, listen to any Calypso record, and the accents will be found to fall into place in a remarkable manner (Brunswick 02623–8 and 04414; Melodisc 1131, 1133, 1134).

Two factors, then, at least, contributed to the Blues lyric form, which evolved into the simple rhyming formula of *a repeated: a*

> I've never seen such real hard times before
> I've never seen such real hard times before
> The wolf keeps walkin' all 'round my door.

is an example of the rhyming twelve bar Blues, and the following shows the use of assonance in print, at any rate, for it must be remembered that many of these traditional lyrics were handed down by word of mouth only, and the attractive slur and elision of final dental-labials is a characteristic of the early Negro speech. 'Mind' becomes 'Min' ', and 'ground' – 'groun' '.

> I'm gonna lay my head on some lonesome railroad line
> I'm gonna lay my head on some lonesome railroad line
> An' let that two-nineteen train pacify my min'.

A more precise use of assonance being this:

> Don't the moon look lonesome shinin' through the trees
> Oh, don't the moon look lonesome shinin' through the trees?
> Don't yo' house look lonesome when your baby packs up to leave?

Although the second line was usually a repeat of the first, considerable latitude was allowed for variations within it, which left the singer scope to embroider it as he or she chose. Thus the last lyric could be varied in dozens of ways as far as the second line is concerned, but as an example:

> Don't the moon look lonesome shinin' through the trees?
> Yes, the moon sure looks lonesome shinin' through the trees, etc.

The words are often crude and banal to our ears, and, when read in the cold light of day, sometimes do not even appear metrical, but the fault there lies in the medium involved and in the eye of the reader. It would be as sane to criticize the banality of the nightingale's song because it might be transcribed to paper as: 'Tweet tweet pripr pripr olly olly olly shreeeeep.' Apparent absence of metre exists only in the mind of the beholder. The executants themselves have an instinctive sense of rhythm which enables them to stress certain syllables and almost eliminate others so that everything falls into place neatly and surely, providing at the same time that element of suspense and achievement which is one of the greatest appeals of jazz.

It would be as well here to draw attention to the importance in African languages of the *manner* in which sounds are spoken: one word can have as many as twenty different meanings, depending on the tone and accent.

Before approaching the musical form of the Blues, let us deal with the reproaches which have been levelled at the various subject matters with which it seems to be involved. These, as was explained earlier in this chapter, centred around the two basic principles of life: self-preservation (eating, drinking, sleeping, keeping warm) and reproduction (finding a mate, making love).

Firstly, self-preservation. When these lines were sung,[1] they

1. *Hard Time Blues*. Ida Cox. Parlo. R.2948.

were a straightforward statement of an economical position
common to poor people the world over:

> I can't go outside to my grocery store [1]
> I ain't got no money and my credit don't go no more.

and

> Ef yo' house catch on fire 'n' they ain't no water roun'
> Throw yo' trunk out the window 'n' let yo' house burn down.

was but a singer's laconic acknowledgement that his personal
possessions, poor as they might be, were of more value to him
than the cheap patchwork cabin which did duty for him as his
home.

Food does not seem to enter into the field of the Blues very
much, probably because hunger does not make for song of any
kind, and in times of plenty the human memory is very short.
Drink, too, except when quoted as an anodyne for unrequited
love, seems to be neglected. It is love, love, love which comes
cascading down through the traditional lyrics of the Blues, which,
by its denigrators, is always depicted as lust, lust, lust.

The shocked attitude towards the frankness of the Blues is
illogical coming as it does from a civilization which has produced,
albeit anonymously:

> My Love in her attire doth show her wit,
>   It doth so well become her:
> For every season she hath dressings fit,
>   For winter, spring and summer.
> No beauty she doth miss,
>   When all her robes are on:
> But Beauty's self is she,
>   When all her robes are gone.

and Lord Chesterfield's *Complete Belle*:

> In Flavia's eyes is every grace,
>   She's handsome as she could be;
> With Jacob's beauty in her face,
>   And Esau's where it should be.

Surely the uneducated Blues-singer was putting as much poetry
into the only vocabulary he knew when he sang with straightforward frankness:

> You can take me, baby, put me in your big brass bed
> Eagle Rock me, baby, till my face turns cherry red. [2]

1. Except when otherwise stated, all examples of Blues lyrics given will
tacitly repeat the first line.
2. *Cherry Red*. Pete Johnson. Parlo. R.2717.

It is after all not so far removed from the Elizabethan

> Christ that my love were in my arms, and I in my bed again.

There is a frank and pleasing atmosphere about many of the early Blues lyrics which is as direct and natural as some of the early English folk songs whose original meanings would scandalize many of the fond mothers who repeat them in the form of nursery rhymes to their toddlers. They have lost sight of their roots, just as they have lost sight of the phallic significance of the May Pole.

Too much stress, however, must not be laid on the sexual flavour of the Blues, except to indicate that a race which had had tenderness and constancy brutally knocked out of it by the enforced separation from loved ones during slavery, had to express itself with a cynical twist which covered to a large extent the hurt and longings which were there:

> Some of these women sure do make me tired:
> Got a handful o' 'Gimme' an' a mouthful o' 'Much obliged'.

and

> Papa, papa, you're in a good man's way,
> I can find one better than you any time of day.

and

> But if you get a good man and don't want him taken away from you
> Don't ever tell your friend woman what your man can do.

and

Can't sleep, can't eat, so weak I can't walk the floor
Feel like hollerin' 'Murder!' an' let the police squad get me once more.

The last lyric quoted is a clear indication of the justice handed out to and generally expected by the descendants of slaves. It is a matter-of-fact acceptance of the give-a-dog-a-bad-name policy. It is expressed even more forcibly in the following:

I sure do hate that wagon, I mean that old police patrol
The best that I can wish it, I hope it falls off in some hole
And if that wagon gets you *make up your mind to go to jail*
You feel just like a hound (hang?) – dog, with a tin can tied to his tail. [1]

This cynical attitude towards the dispensers of white man's law had its parallels elsewhere, and A. L. Lloyd [2] has drawn a nice

1. *Patrol Wagon Blues.* Henry Allen. HMV. 6377 (now deleted).
2. *Social Aspects of Andalusian Folk Music.* William Morris Soc. Bulletin. July 1941.

similarity between the Blues and the *cante jondo* of Andalusia:

> When they saw my mother weep
> The police released me –
> Released me a punch
> Right between the nostrils.

and

> I go to the jail
> But I cannot see him
> Because I have nothing, mother,
> To give to the jailer.

Although most traditional Blues are in the twelve-bar form, there are some variations, but even then, generally speaking, they can be analysed into the classic form.

There are many hazy ideas about what constitutes a Blues number; many people imagining that it is any Tin Pan Alley tune played slowly with an attendant lyric full of lachrymose bleatings. The public can hardly be blamed for its lack of discrimination, for it has had so many *ersatz* versions foisted upon it during the past thirty years that it is in the position of a man who, having been condemned to a diet of tinned salmon for many years, views the real thing with suspicion and a certain conservative alarm. As the composer and conductor, the late Constant Lambert, has said:[1]

. . . although the Jews have stolen the Negroes' thunder, although Al Jolson's nauseating blubbering masquerades as savage lamenting, although Tin Pan Alley has become a commercialized Wailing Wall, the only jazz music of technical importance is that small section of it that is genuinely Negroid. The 'hot' Negro records still have a genuine and not merely galvanic energy, while the Blues have a certain austerity that places them far above the sweet nothings of George Gershwin.

The twelve-bar Blues is twelve bars in common time, and, although the chords can be varied to a certain degree, and can be played in the major or minor according to the requirements of the melody or improvisation, the harmonic progression is three and a half on the common chord of the keynote, which we will take as 'C', half a bar ditto with seventh added; the next two bars 'F' chord; two bars common chord again, two bars dominant seventh of the keynote, and the two concluding bars on the common chord again. Simply put, in the key of 'C' it reads: $3\frac{1}{2}$ C: $\frac{1}{2}$ C7: 2 F: 2 C: 2 G7: 2 C.[2]

1. *Music Hol* Constant Lambert. Pelican A195, Penguin Books. 1948.
2. This book does not purport to be a musical text-book.

Around this simple structure have been built hundreds of thousands of improvisations by different jazz musicians, in a manner which will be discussed later. At present we are more concerned with the vocal elements which went into the synthesis of jazz. To summarize: generally speaking Work Songs were functional without emotion, and the Blues were emotional without a specific function.

The impact of Christianity on the Afro-Americans was, of course, the origin of the Spiritual, and owing to the fact that practically all of the missionary work was done by nonconformist ministers, their evangelical and emotional hymns set the style and flavour of the spiritual as we know it to-day. The great 'Camp Meeting' revival, started by the Presbyterians about the beginning of the nineteenth century, was soon followed by others, and the Methodists, whose appeal to the emotions was even greater than that of their predecessors, made a vivid appeal to the unlettered and sympathy-starved slaves. These meetings were held in rural districts in an improvised chapel formed by an enclosure of tents and covered wagons; the preacher calling upon his huge audience for repentance and leading them in what we would now term 'community' hymn-singing.

That these had a great influence on the spiritual may be seen in *Deep River:*

> Deep river,
> My home is over Jordan,
> Deep river, Lord,
> I want to cross over into campground.
>
> O don't you want to go
> To dat gospel feast,
> That promised land
> Where all is peace?
> O deep river, Lord,
> I want to cross over into campground.

A reference to the Methodist origins may also be noted in *Hard Trials:*

> O, Methodis', Methodis' is my name
> Methodis' till I die,
> I been received in de Methodis' church,
> But I'll die on de 'Piscopal side.

Then even the highly emotional Methodist hymns became too tame for the excited gatherings. As Benson[1] puts it:

1. *The English Hymn.*

But with the tumultuous enthusiasm that soon developed, the old hymns were felt to be too sober to express the overwrought feelings of the preacher and the throng. Spontaneous song became a marked characteristic of the camp meetings. Rough and irregular couplets or stanzas were concocted out of scripture phrases and everyday speech, with liberal interspersing of 'Hallelujahs' and refrains. Such ejaculatory hymns were frequently started by an auditor during the preaching and taken up by the throng, until the meeting dissolved into a singing-ecstacy, culminating in a general hand-shaking. Sometimes they were given forth by a preacher, who had a sense of rhythm, under the excitement of his preaching and the agitation of his audience. Hymns were also composed more deliberately out of meeting, and taught to the people or lined out from the pulpit.

Note the phrase: 'rough and irregular couplets or stanzas were concocted'. This improvisational aspect is also evident in the Work Song and the Blues: a trait of the Negro which is so evident in Jazz.

It must not be imagined that these camp meetings were attended solely by slaves. Far from it, for, as was pointed out in Chapter Two, the opportunity for religious worship was small, and attended by severe punishment. There were some who went, however, and they 'carried the gospel' to their people, both in word and spirit, swaying them with their graphically dramatic presentations of 'de lawd and de debil, Heben and Hell'.

There is little doubt that the purely Negro services thus held were a combination of African tribal rites and third-hand garbled versions of organized Christianity, the leader bridging the gap between witch-doctor and preacher. Zora Hurston refers to 'Shouting' thus:[1]

There can be little doubt that shouting is a survival of the African 'possession' by the gods. In Africa it is sacred to the priesthood or acolytes, in America it has become generalized. The implication is the same, however. It is a sign of special favour from the spirit that it chooses to drive out the individual consciousness temporarily and use the body for its expression.

The regular underlying beat in jazz may be traced to the fervent hand-clapping and foot-stomping which was such a feature of these services rather than to West African drum rhythms which were (and are) far more complicated than those employed in jazz. The clapping and stomping were used as punctuation marks in the rhythmic flow of the preacher's voice, which fell into an

1. *Negro*, by Nancy Cunard.

instinctive rhythmic pattern, gradually rising to a chant at the climax.

Many reconstructions of such services have been recorded in America, both for the Library of Congress and by the commercial companies, but unfortunately there are practically no issues released on English labels.[1] The nearest approach to authenticity obtainable in this country is *The Black Diamond Express to Hell* (Decca F.9720) by the Rev A. W. Nix and his Congregation, in which the imagery of the railroad is used to depict life's journey through such places as 'Drunkardville', 'Liar's Avenue', 'Deceiversville', 'Confusion Junction', 'Fight-town', 'Dancing Hall Depot', 'Gambler's Tower', 'Stealingtown', etc.

I take my text this marning from Matthew seventh chapter and thirteenth verse: 'Enter ye in at the strait gate: for wide is the gate, and broad is the way that leadeth to destruction, and many there be that go in thereat:' (Congregation: 'Amen'). This train is known as the Black Diamond Express train to hell: sin is the engineer, pleasure is the headlight, and the devil is the conductor. ('Amen.')

I see the Black Diamond as she starts off for Hell: ('Amen') her bell is ringin' 'hell-boun', hell-boun' '.

> The devil cries out 'All aboard for Hell!
> First station! is Drunkardville
> Stop there an' let all the drunkards get on board (Right)
> I have a big crowd down there drinkin' Jump Steady
> Some drinkin' Sheneg, some drinkin' Moonshine
> Some drinkin' White Newlyn Red Horse
> Alllll you drunkards You gotta go to hell on the B.D. train.
> The Black Diamond starts off for Hell now.
> Next Station! is Liar's Avenue
> Wait there! An' let all the liars get on board
> I have a big crowd of liars down there
> Have some smooth liars
> Some unreasonable liars
> Some professional liars
> Some bare-faced liars
> Some ungodly liars
> Some big liars, some little liars
> Some go to bed lyin' – get up lyin'
> Lie all day, lie on you and lie on me
> A big crowd of liars.
> You gotta go to hell on the Black Diamond train.
> Next station!' etc.

1. A notable exception has recently been issued, *He's The Lily of The Valley/I shall wear a Crown*, by Rev. R A. Daniels with The Mount Zion Church Gospel Choir – Capitol C.L.13530.

'Next Station!' is shouted with enormous power and then the name is quoted, while the list of various sins is intoned in a natural rhythmic manner which comes to a climax by passing from chant into song, aided by the congregation which discards the interjected 'Amens' and 'That's right' in order to sing the responses.

> And now – the devil sends a despatch to the engineer
> An' tells him to pull his throttle wide open
> An' hit Damnation Switch in the black shade o' midnight
> An' make a fast one for Hell
> Ooooh gambler! Git off the black dimon' train
> Ooooh midnight rambler! Git off the black dimon' train
> Ooooh backslider! Git off the black dimon' train.
> Chillun, aren't you glad you got off the black dimon' train
> A long time ago?
> I'm so glad I got off a long time ago
> Ever since I got off, my soul has been singing.

SINGS: All of my sins
            Been taken away
            Well all of my sins been taken away
            Well all of my sins bin
            Well Glory Hallelujah to his name
            All o' my sins been taken away (taken away)

SHOUTS: Chillun, aren't you glad you got off a long time ago?
            I'm glad I got off a long time ago.
            Amen!

It is impossible to convey the speech syncopation and rhythmic cadence of the sermon phrases by means of the printed word: it could doubtless be scored and analysed, but such a procedure is comparable to giving the wave-lengths of the spectra in a dragon-fly's wings in order to describe the darting beauty of its flight over a pond.

It is an aural experience, and the record should be heard if possible.

The train imagery is a feature of many spirituals, as it was in the case of many Blues. The advent of the railroad from 1830 onwards played a great part in the life of the Negro, for it was bound up with his work as a labourer in its employ. The means of transit to another place was not for him, however, and the railway became associated in his mind with means of leaving his toil – an escape symbolism expressed in *De Gospel Train:*

De gospel train am a-comin',
I hear it just at han',
I hear de car-wheels rumblin',
An' rollin' th'oo de lan'.

I see de train a-comin',
She's comin' 'roun' de curve,
She's loosen'd all her steam and brakes
An' strainin' ev'ry nerve.

De fare is cheap an' all can go,
De rich an' poor are dere,
No second class aboa'd dis train,
No diff'rence in de fare.

Den git on boa'd, little children,
Git on boa'd, little children,
Git on boa'd, little children,
Dere's room for many a mo'.

This 'railway obsession' even gave a name to the famous escape line for slaves across the border to the Northern States – the 'Underground Railway',[1] which was simply a route along which fugitive Negroes were helped by white humanitarians and those of their own race who were living in non-slave States. One of these was the renowned 'conductor', Harriet Tubman, known to the slaves as 'Moses' because of her gift of leadership, and in times of danger the spiritual *Go down, Moses* was sung as a warning signal. There are many verses to this, but the opening one is sufficient to show the obvious parallel between the Jewish oppression in Egypt and the Negro oppression in America:

When Israel was in Egypt's land,
Let my people go!
Oppress'd so hard they could not stand,
Let my people go!

The reiterated phrase 'Let my people go!' builds up an inexorable and dramatic effect, being used as a response to the chanted or sung story of captivity.

The film *Green Pastures* was a remarkably true picture of the manner in which Christianity was accepted, wholly and literally, by the perforce uneducated slaves. 'De Lawd' to them *was* a benign coloured old gentleman in a white nightshirt complete with white wings. What more natural than that he should attend a

1. Ian Hay's play *Hattie Stowe* is a fine presentation of this period and of the work done by Professor and Harriet Beecher Stowe.

heavenly fish-fry and be offered 'Jes' a lettle more custard, Lawd?'
by a fraternal angel? It was a *personal* religion which they created,
and their anthropomorphism – their creating of God in the likeness of man – was no more outside the possibilities of nature than
the creation of man in the likeness of God. As James Weldon
Johnson [1] says:

> His (the Negro preacher's) discourse was generally kept at a high
> pitch of fervency, but occasionally he dropped into colloquialisms and,
> less often, into humour. He preached a personal and anthropo-
> morphic God, a sure-enough heaven and a red-hot hell.

Compare the symbolism of Toplady's *Rock of Ages* with its
smug certainty of salvation, and the 'blessed is he that expecteth
nothing – for he shall get it' attitude of the spiritual *No Hiding
Place*. On the one hand is:

> Rock of Ages, cleft for me,
> Let me hide myself in Thee;
> Let the Water and the Blood,
> From Thy riven side which flow'd,
> Be of sin the double cure,
> Cleanse me from its guilt and power.

and on the other:

> No hidin' place down dere,
>   Hallelujah, chillun!
> No hidin' place down dere,
> I went to de rock for to hide my face,
> De rock replied, 'No hidin' place!'
> No hidin' place down dere.

In thinking of spirituals, the present-day stereotyped and glossy
caricatures presented on concert platforms and over the air must
not be confused with the early forms which were of great beauty
and sincerity. The performance of (say) *Swing Low, Sweet
Chariot*, by Paul Robeson (HMV B.2339), is a musically bowdler-
ized version acceptable in the English drawing-room – it is the
work of an educated Negro singing with a Europeanized outlook.
On the other hand, the work of Louis Armstrong (Decca F.6835)
in *Shadrack*, although recorded fairly recently, in 1938, bears a
closer affinity to the early spirituals.

Again, although of fairly recent vintage, the songs of Sister
Rosetta Tharpe, Sister Ernestine Washington and Mahalia
Jackson give a truer picture of authentic spirituals than most of

1. *God's Trombones* (Sermons in Verse). Viking Press, New York, 1927.

the emasculated versions which obscure the urgency of the spiritual's down-to-earthiness.

Sister Rosetta Tharpe, no mean guitarist in her own right, has a fine shouting quality which displays the spiritual as it was: a personal linking of religion with everyday life. For instance, her rendering of *God Don't Like It* (Brunswick 02784) might be a gospel-shouting extension of the Drunkardsville episode in *The Black Diamond Express*.

> You say you done cut whisky out
> 'N let you have a li'l wine,
> But yet most everybody git on the drunk
> They must be drinkin' moonshine –
> > But God don't like it
> > I know, an' I'm so glad he don' like it
> > I know, an' ain't you glad he don' like it
> > I know: it's a scandalous and a shame.
>
> But they tell me that this yellow corn
> Will make the very best kind
> But you should have turned that corn into bread
> An' stop that drinkin' moonshine –
> > Because God don't like it, etc.
>
> Brother! Ef yo' name is in the church
> An' you drink God's holy wine
> You sure can't walk those Golden Streets
> All staggle (staggered) or look moonshine –
> > 'Cos God don't like it, etc.
>
> Well, this old race is gonna be lost
> If it keeps on like it's goin'
> It's gettin' so weak it havin' a li'l drink,
> For the preacher's drinkin' moonshine.
> > But God don't like it, etc.
>
> I know you don't like my song
> I done made it up in ma mind
> I don't take it back, not a word I said
> 'Cos I sure don't drink moonshine.
> > 'Cos God don't like it, etc.

This represents the admonitory type, but she is equally at ease in singing the praise of 'salvation' in *Rock Me* (Brunswick 02737):

> Now, won't you hear me swingin'
> In the words that I'm singin'
> N'wash my soul with water from on High
> While the world of love is aroun' me

> Evil thoughts divide me
> Ooooh, if you leave me I will die.
> You just hide me in thy bosom
> Till the strife of life is over
> Rock me in the cradle of thy love
> Believe . . .me
> Then you take me to your blessed home above . . .

Even Sister Rosetta Tharpe has a sophisticated ring when compared with Ernestine Washington, who recorded some hymns of the spiritual type in 1945 with Bunk Johnson's Jazz Band (q.v.). They are of academic interest both for the style of singing, which hints at the more secular type of Blues singing, and for the pedestrian accompaniment which might be taken as a sample of the marching bands of New Orleans, particularly in *God's Amazing Grace*.[1]

Mahalia Jackson is a natural gospel singer whose fervent style is heard to advantage in *Since The Fire Started Burning My Soul*, whilst *In My Home Over There* reveals her restrained type of spiritual singing (Vogue 301).

So many influences made their contribution to the formation of classic jazz in New Orleans that once again it will be advantageous to review briefly the geographical situation of that city and its very colourful history.

Its picturesque name of 'The Crescent City'[2] derives from the fact that it was originally founded on the east bank of a bend in the Mississippi in the delta region roughly a hundred miles from its mouth.

John Law, who had acquired from France a charter for the territory thereabouts, founded the small town of about one hundred houses and five hundred inhabitants in the year which is generally given as 1718, but there is some doubt as to the accuracy of that date. Certain it is, however, that it was named in honour of the Regent, the Duc d'Orléans, by the French governor of Louisiana – Jean Baptiste Le Moyne, Sieur de Bienville. Here was no prosperous city, but a collection of cypress-built cabins separated by reptile-infested ponds. Later Jesuits arrived to educate and cultivate and it is probably due to their industry that the sugar-cane became one of the staple crops of the South.

Storms and hurricanes repeatedly swept the site, and the river –

1. *God's Amazing Grace/Where Could I Go But to the Lord?* Sister Ernestine B. Washington. Melodisc 1101.
2. See Map, p. 47.

not the beneficent 'old man' which 'kept rollin' along', but a hungrily rising enemy – covered the area several times.

When the Treaty of Paris was concluded in 1763 between France and England, Louis XV omitted to include New Orleans

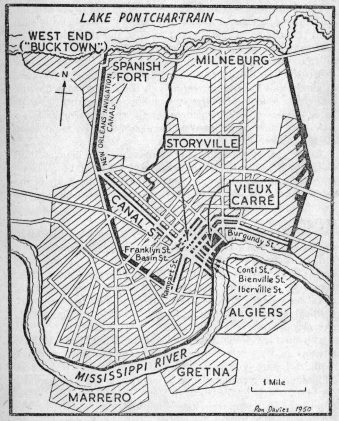

LAKE PONTCHARTRAIN

WEST END ("BUCKTOWN")

SPANISH FORT

MILNEBURG

NEW ORLEANS NAVIGATION CANAL

N

STORYVILLE

VIEUX CARRÉ

CANAL ST.

Burgundy St.

Franklyn St. Basin St.

Rampart St.

Conti St. Bienville St. Iberville St.

ALGIERS

MISSISSIPPI RIVER

GRETNA

1 Mile

MARRERO

Ron Davies 1950

in the transfer of territory to England and had by secret treaty passed that city over to Spain, much to the sorrow of the inhabitants. Their forebodings were unnecessary, however, for it was thanks to the Spanish Governor that great improvements took place in the shape of brick-built houses, shops, the Town Hall, Hospital, and Cathedral. Then the Treaty of Madrid between

Spain and the United States of America laid the real foundations
of a thriving port, for it was agreed that New Orleans should be
open to the Americans as a port of deposit, with no duty payable
but a reasonable storage price to be paid on produce landed.

Then came what was surely the best bargain ever struck between
nations; the purchase of Louisiana [1] by the United States in 1803
– the 'Louisiana Purchase' – and an even greater stimulation of
business. The streets were thronged with a heterogeneous and
polyglot people, and it is interesting to recall that those same
streets still bear the names which commemorate the owners of the
original localities, and, incidentally, is the key to many obscure
jazz titles. Madame Gravier's plantation, for instance, gave its
name to Gravier Street which, in turn, christened *Gravier Street
Blues*, and Camp Street is still a reminder of the slave camp which
existed between Poydras and Girod.

As the years passed, the population more than doubled itself
owing to the influx of emigrants from the West Indies: whites,
mulattos, and slaves, many of the incoming Creoles being of the
same ancestry as those of French stock on the mainland; and
together they formed the major part of the population of this now
prosperous city.

From 1812 onwards the history of New Orleans is colourful to
say the least; even melodramatic: massacres by drunken Choctaw
Indians roaming the streets; rape and pillage by the infamous
Lafitte pirates who held Barataria Bay; regular shipwrecks on the
dangerous bars at the river entrance; yellow fever epidemics;
secession from the Union in 1861; defeat in the Civil War, fires,
political intrigues, and internecine strife – not to mention terrible
river floods.

This brief recapitulation of the geography and history of New
Orleans has been necessary in order to emphasize its importance
as the breeding ground for many of the influences which contributed to the formation of classic jazz. It was the great port and
dockside town of all the Southern States, far exceeding in size and
population all the others for many hundreds of miles, and its urban
character tended to create a more tolerant attitude towards the
slaves than existed in the rural districts. This is proved by the fact
that soon after the Louisiana Purchase they were permitted to
meet on Saturday and Sunday nights for dancing and general
recreation in a field adjoining Rampart Street which became known
as Congo Square, where they chanted and pranced to the accom-

1. This refers to the whole area then owned by the French.

paniment of improvised drums and tom-toms, and such things as the skeletons of asses' jaws, in which the loosened teeth produced a rattling effect. This practice became so ingrained that it was not discontinued after the emancipation, and there are still records of Congo Square dances (although probably performed for the benefit of tourists) as late as 1885, when it was reported in the *New York World*:

A dry-goods box and an old pork barrel formed the orchestra. These were beaten with sticks or bones, used like drumsticks so as to keep up a continuous rattle, while some old men and women chanted a song that appeared to me to be purely African in its many-vowelled syllabification. . . . In the dance, the women did not move their feet from the ground. They only writhed their bodies and swayed in undulatory motions from ankles to waist. . . . The men leaped and performed feats of gymnastic dancing. . . . Small bells were attached to their ankles. . . . Owing to the noise I could not even attempt to catch the words of the song. I asked several old women to recite them to me, but they only laughed and shook their heads. In their patois they told me – 'No use, you could never understand it. C'est le Congo!'

There was always a certain tolerance shown towards the slaves in New Orleans which was conspicuously absent in other Southern areas, partly because of its Gallic history and partly because of that urban 'live and let live' policy mentioned earlier. In addition to this, there was the leavening influence of numbers of 'free people of colour' whose status in Louisiana was settled by Napoleon at the time of the Purchase. Before the transfer, anybody who could prove descent from a French or Spanish ancestor was regarded as a white citizen, no matter what his or her colour, and one of the terms of the sale was that this ruling should still exist under United States law.

These 'free-coloured' people, or Creoles,[1] as they have come to be called, were the coloured aristocracy of New Orleans, and their achievement in the musical world was a far cry from beating an old pork barrel with a bone. Many of them were highly trained and skilled musicians who played in symphony orchestras, and

1. The word has changed its meaning. *Encycl. Brit.* has this to say: '. . . used originally (sixteenth century) to denote persons born in the West Indies of Spanish parents, as distinguished from immigrants direct from Spain, aboriginals, Negroes, or mulattos. . . . It is now used of the descendants of non-aboriginal races born and settled in the West Indies, and in various parts of the American mainland. . . . The use of the word by some writers as necessarily implying a person of mixed blood is totally erroneous. . . .' Where the term is used in this book, it implies the 'erroneous' use of the word.

their names are perpetuated in some of the jazz musicians of to-day – names such as Bechet, Bigard, St Cyr, and Braud. They were doomed to extinction as far as freedom was concerned because of the white political intrigues which followed the Civil War, when the policy seems to have been: 'If the slaves are going to be freed, then that can be compensated by dragging the Creoles down.'

As Jelly Roll Morton[1] says:

As I can understand, my folks were in the city of New Orleans long before the Louisiana purchase, and all my folks came directly from the shores . . . and by shores, I mean from France, across the world – in the other world – an' they landed here in the New World years ago. I remember so far back as my great-grandmother and great-grandfather. Their names – my great-grandfather's name was Emile Pechet – that's a French name, and the grandmother was Mimi Pechet – it seems to be all French and as long as I was able to remember those folks they never was able to speak a word of American or English. . . . I don't know, I don't think they had no slaves back there in Louisiana, don't think so . . . I don't know, but they never spoke of anything like that, but anyway, my great – my grandmother, her name was Laura – she married a French settler in New Orleans by name of Henri Monet – that was my grandfather, and neither one of them spoke American or English . . . well, my grandmother bore sons named Henri, Gus, Meville, and Melascole (?) all French names, and she called the daughters Louise, Viola, and Margaret – that was the three daughters. Louise, her eldest daughter happened to be my mother – Ferd Jelly Roll Morton. Course, I guess you wonder how the name Morton came in, by the name Morton being an English name it wouldn't sound very much like a French name, but my real name is Ferdinand La Menthe. My mother also married one of the French settlers in New Orleans out of a French family, being a contractor. My father was a brick-contractor – bricklayer for making large buildings and so forth and so on. We always had some kind of a musical instrument in the house including guitar, drums, piano, trombone, and so forth and so on, harmonica and jews harp. We had lots of 'em, and everybody always played for their pleasure, whatever it was they desired to play. We always had ample time that was given us in periods to rehearse our lessons which was given to anyone that was desirous in acceptin' lessons. But of course the families never . . . the family, I mean . . . never had imagined that they wanted musicians in the family to make their livin': they always had it in their minds that a musician was a tramp other than the . . . with the exceptions . . . with the exceptions of the French Opera House players which they always patronized. They only thought they was the great musicians in the country and I myself was inspired by going to the French Opera House once, because the fact of it was I liked to play

1. In a Circle recording from Archives of Library of Congress.

piano, and a piano was known at that time to be an instrument for a lady, so I had it in mind that if I played piano I would be misunderstood. . . .

So it can be seen that the late Jelly Roll Morton, one of the greatest names in jazz, had a family tradition of legitimate music which will be more closely followed in a later chapter.

It will be seen from the chart in Appendix One that the phrase 'Instrumental synthesis with human voice' appears in the bridge between 'Early Blues' and 'Classic Jazz'. This needs explanation.

In the same way that West African drum music is an attempt to produce the effects of the human voice by mechanical means, so, when legitimate musical instruments became available to the Negroes, they automatically tried to imitate the sounds of their singing – the sounds of their own voices. By natural selection three instruments became the chosen favourites: the clarinet representing the high-pitched voice: the cornet for the medium-pitched voice, and the trombone[1] for the deep voice. This 'vocalization' of instrumental music affected the whole trend of jazz.

This sounds suspiciously like a truism: all music in its early stages must have been imitative, but in this particular instance the use of slurs, vibrati, and that persistent use of portamenti is directly attributable to the same characteristic elements in Negro speech and song, which were the outcome of African speech-habits being transferred to the American tongue.

In what manner did they acquire such expensive things as clarinets, cornets, and trombones? It is highly probable that the ending of the Civil War in 1865 must have seen many an old band instrument discarded throughout Louisiana, Mississippi, Alabama, Georgia, and South Carolina. These, rescued and treasured

1. James Weldon Johnson in his autobiography *Along This Way* (Penguin Books, 1941) says that he had the greatest difficulty in finding a suitable title for his book of seven sermons in verse. He says: 'I toyed and experimented with "Lord"; "Cloven Tongues"; "Tongues of Fire"; and "Trumpets of the Lord", at least twenty tentative titles. I narrowed them down to "Listen", or "Trumpeters of the Lord". I liked the last two titles, but saw that "Trumpets" or "Trumpeters" would be a poetic cliché. Suddenly, I lit upon "trombone". The trombone, according to the Standard Dictionary, is: "A powerful brass instrument of the trumpet family, the only wind instrument possessing a chromatic scale enharmonically true, like the human voice or the violin, and hence very valuable in the orchestra." I had found it, the instrument and the word, of just the tone and timbre to represent the old-time Negro preacher's voice. Besides, there were the traditional jazz connotations. So the title became "God's Trombones – Seven Negro Sermons in Verse".'

by Negroes, must have been doubly sacred in that many of them were relics of the emancipating Union Army, and it could be that the tremendous popularity of brass bands in New Orleans was a direct outcome of this hero-worship. The very instruments which went 'Marching Through Georgia' – went marching along Canal Street.

These brass bands, which were functional in that they were used for marching purposes in parades and general festive occasions, [1] copied the white man's march music, but added that touch of magic which transformed the clipped starchiness of military strains into something which was approaching jazz. . . . Rudi Blesh says: [2]

Like yellow sunlight the sweetly blatant, brassy sounds float through the streets, echo by day and by night from the old balconied houses, resound in the dim courtyards, carrying the thrilling sounds of the old marches: *High Society, Gettysburg, Panama, If I Ever Cease to Love.* If you turn from the white bands with their military precision to the Negroes playing the same march with their incomparable elastic, skipping, syncopated rhythm, you are hard upon the very source of Negro jazz.

The names of most of these early brass bands have fallen into oblivion, but their later descendants have been remembered by the late Bunk Johnson (that link with the early days of New Orleans jazz), in the following words:

Now during that time parades and funerals were great at hiring brass bands. Here are the brass bands I played with: The Old Teao, Charlie Dablayes Brass Band, The Diamond Stone, The Old Columbis, Frank Welsh, The Old Excelsior and so many other of the old days.

The Negro marching bands were obviously in being some considerable time before 1881, because in that year there were more than a dozen which took part in the procession in New Orleans which mourned the death of President Garfield (an ardent anti-slavery advocate, who rose from log cabin to White House). The transformation of straightforward marches into jazz may be compared with the process which took place when hymns were changed into spirituals, and the general opinion of the many American jazz students who have interviewed elderly Negro musicians of that period places the date of this alchemy of brass band into jazz at about 1890 or shortly after.

1. See Chapter Five.
2. *Shining Trumpets.* Cassell & Co.

This 'jazzing'[1] of marches was achieved partly by the trick of shifting the accent from the strong to the weak beat and partly by allowing solo players to 'decorate' the melody they were playing – *solo improvisation;* or several players to indulge in their extemporization simultaneously – *collective improvisation.* The weaving of patterns by the three melody instruments may be compared with a graph in which the rhythm section lays down the co-ordinates, over which is traced the scarlet line of the cornet; the bright green of the clarinet, and the dark brown undulations of the trombone. A fanciful simile, perhaps, but one which explains the necessity for the beat in jazz to act as a scaffolding.

It is not strictly accurate, however, because the vertical and horizontal lines of the graph are themselves varied slightly in their placing, owing to rhythms within rhythms constructed by the different instruments of the rhythm section. It is as though four fine lines were drawn very closely together; when viewed at a distance of six feet, they merge into one thickish line, but when inspected closely their separation is obvious. This must not be taken to indicate that the rhythm instruments play out of time with each other, but that they have a certain freedom within their own sphere to anticipate or delay the metronomical exactitude of the beat. These instruments were the banjo or guitar, tuba and drums. The substitution of string bass for tuba, and the addition of the piano to the rhythm section will be dealt with in a later chapter.

Before delving into the origins of Ragtime, which must be considered shortly because of its chronological development in the pages of jazz history, let us attend one of the functions in New Orleans where a brass band was a *sine qua non* for every self-respecting Negro family – a funeral.

Let Jelly Roll Morton tell the story:[2]

Of course, everybody in the city of New Orleans was always organization-minded, which I guess the world knows, and the dead man always belonged to several organizations such as Clubs and we'll say secret orders, and so forth and so on, and every time one died, why nine out of ten there was always a big band turn out when the day that he was supposed to be buried: never buried at night, always in the day; and, of course, lot of times right in the heart of the city the burial would take place. Well - that the band would start we would know that the man

1. An excellent example of contrasted *march* and *jazz* treatment can be heard on Part 2 of Louis Armstrong's *New Orleans Function/Oh, Didn't He Ramble.* Brunswick 04541.

2. Circle JM 15. Library of Congress.

was 'ficially to be buried so you could hear the band come up the street before they would get to the place where the gen'l'man was to be taken in for his last ride an' they would play differen' dead marches, and on leavin' this would be the march they would usually start to playin': *Flee is the Bird to the Mountain*. When they would enter the graveyard – some of them call 'em cemeteries and so forth and so on – very suddenly would bury 'em in the deep; they would never bury 'em in the mud, the'd always bury 'em in a vault. They'd leave the graveyard, as they call it, while the band would get ready to strike up – they'd have a second line behind 'em, well, maybe a couple of blocks long . . . the band'd get started, you could hear the drums . . . that would be the last of the dead man – he's gone, and everybody came back home – they b'lieved truly to stick right close to the bible – that means 'Rejoice unto death' and 'Cry at the birth'. New Orleans stick close to the scripture . . . that's the way it always ended in New Orleans – now, the boys from then on, the band would always figure on a big night because they had some money – it wasn't very much, 'cos the band men didn't make very much in New Orleans, the only musicians that made real money was the piano players – the other fellers, lot o' times they'd work for a dollar a night; maybe a funeral procession like that would maybe be two dollars – two dollars and a half, so they had to make the best of it that way. So that was always the end of a perfect death.

The recorded reconstructions of such funeral marches[1] seem irreligious and mystifying to those who hear them without knowing the context. The rolling drums, the shrieking mourners, the chanting of such phrases as: 'Sich a good Man' and 'He rambled and he gambled, but the butcher had to cut him down' were as sincere as the 'shouting' at camp meetings and as sincere a tribute to their dead as were the plumes, mutes, black horses, and cold collations of the Victorian era in England.[2]

The return from the graveyard, when as Louis Armstrong has said 'they'd jess tear their horns apart' was, apart from the psychto logical aspect of expressing joy in their own 'aliveness', a tribute to the music of their time. He was dead. All right – let him hear the music the way he liked it in life.

1. *Oh Didn't He Ramble*. Jelly Roll Morton. HMV B.9217. *New Orleans Function*. Louis Armstrong. Bruns. 04541. *Oh Didn't He Ramble*. Kid Ory (American) Crescent 3.
2. A custom which is still prevalent, especially in some European countries.

CHAPTER FOUR

Ragtime and Early White Jazz

RAGTIME was an immediate forerunner of the period which we have called the 'Classic Jazz of New Orleans', and originated partly in the attempts of Negro pianists in the sporting houses of Basin Street and similar districts to copy the brass bands' trick of shifting the accent from the strong to the weak beat when playing march tunes. Although the white man had imitated certain Negro melodies as early as 1799, when the German singer Johann Graupner appeared in a Boston Theatre with cork-blackened face (to start the minstrel cult which later developed into what were popularly known as Coon Songs), it was the peculiar inflexions of the Negroes' vocalization which created ragtime out of minstrelsy.

Ragtime is *not* just an older name for jazz, any more than swing (q.v.) is a new name for it. It was one of the influencing factors on jazz, but they both ran a parallel course until Ragtime virtually died out after the end of the First World War.

It is now generally conceded that early piano ragtime developed as an imitative art: imitative in that the piano was used to exploit earlier banjo techniques to the full — one piano being able to reproduce the effect of two, three or even four banjos. This banjo effect may be noticed in some of the reconstructions of early ragtime. [1]

Kay C. Thompson [2] says that the earliest *published* rag located is entitled *New Coon in Town*, composed by Gunnar, and published by S. Brainard's Sons, of New York and Chicago in the year 1884, and that this is sub-titled 'Banjo Imitation'. Before this date there were hundreds of pieces of 'raggy' music, if we are to believe the testimony of the *Albany State Register* in 1852. . . .

1. Tempo A. 83, Lee Stafford, *Winter Garden Rag*. Capitol CL. 13381, Marvin Ash. *Maple Leaf Rag/Cannon Ball Rag*.
2. *Record Changer*, April 1949.

... The last Negro melody is on everybody's tongue, and consequently in everybody's mouth. Pianos and guitars groan with it, night and day; sentimental young ladies sing it; sentimental young gentlemen warble at it at midnight serenades; volatile young bucks hum it in the midst of their business and pleasure. ...

What were the stages by which these Negro melodies evolved into ragtime? They have been most succinctly expressed by Ernest Borneman: [1]

Out of this mid nineteenth century vogue of 'Negro Melodies' and 'Coon Songs', there grew the ragtime era which culminated at the turn of the century and merged thereafter almost imperceptibly into the jazz era. ... Five consecutive stages of the Negro's cultural and political development are most clearly recognizable in the changing attitude of the minstrel show towards its protagonist. In its first stage, which might be dated from the time of the Stamp Act, the Negro was treated mainly as a barbarous, comic and somewhat childish figure. ... The second stage began around 1787, when the abolitionist movement started to question slavery's moral status. Almost immediately the minstrel stage turned to the Negro with a new attitude of pity and compassion. ... With the victory of Plattsburg, a third stage of development begins. The Negro ceases to exist as a figure of fun or compassion, and begins to emerge as a patriotic character. ... The fourth stage, minstrelsy proper, starting in 1799 with Graupner's *Gay Negro Boy*, may be considered as a summary of all preceding tendencies. It is characterized, however, by a further advance in social and political awareness which is reflected in the use of actual folk song material, both African and European in origin. *Opossum Up a Gum Tree* in 1822, *Jim Crow* in 1830, *Zip Coon* in 1834 and *Old Dan Tucker* in 1843 represent four significant steps in the development which, in 1862, led to Lucy McKim's *Dwight Magazine* letter and thus to the first recognition of Afro-American music as an autonomous form of American folk music. For whereas the earliest appearance of the Negro on the American stage was but an appearance of burnt cork on a white performer's face, the actual substance of minstrelsy as it developed into a mature art was contributed by the Negro himself and not by his blackface imitators.

From the heyday of minstrelsy, through the transition stage of coon songs, to the emancipation of the Negro idiom which culminated in the application of ragtime to the Blues, the whole movement hinged on a few Negro key figures – James Bland, Gussie L. Davis, Samuel Lucas, Sydney Perrin, Scott Joplin, Tom Turpin, Irving Jones, Ernest Hogan, Shelton Brooks, John Black, W. C. Handy, Clarence Williams, Jim Europe, Will Marion Cook, Walker and Williams, Cole and Johnson, Sissle and Blake.

It is unnecessary to delve more deeply into the antecedents

1. *A Critic Looks at Jazz*. Jazz Music Books. 1946.

of ragtime. It is sufficient to say that published compositions had ragtime strains in them long before the first recorded use of the word itself in 1893, when a Detroit composer by the name of Fred Stone had a song published which he called: *Ma Ragtime Baby*. The word caught on, and within a few years the words 'rag' and 'ragtime' had passed into the American vocabulary, even *Turkey in the Straw* (1896) carrying the designation that it was a 'Ragtime Fantasie'.

The many composers of written ragtime drew for their inspiration from the cakewalks of the Negro, and from the dance tunes of Europe which were currently popular among the white and Creole population of New Orleans and other large cities such as Memphis and St Louis: dance tunes like the polka, the quadrille, minuet, waltz, and mazurka.

The appearance of ragtime in these more northerly towns can be explained by the fact that economic conditions[1] had forced many of the city dwellers of New Orleans to go up the Mississippi, where they naturally gravitated to the towns, in which, as urban dwellers, they found congenial surroundings and company. The entertainment world was given a new impetus by the spate of 'World Fairs'.

In the same way that New Orleans bred the development of jazz, St Louis fostered the growth of ragtime. It was this city, with its population of half a million in 1895, which created the atmosphere of gambling halls and drinking saloons crowded with flashily dressed pleasure-seekers of the naughty nineties. This was the atmosphere which nurtured W. C. Handy, self-styled 'Father of the Blues', who used it as a stepping stone to Memphis and fame; it was also the hot-bed which produced Tom Turpin – one of the greatest names in the history of ragtime.

THOMAS MILLION TURPIN (*died 1922*) was raised in the saloon and club world, but had the advantage of a thorough musical education which enabled him not only to play piano in his own, his father's and his brother's clubs, but to judge the potentialities of other musicians and singers he employed. His first ragtime piece was published in 1897, *Harlem Rag; Ragtime Nightmare* and *St Louis Rag* followed within a few years, but the actual performance of ragtime was his joy, and he continued to delight thousands until his death. It was due to his influence and patronage that many other ragtime players became known to the public of that time; one having received so much publicity that

1. See Chapter Six.

he has often been erroneously quoted as the originator of rag-time – SCOTT JOPLIN (*1869–1917*).

It is difficult to sift the evidence after a lapse of over fifty years, particularly when the subject is one which current writers of the period considered too trivial or too ephemeral to record. One is forced more and more to rely on the testimony of living expon-ents who can recall the history of those days *to the best of their ability*.

With this in mind, no apology is made for the somewhat lengthy quotation from *Ragtime Begins*,[1] in which S. Brunson Campbell recalls his early days with Scott Joplin:

. . . But while this rag (*Harlem Rag*) was a good number it was not in the true ragtime pattern, for it was rearranged three different times, years later, and William H. Tyers[2] (another Negro musician) finally put it in the true ragtime style. But in 1897 a pianist and composer by the name of Scott Joplin, over at Sedalia, Missouri, finally gave birth to ragtime in *its perfected form*,[3] when he wrote his first rag called *The Original Rags*, which was a medley of rags. He wrote it in 1897. . . . Now if that rag was not enough to convince the critics that Scott Joplin was Ragtime's master, then his next rag did, for it was his famous *Maple Leaf Rag* of 1899. It became the classic of all rags.

In the same year he wrote two more rags, *The Sun Flower Slow Drag*, and *Swipsy*, a cakewalk. . . . There were other Negro pianists there (Sedalia) who helped Joplin make ragtime history. They were Scott Hayden, Otis Saunders, Arthur Marshall, Melford Alexander, Tony Williams, Jim Hastings and Ida Hastings. . . . So it was in this musical atmosphere that ragtime was born in 1898, and it was in this same musical atmosphere that Scott Joplin taught me to play his first rags in 1899 when I was fifteen years old. I was the first white pianist to play his famous *Maple Leaf Rag* and his other early rags. . . .

That is one side of the picture. On the other we have the state-ment by those tireless ragtime archaeologists, Dr Bartlett D. Simms and Ernest Borneman,[4] in *History and Analysis of Rag-time* when writing of LOUIS CHAUVIN, one of Tom Turpin's protegés:

Chauvin, nicknamed onomatopeically 'Shove-on', was an im-proviser and piano virtuoso ranking far above Tom himself, but since he could not read or write music, many of his original tunes and

1. *Record Changer*. March 1948.
2. Also received the credit for committing the traditional *Panama Rag* to paper.
3. My italics.
4. *Record Changer*. October 1945.

syncopations were transcribed by Tom and later by Scott Joplin without any due credit. In Tom's case, this was less plagiarism than a conviction, apparently shared by Chauvin himself, that ragtime was a pool of so many men's ideas that proprietary rights were a little out of place and that the credit should belong to the man who had enough knowledge to *write down* what was everybody's common musical property. In this sense, the whole copyright situation as indicated on the covers of the sheet music is somewhat confused and more than a little misleading if taken literally as an indication of the 'composer' in the academic sense of the term. [1]

Scott Joplin's case, in this connexion, is perhaps the most difficult to analyse. It is almost impossible at this date to decide with any degree of confidence which of the many pieces that bear Scott's name as arranger or collaborator were actually composed by him and how many of them were mere transcriptions of rags originally improvised by such men as Chauvin, Otis Saunders, Scott Hayden, and Arthur Marshall. Mr W. P. Stark of the Stark Publishing Company remembers that Scott, unlike Chauvin, was a rather mediocre pianist, and that he composed 'on paper' rather than 'at the piano' as all the real ragtime virtuosos did. This became a real problem when Scott had to play one of his own compositions and found that he had to rehearse it carefully before he could play it convincingly.

Thus it will be seen that there is a considerable divergence of opinion as to the one who can qualify for the title 'King of Ragtime'. One thing is certain, however, that to Scott Joplin must go the palm for fecundity of published rags, for between 1898 when his *Original Rags* came out, and 1917, which saw the issue of *Reflections*, he was responsible for some fifty rags and popular tunes flavoured with the 'rag' idiom.

It will have been noticed from S. Brunson Campbell's recollections of the early days in ragtime that the music was no longer a monopoly of the Negro, for, as he says: 'I was the first white pianist to play his famous *Maple Leaf Rag*.' It is an interesting cycle of events which started with the white man's imitation of the Negro: the Negro's acceptance and transformation of that imitation, and finally, the white man's acceptance of the second phase which was blossoming into a musical form which was to sweep the whole world. The increasing acceptance of ragtime and jazz by white musicians at the turn of the century will be dealt with later in this chapter, but it will be profitable now to devote our attention to JELLY ROLL MORTON, [2] already familiar to readers by the recorded recollections of his youth in New Orleans.

1. Cf. *Tiger Rag* later in this chapter.
2. See also Chapter Seven.

Although he died in 1941 at the comparatively early age of fifty-seven, which would make him about fourteen when *Maple Leaf Rag* was published, his whole life was bound up with music, and, what is of the greatest value to a history of jazz and its tributaries, his recollections and observations were documented in 1938 by Alan Lomax, Folk Music Curator in the Library of Congress, Washington, who found that the few sessions he had planned originally expanded to weeks and weeks of recorded reminiscences and piano examples. At that time Jelly Roll Morton's fame as a jazz man was in eclipse: he was suffering the fate of so many real jazz artists who had been relegated to the background during the worthless swing era which sprang up and flourished then. (See Chapter Ten.)

These recordings remained in the Library of Congress archives until 1947, when, in the words of Rudi Blesh:

It was at this juncture that Circle Sound, a company I had dedicated to the recording of the purist and most authentic jazz and Afro-American folk music, saw the full urgency of the situation. Our Field Director, Mr Kenneth Lloyd Bright, went to California to confer personally with Mr Hugh Macbeth, the prominent attorney who had been Jelly Roll Morton's staunch friend and is now the executor of his estate. Long negotiations began and, at length, the uncompromising musical integrity of CIRCLE, coupled with its expressed desire to make the Morton discs a memorial to the memory and fame of a great artist, won the rights to issue the records.

A limited edition of these was issued in twelve albums under the descriptive title of: *The Saga of Mr Jelly Lord* – a reference to his self-styled 'lordship' which arose from his own composition *Mr Jelly Lord*. The lyric, a little example of *folie du grandeur* to which most of us are prone at one time or another, was as follows:

> In foreign lands across the sea
> They knight a man for bravery
> Make him a duke or a count, you see,
> Must be a member of the royalty.
> Mr Jelly struck a jazzy thing
> In the temple by the queen and king,
> All at once he struck upon a harmonic chord,
> King said: 'Make Jelly a Lord'.
>
> Oh, Jelly Lord,
> He's simply royal at the old keyboard,
> You should see him when he plays jazz music as a rule,
> God knows he's an ivory fool.

With him, melodies have made him Lord of Ivories,
Just a simple chord,
And at home as well as abroad,
They call him Mr Jelly Lord.

Now, what can we learn from this unique autobiography with regard to the advent of ragtime? Let us travel back in time, and re-live, through him, some of the atmosphere of those faraway days.

Jazz started in New Orleans, and this, er, *Tiger Rag* happened to be transformed from an old quadrille that was in many different tempos, and I'll no doubt give you an idea how it went. This was the introduction meaning that everyone was supposed to get their partners. . . . *Get your partners, everybody, get your partners!* And people would be rushin' aroun' the hall gettin' their partners, it may be five minutes' lapse between that time, an' of course, they'd start it over again, and that was the first part of it . . . then the next strain would be a waltz strain I b'lieve . . . that would be the waltz strain. Also, hey'd have another strain that comes right belong – er – right beside it . . . mazooka time . . . of course, that was that – er – third strain, an' of course, they had another strain, an' that was in a differen' tempo . . . a two-four time . . . of course, they had another one, yeah . . . now I'll show you how it was transformed – it happened to be transformed by your performer at this particular time – Tiger Rag for your approval I also named it. It came from the way that I played it by 'makin' the tiger' on my elbow. I also named it: a person said once: 'It sounds like a tiger house.' I said: 'Fine.' To myself I said: 'That's the name.'

*

. . . I happened to invade that district, one of the sections of de district where the birth of jazz originated. At that time that was the year of 1902, I was about seventeen years old, I happened to go to Villere and Bienville: at that time one of the most famous night spots after everything was closed. Was only a back room where all the greatest pianists frequented after they got off from work in the sporting houses, and around four or after, unless they had plenty money involved, they would go to this 'Frenchman's' – that was the name of the place – saloon – and there would be everything in the line of hilarity there: they would have even millionaires to come to listen to the different great pianists what would no doubt be their fav'rites maybe among 'em.

*

You see *The Animule Dance* was s number that eas ages old: I wrote the number and ten thousand claimed it. I don't believe it's ever been published – I don't guess it ever will be published, or maybe it will – but since so many claimed it I thought I wouldn't try to claim it, but there's nobody has been able to do it so far but myself. All that was wrote around 1906, right after the *New Orleans Blues* was wrote, and *The Winin' Boy* – of course, that's unknown too right now – de *Winin' Boy*, but it was a very big hit for the time in Noo Orleans around the tenderloin district. That was one of the numbers I made a lot of money on: *Winin' Boy*. I also made a lot o' money on this number, too, which is known as *The Animule Dance* – of course that means ani*mals*. . . . Oh, I'll sing some scat songs. That was way before Louis Armstrong's time. Er, by the way, 'scat' is something a lot of people don't understand, and they begin to believe that the first scat numbers that was ever done was done by one of my home town boys, Louis Armstrong, but I must take the credit away since I know better. The first man that ever did a scat number was a man from Vicksburg, Mississippi, by the name of Joe Simms, an old comedian, and from that Tony Jackson and myself and several more grabbed it in Noo Orleans and found it was pretty good for an introduction of a song.

*

All of 'em, everybody had a different style – of course there was some more acc'rate than others. Of course, that style that I jes' got through playin' was the style of the ones that couldn't play very well – they'd have an inspiration they would be doin' better to continue increasin' the tempo . . . well, I decided that was a mistake, and I b'lieve it *was* a mistake, 'cos everybody grabbed the style. I thought that acc'rate tempo would be de right tempo suited for any toon regardless to any tempo that you would set, fast or slow, you should end it up specially if it was meant for a dance toon – so that was the idea I decided on when I found that the slow toons did more in the development of jazz (that is the medium-slow toons), than any other thing, due to the fact that you would always have time to hit a note twice when ordinarily you would only hit it once, and that gave it a very good flavour . . . well, of course, my theory is, er, never discord the melody: always have the melody goin' some kind of a way, and, of course, your background would always be with perfect harmony with what is known to-day as riffs, meanin' figures – musically speakin' as figures . . . a riff is somethin' that gives any orchestra a great background, and de main idea of playin' jazz – there's no jazz piano player can ever really play jazz unless they try to give a imitation of a band.

*

You may have noticed that in playin' jazz the breaks are one of the most essential things that you can ever do in jazz. Without breaks and without clean breaks; without beautiful ideas in breaks, you don't need to even think about doin' anythin' else. If you can't have a decent break

you haven't got a jazz band and you can't even play jazz. . . . Without
a break you have nothin'; even if a toon hav'n' a break in it, it is always
necessary to arrange some kind of a spot to make a break because as I
said before, you haven't got jazz, and, er, your acc'rate tempos with
your backgrounds of your figures which is called riffs to-day. . . . A riff
is a background – a riff is what you would call a foundation (as like you
would walk on), and a break is something that you break: when you
make de break that mean all the band break, with maybe one, two or
three instruments – it depends on how the combination is arranged, and
as the band breaks, you have a set given time, possibly two bars, to
make the break.

A fuller appreciation of the influence which Jelly Roll Morton
had on ragtime and jazz will be found in Chapter Seven where
his life and recordings are discussed at length, but these actual
observations of his were relevant at this point inasmuch as they
give us some first-hand information of the manner in which ragtime merged into jazz.

It would be as well to attempt a definition of ragtime, and to
suggest records which will help the reader to identify the style.
As this is not a musically technical book, the definitions will
therefore be confined to terms acceptable to the average reader as
distinct from the musician. Ragtime is characterized by a highly
syncopated air played against a regularly accented beat in the
bass. This rigidity of the beat was much more pronounced in the
work of the northern rag pianists, who preserved a steady two
beats in the bar for the left hand. *It was the New Orleans ragtime
pianists, with their closer proximity to jazz* who 'ragged' the bass
and at the same time syncopated the melody; thus creating
rhythms against rhythms. This accounts for the fact that the rag
compositions of Jelly Roll Morton and Tony Jackson lend themselves much more readily to jazz treatment than those of, say,
Scott Joplin, with their more stereotyped pattern. It is particularly noticeable in the case of the famous *Maple Leaf Rag*, a Scott
Joplin and Otis Saunders collaboration, which was originally
intended to be played at a moderate speed. [1] When interpreted by
a ragtime player of that early period the correctness of the slower
speed is felt very clearly, and the full flavour of the composer's
intentions are disclosed. [2] Most jazz interpretations, however, are

1. Most of Joplin's published sheet music carried the instructions: 'Do
not Play Fast'.
2. *Maple Leaf Rag*. Brunson Campbell. West Coast Label (Amer.).

given at a breakneck speed, which obscures the value of the original melodic figures. [1]

Jelly Roll Morton's *King Porter Stomp*, [2] on the other hand, in which the 'ragging' of the left hand is most noticeable, and which is also taken at a moderate speed, has proved itself a jazz evergreen since it was composed in 1906 as a compliment to the Gulf Coast pianist Porter King, and receives successful treatment from small and even large bands of the Fletcher Henderson type. [3]

A revival of interest in ragtime began in the early forties, and will be dealt with in the chapter devoted to The New Orleans Revival, but before passing on to the integration of ragtime and jazz by the white musicians at the beginning of the century, let us see what R. W. S. Mendl [4] had to say on the subject in 1927, in one of the first books about jazz to be published in this country. Writing of ragtime tunes, he said:

If anything they were welcomed as a refreshing change from the conventional music-hall song of a previous generation, with its square cut, regular rhythms and its often commonplace melodic outline. Ragtime was regarded at any rate as a harmless innovation. It was interesting to find something unusual – in the form of broken time – being introduced into popular music, and on the other hand there was nothing in the way of discordant effects or weird instrumentation which could give offence even to the conservative lover of music.

A singularly clear-sighted attitude at a time when ragtime and jazz were terms of opprobrium to both classical musician and layman.

In such a cosmopolitan population as that of New Orleans, it was natural that a tradition of music making should have been brought from France, Italy, Germany, and other European countries by the white emigrants who settled there, and there is ample evidence to show that the performance of classical music by families and friends of the family was a feature of their life.

As ragtime and jazz impinged more and more upon the consciousness of the younger members of these families, they began to experiment with the idiom, much to the horror and consternation of their elders, whose devotion to the 'written note' in music was equalled only by their antagonism to a music which they

1. *Maple Leaf Rag*. Sidney Bechet. HMV B.9408.
2. *King Porter Stomp*. J. R. Morton. Brunswick 03564.
3. *King Porter Stomp*. Fletcher Henderson. Columbia CB 701.
4. *The Appeal of Jazz*. R. W. S. Mendl, M.A., Oxon. Philip Allan & Co. 1927.

associated with vice and debauchery. (In passing, it would be as well to reiterate that jazz did not arise from the gutter, as so many of its opponents have insisted: it was forced *into* the gutter by its non-acceptance in polite society.)

Doc Malney's Minstrel Show in 1896 must have been the cause of heartburnings in many a home after the visiting youngsters had seen and heard the Spasm Band led by 'Stale Bread', whose real name was Emile August Lacoume (Senior). This was a band which played raggy music on instruments which, to say the least, were unusual. Stale Bread himself played a zither (a typical instrument of the Tyrol), and 'Cajun' (Willie Bussey) the harmonica. The others, all of whose real names indicate their European ancestry, used home-made instruments. There was Albert Montzulin, who, in common with the others, adopted an arresting pseudonym – 'Slew-Foot Pete' – played a guitar which was built from a cigar-box; 'Whisky' or Emile Benrod, whose string bass was engineered out of a half-barrel; and 'Warm Gravy' (Cleve Craven), whose banjo first saw light as a cheese box.

It was not only in the minstrel show that this and other Spasm Bands appeared. They played in clubs, saloons, on riverboats and on the streets, and if 'street music' has any gutter implications, it must be remembered that street music was a feature of Italian and German life for many years: many of the great Bach's ancestors and relatives being employed as street musicians.

Imitative spasm bands by children who formed a second line for the marching brass bands became a feature of the streets, and it was this hero-worship of the brass bands which brought the 'papa' of white Dixieland music into the jazz field – JACK LAINE (born *1873*).

As this is the first time that the word *Dixieland* has been used it must be indicated that the word has no precise meaning but is generally used for jazz which is played in a quasi-New-Orleans style by white musicians. The word *Dixie* is said to have originated in the issue by a New Orleans Bank of a ten dollar note with a prominent DIX displayed.

Jack Laine led a double life in that he formed a brass band and a ragtime band, switching key men from one to the other as the occasion arose. He himself played alto saxophone and, at times, the drums, whilst the key men of his band played respectively cornet, valve trombone, and clarinet; violin, string bass and guitar being added for dances, and other brass instruments for march parades.

J–3

This band, 'Jack Laine's Ragtime Band', set the style of Dixieland jazz which later swept across America and fascinated the entire world, and although the personnel of this group varied from time to time as it does in most jazz combinations, he himself has recalled the following names as being the most important ones in his early days:

Jack Laine	Leader and Drums
Lawrence Vega	Cornet
Achille Baquet (Creole)	Clarinet
Dake Perkins (Creole)	Trombone
Morton Abraham	Guitar
Willy Guitar	String Bass

Two points of interest arise from this: firstly, there was no use of the piano, and secondly, that two Creoles were included in a band from which most 'white' jazz stemmed.

Gradually, the dancing public's taste began to swing round to the new rags which Jack Laine played, and as the demand grew, so the quadrille and the 'mazooka' lost their popularity. The waltz, probably by reason of its three-four time acting as a relief for the rag numbers, remained in public favour for a much longer period.

His first brass band venture was the Reliance Brass Band, but this was the forerunner of several; indeed, as time went on he had several dance and brass bands running at the same time, and he employed many of the white New Orleans musicians including 'Stale Bread' and the Brunis brothers – one of whom, GEORG BRUNIS, is still well known in American jazz circles.

Other early bands of the time included one led by Jack Laine's son – ALFRED LAINE, which included HENRY RAGAS on piano and EDDIE EDWARDS the trombone player. Then there was 'Ernest Giardina's Ragtime Band' which was at its height in the year 1908 or 1909, and others led by Johnny Fischer, SCHILLING, 'YELLOW' NUNEZ and TOM BROWN.

'Tom Brown's Band from Dixieland' is the one which takes the thread of our story one stitch further in the spreading tapestry of jazz, for it was this band which was heard in New Orleans by talent scouts during 1913 and went north to Chicago to appear at Lamb's Café in the summer of 1915.

This, as far as can be ascertained, is the first appearance of the word 'jazz' or 'jass' as it was then spelt. Many theories have been advanced as to the etymology of the word, but its significance in Chicago at that period was distinctly copulative, and it is said that the word was applied to Tom Brown's Band by a rival café in a spirit of derision. Derisive it may have been, but it caught on, and, making capital out of it, Lamb's Café put out a new sign which stated: 'Added attraction – Brown's Dixieland Jass Band, Direct from New Orleans: – Best Dance Music in Chicago!'

It was a great success, so much so that other cafés began to look around for similar bands to stimulate their business, and in 1916 one went to Chicago with what proved to be the nucleus of the 'Original Dixieland Jass Band'. The personnel consisted of:

Dominick James La Rocca	Cornet
Eddie Edwards	Trombone
Alcide Yellow Nunez [1]	Clarinet
Henry Ragas	Piano
Tony Sbarbaro	Drums

(Note the preponderance of names with Latin origins.)

The following year, LARRY SHIELDS replaced Nunez, Tom Brown's Band broke up, and the 'Dixieland Jass Band' added the word 'Original' to its name, so that there would be no misconceptions on the part of the public, and moved into Reisenweber's Restaurant in New York, where the patrons, after sniffing at it suspiciously like a cat with a saucer of strange food, suddenly decided that it was good and lapped it up.

The music was a sensation: Dixieland music had come to stay, and it grew in stature despite the cheap publicity it was given at the time: 'The Famous Original Dixieland Jazz Band – Untuneful Harmonists playing Peppery Melodies.'

Because of the vision of the Victor and Aeolian Recording Companies, we can still hear the band as it was playing in 1917 – collectively improvising along ragtime lines. The reproduction is poor, and the record which you can hear to-day is a dubbing from an acoustically recorded master, but through it all comes echoing the spirit of a remembered New Orleans, with Larry Shields' imaginative clarinet weaving patterns against the rhythmic drive of Edwards' trombone, and La Rocca's staccato cornet.

For convenience, some of the O.D.J.B's early recordings which are available in Great Britain are listed below:

New York, 1917
    Tiger Rag/*Reisenweber Rag*   Brunswick 02500

1. TONY PARENTI (*born* 1900) was originally chosen, but his parents would not give permission because of his youth. He has said that the band in which he played – Johnny De Droit's – was the first Dixieland band to play for New Orleans White Society.

Barnyard Blues/At the Jazz Band Ball   Jazz Collector L.53 1918
Ostrich Walk/Bluin' the Blues   HMV B.8485
Clarinet Marmalade   HMV B.8500

They visited England in 1919, and made many records for Columbia, but these are now unfortunately deleted from the catalogue. Their impact on the British public, upon which only a drip of ragtime had previously fallen, was phenomenal, and adjectives, both laudatory and condemnatory, were lavished upon them. Their influence on the English school of jazz will be discussed in Chapter Twelve.

It should be mentioned that the trombonist they brought to England was not Eddie Edwards, but another New Orleans man, Emile Christian, while their pianist, Henry Ragas, having died a month before they were due to sail, was replaced by Russell Robinson. He however, did not stay with them, and for most of their spell here, the piano was taken over by ragtime pianist Billy Jones, now proprietor of 'The Cross Keys' in Lawrence Street, Chelsea, where he can still be persuaded to re-create *Sensation Rag* or *Ostrich Walk* at the piano.

But we have encroached far into the later years of jazz. Before returning to the pioneer jazzmen of New Orleans, though, reference must be made to the 'New Orleans Rhythm Kings', a group which went to Chicago in 1920, and which filled the white musical vacancy left when the O.D.J.B. went eastwards to New York. Their music was a closer approximation to the Negro jazz of New Orleans than that of most white groups: it was nearer to jazz than to ragtime, and was taken to Chicago by the riverboat trumpet player PAUL MARES (*1900–1949*), in 1919. He was accompanied by GEORG BRUNIS (*born 1900*) trombone, and LEON RAPPOLO (*1902–1943*) the clarinet player of eccentric habits: all New Orleans men who had spent many nights listening to the great Negro exponents of jazz.

Through an agent named Husk O'Hare, whose name is remembered for his insistence on its inclusion in the band's original title, they were engaged to play at the Friar's Inn – hence the recording name of the Friar's Society Orchestra for their first session in September 1922, when they made the following sides, still available:

Eccentric/Farewell Blues   Brunswick 02211
Tiger Rag/Panama   Brunswick 02212
Bugle Call Blues[1] Brunswick 02213

   1. The reverse is Husk O'Hare's Super Orchestra of Chicago.

All these have a well-knit atmosphere, a strong drive from Mares' growling trumpet, and beautifully conceived breaks and solos from the clarinettist (who is reputed to have spent much time leaning against a telegraph pole and playing choruses to the accompaniment of the harmonies humming in the wires overhead). Most of the tunes were jazz melodies which they had heard since childhood, and when they did copyright a title, it was usually the whole band which received the credit. They lived, drank, ate and slept jazz, and spent what time they could listening to King Oliver and absorbing the Negro style. It must not be imagined that they copied his tunes note by note: they merely wanted to drink at the fountain head of the jazz which was available to them at the time.

They themselves had their own admirers, including a youngster who sat entranced as they played, listening avidly to the wealth of ideas which flowed from Rappolo's clarinet. Occasionally he was even allowed to sit with the band and add his quota to the music. His name was Benjamin Goodman. [1]

By March 1923, some changes had taken place in the personnel of the band, and the rhythm section was formed by Mel Stitzel (piano) and Frank Snyder (drums). Brunis had developed a firmer, more forthright trombone style by then, but in the several examples of their music at that time, Rappolo is the one who carried the band by his brilliant melodic invention, as shown in *That's a Plenty* (Brunswick 02208) and *Weary Blues* (Tempo R.2).

In common with most of the early New Orleans jazzmen, white or coloured, the members of the band were not familiar with printed music, and their troubles arose when the management of Friar's Inn decided that it would look better if they played from music. They went through a bad period, even being asked to play light music and romantic ballads. This was the last straw, and they left. It was the management's loss, for it was soon noticed that the bandstand was not the only part of the Inn which was empty. They were approached, and agreed to return on the strict understanding that there would be no repetition of the *Bells at Eventide* routine. So they went in this time augmented by the riverboat trumpet player EMMETT HARDY and three others including the bass man CHINK MARTIN. They were hired, however, on the distinct understanding that they could read music, and it is one of the hoary old chestnuts of jazz that Martin was asked to point out the notes he was playing at the audition, and was un-

1. See Chapter Ten.

lucky enough to point firmly to a place in the music where no bass
part was marked! He got in, however, and this larger outfit kept
its job until 1925, when Ben Pollack, the drummer, left owing to
family pressure.

They offered him a trip to California if he would only give up
'this jazz mania'. He went, but settled down in Los Angeles with
another band almost immediately.[1]

Georg Brunis left in order to join Ted Lewis, and an even worse
fate befell Rappolo whose eccentricities had begun to extend
beyond the wearing of white socks with his dinner jacket. He was
sent to a sanatorium shortly after the break-up of the band, and
died there in 1943.

Thus ended the stem of New Orleans jazz as far as the white
musicians who comprised the New Orleans Rhythm Kings is concerned. Their separate activities will be considered in Chapter
Eleven.

---

1. This is a strange parallel with the early life of Frederick Delius, o
whom Ralph Hill writes in *British Music of Our Time:*
 . . . But the more he became infatuated with the idea of making music his
career, the more his father put obstacles in his way. Having tried his hand in
the woollen business. . . . Delius prevailed upon his father to buy him an
orange-grove in Florida. Recalling those days, Delius told Eric Fenby that
when he left England for Florida he was demoralized. . . . Then Delius struck
up a friendship with an organist and music teacher named Thomas Ward,
from Jacksonville. Ward was invited to stay at the orange-grove with the
result that a course of composition appeared to Delius a more fruitful occupation than growing oranges.

CHAPTER FIVE

The Pioneer Jazzmen

THE conclusion has already been reached that, if a new music or art form was to be born anywhere in the Southern States of America, then it had to be in New Orleans, by far the largest city south of St Louis and the entrepôt of trade for the whole of the Gulf region and the Mississippi hinterland. We have seen how the atmosphere of this city was predominantly Latin and that musical entertainment took an important part in everyday life. The cosmopolitan and Creole population were anxious to make their city as easy to live in as the Paris of their ancestors – and well they succeeded – the Vieux Carré or French Quarter became a raw and lusty Montmartre. The centre of artistic and social life was the Opera House where the Mardi Gras balls were held until 1919, when the building was burnt down. These Mardi Gras festivities were, and still are, part of a prolonged carnival season which lasts from Twelfth Night until Lent. After a hectic period of celebration and ceremony the climax is reached on the eve of Ash Wednesday, with a huge procession and the crowning of King Carnival. In 1949 Louis Armstrong was crowned King and some idea of the honour which the title carried with it may be judged from Louis's words: 'After that, I'll be ready to die.'

New Orleans was indeed a happy city (the tolerance towards the Negroes has already been referred to); processions, concerts, marches were indulged in at the slightest excuse, instigated by some society or lodge, akin to our Oddfellows; or even by a marching club, in which parades with a brass band and the organizing of a funeral procession for a deceased member was the chief activity. Advertising by means of a band was also the custom in those days, more often than not on a wagon of some sort. The band would squeeze themselves on (the trombonist at the back, pointing his instrument over the tailgate),[1] and it was their duty

1. Hence the term: 'tailgate' trombone

to attract attention by creating as much noise as possible. Later on in this chapter will be mentioned the 'cutting' contests which occurred when two rival bands met at, perhaps, a road junction. The bands would fight it out musically, the wagons often being tied together so that neither could escape until victory had been won by one or the other – a survival of the fittest and a feat of endurance indeed.

When it is considered that New Orleans is a city about the size of Bristol, no more, some assessment can be made of the way in which life was really lived – to the full. Here was the spawning ground of jazz; what more natural than that a new musical way of expression should find a definite form when there was a demand for so much music; when so much latent talent among the Negro musicians was straining for self-expression, with nothing but their own instincts to guide them – for hardly one could read music; when quality of performance reached a high standard, forced upward and still upward by dint of cut-throat rivalry; and when ultimate success brought with it a popularity and prestige comparable with that of a Babe Ruth or a Denis Compton?

We enter, then, into the formative years of classic jazz, when the music took its final shape; the rest of this book is mainly an account of the jazzmen who played in this shape. The music was never written down; the exponents themselves drifted into obscurity more often than not, so that the majority of the early history has been handed down from mouth to mouth. Nevertheless we are able to piece together the main facts about the pioneers of New Orleans who created their music between 1890 and 1920. And in so doing, in writing an account of the activities of Manual Perez, Buddy Bolden, John Robichaux, Freddy Keppard, and Kid Ory, we are at the same time explaining how the many fragments of influence were finally welded together to form the whole – Jazz.

Of this short list of early jazzmen that of Buddy Bolden was certainly the best known name, if only because of his spectacular, almost lurid career. A legend has been built around the name of Bolden, mainly through the romantic account in the pages of *Jazzmen* (extracts of which are quoted later in this chapter) and this legend of the barber of Franklin Street has impinged itself upon the world of jazz knowledge to such an extent that little or no attention has been paid to one who was, in all probability, a greater cornet player, a better all-round jazzman and one who certainly influenced many more than did Bolden.

MANUEL[1] PEREZ (*born 1873*) could have been successful in any field of music, if social conditions had allowed, for he was excellent both as a reader and as a teacher. He played with John Robichaux in the very early days, around 1895, but in 1898 formed his own band, the Imperial, along with Alphonse Picou, and later organized the magnificent Onward Band. In an interview with Robert Goffin[2] both Picou and Louis Nelson confirmed emphatically that Perez was the first jazz trumpeter. Nelson, in fact, was able to give more positive proof of the claim; he produced a newspaper cutting about his father's death in 1900 and remembered that he was playing then with Buddy Bolden who, at that time, not only did not have his own orchestra but was only playing an accordion and making his first attempts on the trumpet. Bud Scott says about Perez: 'A great trumpet player and a jazz man – everything, anyway you pick it; he could do all the tricks.'[3] These testimonies must be taken as of at least equal importance to those of Bunk Johnson, who, because he played with Bolden, may be expected to have shown a little bias in Buddy's favour. Undoubtedly both the Imperial and the Onward were magnificent marching bands, the Onward probably the greatest of all the New Orleans marching bands and one held in an esteem approaching reverence by most New Orleans musicians who can remember it.

Perez led his marching bands right up until the general exodus from the South. There were no exciting incidents in his life which served to preserve the memory of the Onward Band; compared with most other New Orleans jazzmen, his habits were temperate and he led a quiet life. Moving north even before Oliver, his band which played at the Pekin Cabaret in Chicago, consisted of Picou, clarinet, A. DesVerney, trombone, Frank Haynie, piano and Ed Garland, bass. This band was as talented and renowned as the Oliver group, but it so happened that Oliver made the first records, thereby staking an unimpeachable claim to fame, whilst Perez returned to his native New Orleans, having saved enough money to start a grocery business. If the collectors who still search for the fabulous Bolden cylindrical record shift their attention to the possible (and more probable) recorded evidence of Perez, they will be searching for something of greater historic importance and they will stand a greater chance of success – for Perez lived

1. Also spelt Emanuel.
2. *The Jazz Record*. June 1946.
3. *Record Changer*. September 1947.

through a period of more recording activity. With a different
temperament, a more striking personality, like Bolden, Perez
could have become King Perez; yet even in 1945, when Eugene
Williams wished to speak to him, he shunned publicity of any
sort, claimed he was ill and refused even an interview, and there
have been no recent reports as to whether he is well again or
whether he is alive or dead.

During his career he received acclaim and respect wherever he
played; yet his fine musicianship was never honoured in New
Orleans by the royal 'title'. This recognition fell to CHARLES
BOLDEN (*1868–1931*), nicknamed Buddy, Kid, and finally King
Bolden, and most handed-down accounts and many first-hand
witnesses are definite on the point that, if musical *personality* is
deemed a passport to investiture, Buddy was entitled to his crown.
Because of this personality, a great deal of the way in which he
played and lived has been remembered, and through these memor-
ies can be gleaned a reasonably true picture of the colourful life of
New Orleans jazz at the turn of the century.

Bunk Johnson, who has related so much to our generation of
the early history of jazz, says:

Buddy could not read a note, but he surely played a good stiff lead
and would have you in maybe six sharps before you finished, but I
could always go anywhere the King went. We played parades and
advertising wagons and, excuse me for the expression, honky tonks,
and together we made many famous blues. Until the King went crazy
we killed all the other best Bands in New Orleans.

At that time, towards the end of the nineteenth century, the
important bands of the Crescent City were Adam Olivier, The
Golden Rule, Bob Russell and JOHN ROBICHAUX. The last-
named was the most prominent, playing in a more 'legitimate'
style, and capable of providing the musical accompaniment for
both open-air concerts and polite society balls, and, at the time
Bolden entered the scene, was at Antoine's Restaurant and the
Grunewald (later the Roosevelt). Robichaux's band was accomplished in playing the dancing music of the period, quadrilles,
cake walks, and square dances, and the band contained many
famous hot players of the time. Robichaux might be compared
with Fletcher Henderson of a later period in jazz; the fact that he
played a good deal of straight dance music need not necessarily
result in his contemptuous dismissal as a 'sweet' band. Manuel
Perez, Lorenzo Tio, Batiste Delisle, and Bud Scott played with
Robichaux and these men, whilst lacking Bolden's scintillating

personality perhaps, can hardly be described as mediocre. Indeed, Bud Scott has said that, on occasion, in one of the many 'cutting' contests in Lincoln Park, Robichaux came out the winner. But this was not often and Scott gives full credit to Bolden for his dynamic execution. He says:

Bolden was still a great man for the Blues – no two questions about that. The closest thing to it was Oliver and he was better than Oliver. He was a great man for what we call 'dirt music'. Let me tell you he was plenty powerful. Even with all that power, the trumpet players of that day would have their notes covered and they would not hurt the ear the way rebop does now. You could hear every instrument in these bands and the drummer had his drums tuned – he would tune those drums like they were a piano.[1]

Buddy Bolden was a barber in Franklin Street and, in addition to leading his band, he seems to have been quite a character, publishing a gossip and scandal-sheet called *The Cricket* in which stories gleaned from New Orleans lower life found print. It is highly probable that Bolden's personality did much to ensure his supremacy over other trumpeters. It must be borne in mind that in these days there was no radio, no gramophone, no high-powered publicity, and no booking agents; a musician had to succeed on the strength of his reputation, ability, and personality alone. Buddy played at places like the Tin Type Hall, the Perseverance Hall, and the Longshoreman's Hall, for such nefarious organizations as the Mysterious Babies and The Buzzards. He played regularly at Johnson Park, not far from Lincoln Park, where Robichaux played, and it was here that Buddy used to 'call his chillun home'. If he arrived at Johnson Park late, when the prospective audience was over in Lincoln listening to Robichaux, he would stick his cornet through the fence and blow like mad until Lincoln Park was empty and the crowd was in Johnson Park listening to the King. At this time, in the early 1890s, Bolden's Band consisted of William Warner or Frank Lewis on clarinet, Willy Cornish, valve trombone, Jeff Mumford, guitar, James Johnson, bass, and Cornelius Tillman, drums. Later on, Bunk Johnson joined the band as second cornet, Frank Dusen was trombonist, Bob Lyons, bass, Sam Dutrey, clarinet, Henry Baltimore, drums, and Jimmy Palao, violin. In the early band Cornish was the only one who could read music and the presence of Palao in the later band is probably explained by that same reason. For Bolden was unique in that he scorned written notation and even

1. *Record Changer*, September 1947.

the desire to learn the notes.[1] He fashioned his music according to his own creed, which was to overprint his personality and inspiration of the moment on to the traditional basis of the march and dance music which he played. Cornish, having learned the new numbers, passed them on to the rest of the band, and then, after Buddy had finished with it, it was Bolden's jazz music (though, of course, the term *jazz* was as yet unknown in this context). Once again, to quote Bunk Johnson, in his letter to Fred Ramsey, printed in *Jazzmen:*

Here is the thing that made King Bolden Band be the first band that played jazz. It was because it did not Read at all. I could fake like 500 myself; so you tell them that Bunk and King Bolden's Band was the first ones that started jazz in the City or any place else.

In his rough and ready way, Bolden and his band had discovered the vital clue to an embryo music which was maturing into jazz. By force of circumstance, they were compelled to improvise; by the hand of Fate they were inspired enough not only to emulate their academic contemporaries, but, by sheer brilliance, to forge further ahead and crystallize a new musical art form.

It was during Bolden's reign that the notorious Storyville was created. Named after the alderman who drew up the necessary civic regulations, it consisted of an area off the French Quarter which was designated a legal 'red light' district. The Crescent City had always been notorious for its tolerance to an extreme of waywardness – it had once sent an S.O.S. to Paris for a consignment of *good* women because all the female population were bad. But even those who had known New Orleans in its earlier days could not have condoned the practices which obtained around Iberville, Franklin and Basin Streets. Already known for political corruption and vice in general, Storyville became a showplace of the city and the scandal of the whole South and, indeed, America. Organized prostitution had never been conducted in such a grandiose manner, nor at such a sordid level.

Tom Anderson was 'boss' of Storyville; in addition to running the Arlington Annex, he published the twenty-five cent *Blue Book*, which was a brothel Baedeker. A directory of all the prostitutes and sporting houses, it carried advertisements from the ornate palaces of joy like Lulu White's Mahogany Hall, Countess Willie Piazza's place, which specialized in Octoroons,[2] and Josie Arling-

1. Cf. Perez, who was an improvisor, but nevertheless could read music.
2. Octoroon – person having one-eighth Negro blood.

ton's Five Dollar House. Starting life in 1897, there were, in 1910, 200 houses of pleasure in the district. And not until this date when Billy Phillips decided to go one better than the others, replacing the single pianist in his *101 Ranch* by a whole band *playing regularly*, did jazz really move into Storyville. This point is mentioned here as one of some importance; jazz may have flourished in the gutter but it was not born there; and it took to the gutter because the pavement ostracized it. Bolden himself, playing in a previous decade, performed mainly in club halls, at open-air concerts and in marches and did not rely upon vice for a livelihood. This is not to whitewash Buddy, who loved women at all times and in great numbers, but to underline the fact that jazz was not born in the honky-tonk. It went there because it provided work with remuneration: if society balls had been such that they required Bolden's powerful cornet instead of string quartets then jazz would have flourished in the 'dicty' houses of class among the New Orleans upper set. Whatever theories we may hold as to the origins of the music, the fact remains that jazz, like any other art, has followed its sponsors. In the Middle Ages Michelangelo and Raphael painted for their sponsors, the Church; but their Florentine art was eclipsed when the merchant class of Venice sponsored Titian and Giorgione. Similarly jazz went to the vice district when it offered regular and well-paid employment – and moved on to Chicago, St Louis, and Los Angeles when Storyville closed down.

Bolden sailed through his musical career in the most enviable of fashions. All the girls flocked around him on marches when it was a privilege indeed to be honoured as coat-carrier; and sometimes in dance halls he was mobbed in true bobby-soxer tradition. But women and overwork eventually went to his head, literally. The man who could blow his horn so loudly that he could be heard two miles away on a quiet night, finally went insane in a spectacular manner at a Mardi Gras Carnival and was committed to the East Louisiana State Hospital in 1907, where he died in 1931, completely unknown and unwanted by the world at large, but not forgotten by such as Jelly Roll Morton, who, in 1939, sang

> I thought I heard Buddy Bolden say
> You're Nasty but you're Dirty; Take it away!
> You're Terrible! You're Awful! Take it away!
> I thought I heard him say . . .

*

After King Bolden's death there was a struggle for the vacated throne. Many bands had followed his lead in triumphing over academic failings by a combination of sheer technique, inspired improvisation and memory. John Robichaux carried on, but he still had many rivals. Frank Dusen, trombonist with Bolden's band, together with some other members, formed the Eagle Band. They had brown military uniforms, like most of the brass bands of the period, and soon enrolled Bunk Johnson, who had played with Bolden from 1895 to 1898. Bunk was an accomplished cornet player, but immediately after the King's departure he was not at the top of the ladder.

The man who succeeded Bolden was FREDDIE KEPPARD (*1883–1932*). He began by playing violin, or 'alley fiddle' as the rougher style was called, but soon took up the cornet, with which he could better demonstrate his prowess, and from then on fairly rocketed to the forefront. By 1903 he was playing with the best and it was his Olympia Band which became the natural successor to Bolden's. An exuberant technician, he is said to have sounded sometimes like a trombone, yet could exploit the higher register, going above high E. Like Bolden he was tremendously powerful, robust, rough, almost coarse, yet, strangely enough, he associated with the more finished Creole musicians of downtown New Orleans. Mutt Carey has this to say about King Keppard:

When Freddie got on the street it was the King on the street, Louis will tell you that. Keppard was the first man I ran into in a band battle, and it was just my hard luck to run into the King. It was certainly an experience for me I'll never forget. Freddie had a lot of ideas and a big tone too. When he hit a note you knew it was hit. I mean he had a beautiful tone and he played with so much feeling too. Yes, he had everything; he was ready in every respect. Keppard could play any kind of song good. Technique, attack, tone and ideas were all there. He didn't have very much formal musical education but he sure was a natural musician. All you had to do was play a number for him once and he had it . . . he was a natural![1]

ALPHONSE PICOU was the clarinettist of Keppard's Olympia Band, the same Picou who first played the clarinet part of *High Society* in Perez's Imperial Band. Taken from a standard street parade march, it became a test piece for all clarinettists from then onwards. Picou composed many other classics – if composition is the word: it's a dangerous one to use in connexion with classic jazz. It meant virtually that Picou set out the broad outlines of a

1. *Jazz Music*, Vol. 3, No. 4, edited Max Jones.

number and the rest of the band picked it up; it was a case of variation upon the tried themes, the introduction of new tunes. Keppard, of course, being Keppard, took about five seconds to pick up anything, blasting out a new tune on the first playing as if he had known it all his life.

When Picou left the Olympia Band, Louis Nelson Delisle, known as BIG EYE LOUIS NELSON (*1885–1949*) replaced him. He too had played with Manual Perez and:

... his C clarinet inspired many of the younger players, including Jimmie Noone, Sidney Bechet, and Johnny Dodds. A little on the French side in appearance, genial in a quiet way, Louis became a changed person when he put a clarinet to his lips. He had a big tone and while he played in the fluid style characteristic of New Orleans, he brought to it a broad inventiveness. As with Bechet, he had a vibrato that was in keeping with his sweeping crescendoes and just a touch of blue quality. While he played he seemed oblivious of the smoke-filled room and of the dancers. He sat hunched forward, his clarinet pointed towards the floor.[1]

The validity of Bud Scott's claim that Keppard's band was the greatest of them all is readily understood, when the other members of the Olympians are listed. Trombonists were either Joseph Petit, who also managed the band, and the fabulous ZUE ROBERTSON (*1891–1943*). Zue never settled down for very long in any one place, making frequent road trips all over the States with Wild West shows and the like. But when he did stay in New Orleans for a while on a regular engagement there was no trombonist to approach him in technique or feeling for the jazz style. Zue caught up again with Keppard in his travels in 1917 and played at the de Luxe Café in Chicago. Five years later he made his only visit to the recording studios, with Jelly Roll Morton.

The rhythmic part of this band was the forerunner of all rhythm *sections:* John Vigne combined a flamboyant showmanship with a tremendous drum rhythm – perhaps he was the first to establish the four-beat rhythm which is the foundation of New Orleans style playing – contrary to the sneering references that are made to its being a 'two-beat' music. John soon played himself out, however, with the usual ailment, wine and women, and later Louis Cottrell, Ernest Tripania, and Zeno Baltimore were the strong men of the Olympian rhythm. Louis Keppard, Bud Scott, and Willie Santiago were the guitarists, Billy Marrero, Pops Foster, and John Lindsay the bassists at various times. It is worth noting at this

1. *Jazzmen.* Fred Ramsey, Charles E. Smith.

point that the rhythm section of what was probably the greatest New Orleans band of the early classic period consisted of guitar, string or brass bass, and drums. The guitar was invariably preferred to the banjo; the bass was a matter of personal preference or it was determined by the need, either for concerts or for marching; and there was seldom a piano.

Eddie Venson, trombone, Lorenzo Tio Jr. and Sidney Bechet, clarinets, were others who played with Keppard in the old Olympia days. With so much talent in rivalry for the five places to back Keppard, it is not hard to believe Bud Scott's claim that this was the greatest band of them all.

Actually, Keppard's greatest period was when he went on tour all over America with the Original Creole Ragtime Band.[1] This band was organized in 1911 in California by Bill Johnson, one of the earliest string bass players, who is reputed to have discovered the plucking and slapping technique by accident one day in Shreveport when his bow broke. Bill's brother, the versatile Dink, played drums for the Creole Band and Norwood Williams was the guitarist. But the backbone of the band was recruited from New Orleans in the persons of Eddie Venson, Keppard, and GEORGE BAQUET (*1870–1949*).

Baquet was a veteran already; he was one of the early members of John Robichaux's first band and had played with Manuel Perez's Imperial Band as well as with Keppard. He was an expert legitimate musician with a finished technique and excelled in executing a beautiful melodic line, full of expression, his E Flat clarinet a perfect foil for Keppard's inspired variations. Unfortunately, the only recorded band work of George Baquet is a session with Jelly Roll Morton which came about ten years after the Creoles disbanded and then only by the coincidence that he had settled down in Philadelphia, just across the river from Victor's recording studios at Camden, New Jersey.[2]

To get back to the Original Creole Orchestra; they barnstormed their way across America well before the white Brown's Band left New Orleans for Chicago. As Charles Payne Rogers puts it, 'Crowds of Chicagoans fell out when the Creoles included the South Side in their tour, and thus an important beachhead of hot music was established.' They would probably have been the first jazz band to record, for Victor offered them a date in 1916

1. Note that the terms 'Creole' and 'Ragtime' were the predecessors of 'Jazz'.
2. *Tank Town Bump*. J. R. Morton and R.H.P. HMV JF. 56.

but Keppard refused on the grounds that everybody would steal their music; Victor got the Original Dixieland Jazz Band on the rebound.

The Creoles finally disbanded in 1918, by which time only Keppard and Bill Johnson of the original band and Jimmie Noone, who had replaced Baquet, were left. Keppard was no longer King; Oliver had by now usurped his position, but he was still a fine player and had no difficulty in getting jobs, with Sugar Johnnie, with Doc Cook and Lil Armstrong. But before long Freddie Keppard drank himself to death.

Few identified records remain to testify to the quality of his playing; the best of these, Stockyard Strut/Salty Dog (Jazz Collector L.8), while giving evidence of the rough tone and attack, does not preserve for posterity the power and range for which Keppard's cornet was famous.

*

The account of Keppard's career has taken us beyond the pale of New Orleans, both geographically and chronologically, and so we must recapitulate somewhat and view the position down in the Crescent City when the Original Creole Orchestra tempted three of the stars away from their firmament, leaving in 1911, as Bolden's incarceration had done four years before, a state of flux in the jazz band fraternity, with several bands and musicians vying for supremacy.

There were the existing bands. ARMAND PIRON, a violin player, led a band which was modelled on the style of Robichaux's band of earlier years. Piron was a barber, like Bolden, but his talent lay more in organizing and managing than in an individual jazz technique. Later, he went into the music-publishing business with Clarence Williams and his band which recorded for Columbia in 1923 included such old-time names as Pete Bocage, trumpet, John Lindsay, trombone, Lorenzo Tio, clarinet, Steve Lewis, piano and Louis Cottrell, drums.

The Bolden Band was still in existence, under Frank Dusen's leadership, and called the Eagle Band. Bob Lyons and Brock Mumford were still with Dusen and so was BUNK JOHNSON (1879–1949). William Gary Johnson, to give him his full name, was a fine cornettist; he had come up the hard way, playing second to Bolden and having his cornet knocked out of his mouth if he played the wrong notes; yet he had good taste; he was not raucous and coarse, like many other New Orleans born men. His range was not remarkable, but he played in a fluid style. In his own words, with no false sense of modesty, Bunk says: 'When I became the age of fifteen years old I was good to go and I really have been going ever since. Now for faking and playing by head I was hard to beat.' This must have been so; otherwise Bolden would never have tolerated him. A fair assessment of his rank in New Orleans trumpeters would be that of Bud Scott, who says Bunk 'was a good trumpet player – no two questions about that. He was popular but didn't have half the popularity of Keppard or Perez.'[1] The Eagle Band played through a halcyon period; work of all kinds was plentiful. There were marches around town for advertising; funeral parades, when, after the mourning and the dirges on the way to the cemetery, the return from the grave would be marked by the hottest of music; and picnics in the summer months in the amusement centre out on the shores of Lake Pontchartrain. The district called Milneberg contained a prosperous area which must have been something approaching the modern conception of a holiday camp, in which there was always a demand for the sort of music which was conducive to dancing and relaxation. Though the lake front of Pontchartrain has since changed its aspect, the tune *Milenburg Joys* recalls past memories of the heyday of classic jazz bands such as the Eagle.

After a few years with this band, Bunk, like many other New Orleans musicians before and after him, got the wanderlust and toured America. By a turn of fate, he never visited Chicago, where, of all places, there was most chance of his building for himself a great musical career. Instead, he gradually withdrew into obscurity and, in the same year that his former leader Buddy Bolden died, he retired to the Louisiana rice-growing centre of New Iberia, a small enough place to bury him completely. Not until 1938 was Bunk traced, by Fred Ramsey, Jr., on the suggestion of Louis Armstrong, and then the name Bunk Johnson became the symbol of the great New Orleans jazz revival of the 1940's, the story of which is told in Chapter Thirteen.

Mention should be made of two of the many Carey Brothers, Jack and Tom. JACK CAREY was from the brass band school, having played with Henry Allen's Brass Band in Algiers, just across the river from New Orleans. He became the leader of his own band, the Crescent, which had at one time, in addition to the Carey brothers, Sidney Bechet (of whom much more later) as clarinettist, Jim Johnson, bass, Charles Moore, guitar, and Ernest

1. *Record Changer*. September 1947.

Rogers, drums. In his repertoire was a number derived from an old French quadrille, which was known vaguely as *Jack Carey*. This tune was, in fact, the same one that was later copyrighted by Nick La Rocca as *Tiger Rag*.[1] It is doubtful whether Jack ever thought his tune might be played, albeit adulterated, by the Boston Promenade Orchestra.

Jack's younger brother, Tom, known as PAPA MUTT CAREY (*1891–1948*), played a cornet, and his early career contained one or two set-backs, not the least of which was the occasion when, in a cutting contest aboard two wagons, he was 'cut to pieces' by the accomplished Keppard. But Tom made good; apart from his all-round ensemble playing he was clever with muted effects and it may well be that King Oliver himself copied some of Tom's tricks. He was associated for the most important period of his jazz life with Kid Ory, with whom he played in New Orleans and, in the early 1920's, in California, when the Spikes Brothers recorded the Ory Band. Papa Mutt was lost to jazz for many years after this, until the Ory Band took part in the great Revival movement.

Then there was OSCAR CELESTIN (*born 1880*), known also as 'Papa', who played quite regularly at the Tuxedo Hall with a band which included, in 1910, Peter Bocage on cornet, George Filhe, trombone, Alphonse Picou and Lorenzo Tio, Sr., clarinets, and Louis Cottrell, drums, all good exponents of the New Orleans style. After their contract with the Tuxedo came to an abrupt end when the manager was shot in a brawl, Celestin and William Ridgely, a trombonist, perpetuated the name of the Tuxedo by adopting it as the name of their band and many were the great jazzmen, even Louis Armstrong himself, who played with it. Kid Shots Madison was his regular trumpeter for several years, recorded with Papa in New Orleans in 1924, and was still with the band in 1946. Papa was a leader, a composer in a small way and a player; his Tuxedo Orchestra has been in existence, with few gaps of complete inactivity, from 1910 to this day; and that in itself is a striking tribute to the sincerity of the leader and his belief in his kind of music.

But in the period which followed Keppard's departure with the Creole Orchestra in 1911, though Bunk Johnson may have reached the top for a short while and Carey, Perez, Piron, Celestin, and others received attention, one band stood out above the rest in popularity – that of EDWARD 'KID' ORY (*born 1889*).

1. Jelly Roll Morton also lays claim to the composition of this tune.

Like several of the great pioneers, Ory was a native of Louisiana, but not of New Orleans, coming from La Place, about twenty miles away. While Bolden was in his prime, Ory was still playing in rustic bands in his home town, visiting the city at weekends so as to listen to the King. It was not long before his ambitions became realities and in 1910 he brought his first ragtime band to New Orleans, with Lawrence Duhé on clarinet, Louis Mathieu on cornet, Joseph Mathieu on guitar, Alfred Lewis on bass and Eddie Robertson, drums. Changes were made in the band, as happens with all jazz bands, but the changes that were made in Ory's Brownskin Babies were more than mere substitution; they were almost major events in the jazz calendar.

After Lawrence Duhé dropped out all the greatest clarinettists played with Ory. Big Eye Louis Nelson, Sidney Bechet, [1] Johnny Dodds [2], and Jimmie Noone, [3] all were great. If any critic or enthusiast of clarinet playing is asked to-day who was the best of them all, the chances are he will name one of those four. Dodds had only just bought his instrument when Ory heard rumours about him, gave him a trial and took him on, in the Come Clean Hall over in Gretna, at top salary. When Dodds moved northward, Ory found Jimmy Noone playing in trios and quartets, but Jimmie soon settled down under the influence of Ory's great flair for ensemble work. When Noone followed Dodds to Chicago, Kid Ory took on Wade Whaley and later George Lewis; Wade is one of the great unrecognized jazzmen and George, of course, found fame thirty years later with Bunk Johnson's great rejuvenation.

The Brownskin Babies were no less fortunate in their choice of cornettists. As soon as Mathieu dropped out, in came Papa Mutt Carey; when Papa Mutt joined the Dodds brothers in Mack's Merrymakers, a touring vaudeville show, Kid Ory took on Joseph Oliver. When Joe Oliver, [4] crowned 'King' Oliver by Ory, made the Chicago journey in 1917, Ory found another trump card, a youngster in short trousers, one Louis Armstrong, [5] who stayed about a year, to be replaced by HENRY KID RENA.

Rena was not, perhaps, one of the greatest trumpet players, but he was good enough to take over Louis' chair, which was no mean test, even then. Rena played in and around New Orleans long after the Great Ones had left. Years afterwards, in between

1. See Chapter Seven.　　4. See Chapter Six.
2. See Chapter Six.　　　5. See Chapter Seven.
3. See Chapter Six.

bouts of illness, he took part in a remarkable recording session, a private one for the American Delta label, owned by Heywood Broun. The personnel included Big Eye Nelson and Alphonse Picou and the year was 1940; this was to be the first exciting taste of real New Orleans music to be experienced by the stalwarts of the revivalist movement of the decade which followed.

But to get back to Ory. Max Jones has written:

> Ory was never a virtuoso but he was unequalled as a band player. Not too happy in long solos he makes more out of a break than almost anyone, and enriches the music's bass harmonies, adding to the rhythmic strength when needed.

That, of course, is the essence of the trombone's part in New Orleans jazz and Kid Ory performed the role to perfection.

In 1918, when Storyville was closed down, Ory did not follow the custom by moving straight to Chicago. He preferred the climate of California and it was here that the Brownskin Babies settled for a while, with Papa Mutt back on cornet and Wade Whaley on clarinet. They were an immediate success; Keppard had already broken the ice, as it were, whilst on tour with the Creole Orchestra, and in fact there was a jazz band called the Black and Tans who were making a good thing out of the new music. But not after Ory hit the Pacific coast; experienced as they were in the technique of cutting contests, Ory's boys just wiped the Black and Tans off the map.

And here in Los Angeles, on Santa Monica Boulevard, Ory and his band made the first records by a New Orleans coloured band. Let Ory himself recall the occasion:

> In June 1921, the Spikes Brothers hired me to make some records on their Sunshine label. I made a special trip down from Oakland where my band was playing to make the records. They were made out on Santa Monica Boulevard near the beach. The studio was just a small room, nothing fancy. We made them all in one day – one afternoon. They put a mattress under Dink Johnson's feet, he was stomping so hard. We made six sides so quickly we didn't know who was there, playing each tune just once. We didn't get excited. We got fifteen or twenty dollars apiece and expenses for travelling. I got four dollars royalty check from *Ory's Creole Trombone*.[1]/[2]

Kid Ory claims another first too; he made radio broadcasts in 1923, surely the first airing by an authentic New Orleans group.

1. *Record Changer*. November 1947.
2. *Ory's Creole Trombone*: Ory's Sunshine Orchestra. Jazz Collector L. 33.

Two years later, however, when the band were not exactly achieving nation-wide acclaim, he finally went the same way as the others, to Chicago, where he joined King Oliver's Creole Jazz Band.

The remainder of Ory's story belongs to other chapters in the book. And here we must bring to a reluctant end the account of the great jazz pioneers. For great they indeed were. The carefree yet vital instincts, the dominant personalities and creative genius of these early exponents of the new improvised music started a movement which has spread throughout the globe. They brought about the miracle of the rhythmic foundation for the melodic instrumental synthesis of the human voice which matured into the form we now know as jazz.

As Jelly Roll Morton said in another context, they 'played more music than you can write down on paper'.

CHAPTER SIX

Exodus from New Orleans

IN the last chapter the history of the very early days of jazz in New Orleans has been dealt with, in chronological order as far as overlapping of the life stories of individual musicians has permitted. It began, as all jazz histories must begin, with Manuel Perez and Buddy Bolden. Then Bolden went mad and Keppard was crowned King. King Keppard's departure to Los Angeles left behind several contesting bands: Piron, the Eagle Band with Bunk Johnson, Jack Carey's Band, Papa Celestin, all of which had to give way to Kid Ory's Brownskin Babies, who were supreme from about 1913 until the closing of Storyville in 1918. The account of Ory's activities until he went to Chicago in 1925 completes the saga of the pioneers, though, in the scope allowed by this book, it has been far from exhaustive and by no means detailed. Considerable research has been undertaken in order to sift fact from legend, and, having satisfactorily come to a decision, I have tried to present these facts in a brief yet readable manner.

An attempt has been made to retain a sense of proportion in the assessment of individual values; and a sense of perspective in the linking of events. The conclusion has been reached, for example, that John Robichaux was not such a fool as many reporters have led us to believe, that Bunk Johnson, leader as he may have been of the revivalist movement in the 1940s, [1] was a trumpeter of only equal importance at most to half a dozen others, and that Manuel Perez's failure to make any gramophone records (as far as is known) is the only reason why he has never been acclaimed the greatest of the pioneers.

The fourth main conclusion which has been reached is that the popular conception that King Oliver was one of the *great pioneers* of jazz is fallacious. King he may have been; his greatness as a cornettist is not disputed – as a later section of this chapter will

1. See Chapter Thirteen.

show; but on the evidence his achievements in New Orleans do not warrant his description as a pioneer in the *great* category.

Oliver was born in 1885, and though he played in a children's brass band while in his teens, he did not enter a jazz group until around 1905. For the next ten years, roughly, he improved, and when he joined Ory's Brownskin Babies in 1914 or 1915 he was good enough to take over from Papa Mutt Carey. It was only after he joined Ory that he eventually became 'King' Oliver and shortly afterwards he went to Chicago, where he found fame. Bunk Johnson says 'Now Joe was a poor cornet player for a long time'[1]; Ory said about Joe when the latter joined the Brownskin Babies, 'He was rough as pig iron'[2]; and witnesses like Preston Jackson affirm that in the early part of his career he was only one of many good trumpeters. If, therefore, Oliver were considered great as a pioneer, it would be only reasonable to include also Willie Hightower, Tig Chambers, Buddy Petit, Sidney Desvigne, and a host of other lesser known men. Joe Oliver may have achieved greatness for a fleeting period in the Crescent City; he was certainly not born great, as was Buddy Bolden; and so for the purposes of this book his life and the analysis of his contribution to jazz will be dealt with in this chapter, which takes in the period when King Oliver achieved greatness in Chicago – and even posthumously, when he had further greatness thrust upon him.

*

The occasional movement northwards early in the twentieth century in the general direction of Chicago by some New Orleans jazz musicians became a flood in 1918 when the cabarets and sporting houses of the Delta City closed down. It was a bold step indeed on the part of the United States Naval authorities to get the closing of Storyville sanctioned from Washington. For years the place had been accepted as a necessary evil and the local New Orleans councillors, who had never been completely free from corruption of various kinds, had seen no reason why they should put hundreds of flourishing concerns out of business. The sudden order from higher authority came as quite a shock, therefore, and the watchword of the day became 'quit New Orleans'. Rumours had already filtered down from Chicago of better living conditions, and when all the jazzmen were suddenly deprived

1. *Jazzmen.* Fred Ramsey and C. E. Smith.
2. *Record Changer.* November 1947.

of their main source of income they naturally thought of the Windy City at the bottom of Lake Michigan.

There were other contributory factors to this general exodus. Firstly there was the statistical fact that Chicago is a much bigger city than New Orleans. Just as in England musicians gravitate from smaller towns to London, so musicians were inclined to seek better terms of employment in the thriving city of the north – where the Slave Code had never been a law, written or otherwise. Secondly, a few years after the closing down of Storyville, just when, perhaps, many were beginning to rehabilitate themselves, one of the basic industries of the South – cotton production – received a severe set-back. In 1921, the boll-weevil, the little quarter-inch-long insect which had been the scourge of the cotton-fields ever since it trekked across the Rio Grande in the late nineteenth century, found its appetite and consumed half the cotton crop. It was three years before production reached anything like normality and, during this time, hundreds of thousands of people, white and coloured, moved northward in search of other and perhaps better employment. The shift of focus of jazz from New Orleans to Chicago was but a part of a wide transfer of population; this, coupled with the growing popularity and demand for music of the jazz type in the Chicago of the Roaring Twenties, gave the necessary direction of flow to the music from Storyville.

The majority of the musicians lived a precarious life financially and few could afford to speculate on the train fare and the chance of a permanent job in Chicago. Fortunately for them, however, there was a ready-made stepping-stone to the north – the fleet of Mississippi river-boats, which forged their way far into the heart of the continent. New Orleans was the southern terminal point for the boats and furthermore was a base during the winter months. Traffic on the river was less from about November until April, and during this time, when the weather was quite warm in the South, they were used for excursions, mainly at night. When the work of the city was finished, the dockers, porters, and warehouse-men would take their girls on the excursion boats, invariably fitted with large dance-floors, with a band in attendance. The musicians left over from Storyville found work on the boats during the winter and, as often as not, stayed with them when they resumed their longer trips up the Mississippi. In this way the new music spread to practically every stopping place of note, Memphis, St Louis, Davenport, distant Minneapolis, even to the cities on

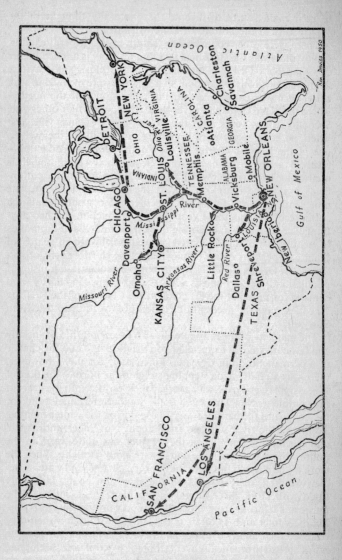

the larger tributaries of 'Old Man River', Omaha and Kansas City on the Missouri, Pittsburg on the Ohio and Shreveport on the Red River.

The Mississippi paddle-wheeler, it must be remembered, is an institution peculiar to the U.S.A. Its business is not only to carry people up and down the river but also to provide entertainment at the stopping places *en route*. At these halts, places with romantic-sounding names, Baton Rouge, Natchez, Vicksburg, Arkansas City, Memphis, Cairo, Paducah, right on to St Louis and beyond, the boats would pull in for excursion trips, staying an evening, a day, or even many weeks at a big city like St Louis.

It will be remembered that, immediately after the Abolition in 1865, one of the main occupations of the ex-slaves was railroad building, this being the reason why the theme of the railroad is common in Negro song and even in jazz. St Louis was almost like a promised land to the embittered Southern Negroes; it has been eloquently stated that the Negro would rather be a lamp-post on Targee Street, St Louis, than Mayor of any city of Alabama or Georgia.[1] Here, in the city where forty-two railroads meet, he was essentially a free man and money was more easily earned. There was no lack of a musical environment, for a high proportion of the three-quarter-million population was of French and German extraction and consequently musically minded. Not far away, as a matter of interest, in the Ozark region to the south-west, were the original settlers who still used Elizabethan words, and sang in a distinctive, archaic ballad style. Musical knowledge was of a generally higher standard, technically, than in New Orleans – Barlett D. Simms has remarked: 'St Louis musicians, both white and coloured, were used to carrying their portfolios around, could read music on sight as well as give with the jazz hokum.'[2]

Against this background Captain Joseph Strekfus, owner of the big river-boats, decided around 1910 that he wanted some bands on his boats which could not only read music but could put more life and rhythm into their playing. He had heard of the vitality and drive of the music down in New Orleans and he decided to try to assemble the best musicians available. FATE MARABLE (*1890–1947*), pianist and leader of one of Strekfus's bands, was appointed chief talent-spotter and it was through him that many of the famous jazz musicians came up the Mississippi. It was

1. *They Seek a City*, by Arna Bontemps and Jack Conroy.
2. *Record Changer*. November 1945.

Marable who, in 1918, finally lured Louis Armstrong away from
his home town, to play on the *Dixie Belle* with, incidentally, one
of the first of the coloured river-boat orchestras; their predecessors having been almost entirely white.

The sort of impression that Fate Marable's star-studded[1]
orchestra made on the night life of St Louis is well described by
Louis Armstrong:

It was the first time that coloured 'cats' had ever come North to play.
The people learned to like us right away. Every night, at the top of the
programme 'Fate' would swing us into the *St Louis Blues* and they
would go crazy about our music. It was good all right. Just a few days
after we arrived the boys in the band began to get invitations to parties
in the city and some of the best players were invited to be guest per-
formers with local bands in the big cabarets. We usually had some
place to go every night when we got in from the evening trip.[2]

Yes, jazz was gaining popularity all right, and nowhere more
than in St Louis. There were many good bands, but unfortunately
it is hard to assess their undoubted quality because few of them
recorded. The 'Mound City' did not possess a recording industry
on the scale of Chicago and the fact that many of the bands
played up and down the river meant that they were seldom available. What few records were made are now rare and the only ones
reissued during recent years have not, as yet, reached the English
catalogues.

Marable's bands were composed of rolling stones, and his star
men, Louis Armstrong, Johnny and Baby Dodds, Boyd Atkins,
Pops Foster, Johnny St Cyr, and Joe Howard finally rolled on to
Chicago. In St Louis, however, there were several bands who
could hold their own against impressive personnels such as the
Strekfus Line provided. CHARLIE CREATH, a cornet player, soon
made a name for himself, being engaged in 1910 by Strekfus to
play in his boat the *St Paul* for the season. Barlett Simms says
that Creath's Band was the finest to play on the river and a glance
through the names shows that this is probably no idle claim;
Cecil Scott, clarinet, Leonard Davis, trumpet, Charles Lawson,
trombone, Zutty Singleton, drums, and Lonnie Johnson, guitar,
all played with Creath. Simms recalls the occasion when Fletcher
Henderson and McKinney's Cotton Pickers were engaged in a

1. Armstrong, Norman Mason, trumpets, Sam Dutrey, clarinet, Baby
Ridgely, trombone, Davey Jones, mellophone, Paul Dominguez, violin,
Johnny St Cyr, banjo, Pops Foster, bass, Baby Dodds, drums.
2. *Swing That Music*. Louis Armstrong.

battle of music at the Coliseum Theatre. Creath's Band happened
to be in town that evening, and, spotted by the audience, were
persuaded to play during the intermission. Henderson and the
Cotton Pickers came second and third in that competition; they
had nothing to approach Creath's *Market Street Stomp*.

DEWEY JACKSON (*born St Louis 1910*), was a fine trumpeter
who played with Creath and Marable and later led his own band
for the Strekfus Line. His recordings were limited to one session
for Vocalion in 1926, but his *Capitol Blues*, which has been re-
issued on American Brunswick, proves him a good musician – as
good as dozens of the much recorded trumpeters. Another good
cornettist who led a river-boat band was ED ALLEN, the same
who later played on so many of Clarence Williams's records.
His Whispering Gold Band, playing in St Louis in the early
1920s, included Eugene Sedric and Walter Thomas, saxophones,
Pops Foster, bass, and Sidney Desvigne, trumpet. It will be
noticed in all these St Louis bands that a reed section has added
itself to the brass and rhythm. A direct result of the merging of
the more legitimate approaches to the music with the bold individualism of New Orleans, it is probably the main reason why
the brand of jazz from St Louis never settled down to a sound and
robust style good enough to stand the test of time. The place of
this city in the annals of jazz music has been so associated with
ragtime that its separate development of band music has been
overlooked. Nevertheless, this book is content to leave it at that;
for no resurrections of the past can obscure the fact that Chicago
was the focal point of jazz in the early 1920s and that, when the
uncertainty in the jazzmen's world which followed the closing
down of Storyville had cleared, it was to America's second metro-
polis that they made their eventual pilgrimage.

Some bands, white bands playing the staccato 'dixieland' style,
had reached Chicago as early as 1915 and there had been spasmodic visits from Perez and other coloured bands. The Windy
City was just beginning to acquire a liking for this new kind of
music and it was a potential audience of three million souls which
brought Tom Brown's Band up from the Delta. A strange twist of
fate that the white copyists and adulterators of the pure style
should have been instrumental in popularizing the true music, but
popularize it they did. The dance hall patrons found bands like
Tom Brown's to their liking during the frantic period occasioned
by the end of the First World War. They had even given the music
its name, Jazz, and the Original Dixieland Jazz Band had re-

corded the first tunes, to the delight of the record-buying public, who had not, as yet, the radio as a means of musical diversion. That first O.D.J.B. session had a profound effect upon the spread of jazz appreciation and it was not necessarily a good one. Being the first record of this new music, millions of copies of *Tiger Rag* were sold, and the first impression created thereby was quickly accepted as the authentic jazz. Even now, thirty years later, any fast and untutored music passes as jazz, especially when accompanied by the symbolical wearing of funny hats.

But one man soon put an end to any misapprehensions there may have been as to which race, white or coloured, was the true exponent of Hot Jazz. JOSEPH 'KING' OLIVER (*1885–1938*) hit Chicago in 1917 and for the next eight years or so he was undisputed King of Jazz anywhere in America. As has been noted at the beginning of this chapter, though King Oliver came to the throne while still in New Orleans, he really belonged to a second generation of early jazzmen and was not one of the first pioneers. For many years he was a moderate player and his own bands, such as the Magnolia, were not so good that he could afford to refuse an offer by Kid Ory when it was made. After he joined the Brownskin Babies, however, he made great progress, mastering all the styles and moods of New Orleans hot playing and introducing some original methods and techniques of his own, chiefly with an assortment of mutes. He and Papa Mutt Carey were the top men at muted effects and the latter gives Joe full credit for introducing them. He says:

He was the greatest freak trumpet player I ever knew. He did most of his playing with cups, glasses, buckets, and mutes. He was the best gut-bucket man I ever heard. I called him freak because the sounds he made were not made by the valves but through these artificial devices. [1]

Joe came to Chicago when Bill Johnson (who, it will be remembered, had organized the Original Creole Orchestra) sent for him with the offer of a steady job at the Royal Gardens Café. But the rival band over at the Dreamland Café had the same high opinion of Oliver and they decided to try to persuade Joe to play for them. There must have been some tense moments at the railway station when two reception committees met the King off the train, but the *impasse* was eventually settled by a delightful compromise. Joe played for both bands. At the Royal Gardens he played with Johnson, Jimmie Noone, Eddie Venson, Paul

1. *Jazz Music*. Vol. 3, No. 4. Ed. Max Jones.

Barbarin on drums and Lottie Taylor, piano; at the Dreamland he took over the trumpet chair from the debauched Sugar Johnny to front Lawrence Dewey and Sidney Bechte. Shortly after winning a battle of cornets, Joe was offered a permanent engagement at the Dreamland within two years of leaving the South. In this short time he had proved himself King in Chicago as well as in New Orleans; he was acknowledged better than the once supreme Keppard.

King Oliver's Creole Jazz Band opened at the Dreamland with Honoré Dutrey on trombone, Ed Garland, string bass, Lottie Taylor, piano, Minor Hall, drums, and Jimmy Noone, clarinet. And thus began the life of the band which has influenced jazz more than any other, if only because it was the first to make gramophone records of the real music. It has probably been noticed that it was the custom in the New Orleans style groups to have a female pianist, if they were to have a pianist at all. There may well be a psychological reason for this; when the bands accepted the innovation of a fourth rhythm instrument they probably considered that the comparatively simple chording required of the piano could be executed equally well by a girl who would also provide feminine attraction; also piano players of real value were able to maintain solo jobs, paid as solo artists and would consequently be loath to accept usual band rates. In these days there were seldom any male pianists who regarded themselves as bandsmen. They were either artists in their own right, like Jimmie Blythe, or Earl Hines – or they were women.[1]

This was the Chicago of the Roaring Twenties; the Chicago of 'Scarface' Al Capone, of Prohibition and liquor rackets; of 'speakeasies', easy money earned or chiselled and money extravagantly spent. Dance halls, night clubs and 'dives' sprung up in hundreds and here in Chicago's 'Black Belt' were duplicated similar conditions to those the jazz musicians had left behind in New Orleans, with the difference, however, that life was even more hectic. The jazzman started work at 7 o'clock in the evening and finished around 7 o'clock next morning. Oliver's first band played at the Dreamland until 1 a.m. and then moved on to the Pekin Cabaret, with its large gangster patronage, where they continued to play until morning.

This was in 1920 and for the next few years the story of King Oliver's Creole Jazz Band is one of success following success. As a form of recuperation after the broken bottles and shot-guns of

1. See Jelly Roll Morton's remarks in Chapter Three.

the Pekin, the band went on a triumphant visit, in May 1921, to California. With Johnny Dodds, clarinet, and pianist Lil Hardin, a bright young girl from Memphis who had studied music at Fiske University, they played a six months' contract at the Pergola Dancing Pavilion in San Francisco. When Minor Hall fell out with Oliver, Baby Dodds was persuaded to leave the river-boats, where he was still with Marable, to join his brother in Los Angeles. The Creole Jazz Band was right at the top of the tree; many a musician would have given his right hand to play with it; it was an honour to be asked to join the band and there were remarkably few changes in personnel; Joe himself was not a hard man to get on with and he encouraged many musicians on their way up; but he was a stern disciplinarian, believing at all times that the success of his band depended on social harmony within. He once wrote the following, which could well be a criterion for young jazz musicians of to-day, to be hung, suitably framed, in the spot over the bed where 'Home Sweet Home' used to be:

I mean I wants you to be a band man, and a band man only, and do all you can for the welfare of the band in the line of playing your best at all times.[1]

King Oliver set Los Angeles on fire, according to the *Chicago Defender*, and was offered a fabulous salary to stay on; but the band were a little homesick for the old Windy City and back they came to the Royal Gardens Café, by this time renamed the Lincoln Gardens. It was a strange coincidence that the great liberator of the Negro slaves sixty years before should give his name to the scene of the greatest triumphs of Buddy Bolden, jazz King of Lincoln Park, New Orleans, and King Oliver, jazz King of Lincoln Gardens, Chicago. The Lincoln Gardens, on 31st Street, was an ugly, ornate place, but with the Creole Jazz Band in residence it became the mecca of all the enthusiasts of hot music in Chicago. Then when Joe sent for Louis Armstrong, all the way from the Tuxedo in New Orleans, the management had to reserve a section for musicians and listeners as well as the space for dancers. How parallel is this phenomenon in 1922 with the state of things at the London Jazz Club in 1952, where a similar division of listeners and dancers exists!

There has been speculation about the motives which prompted King Oliver to send for Louis Armstrong (whose full story is told in Chapter Seven), in view of the fact that young Louis quickly emulated, and then surpassed his leader in the never-ending

1. Quoted from *Jazzmen*. Fred Ramsay, C. E. Smith.

battle for the highest honours. The King has often been quoted as inferring that as long as Louis was with him he could not be hurt by him; but a study of Oliver's character does not support such an attitude on his part. The reason is far more simple; Oliver knew a good man and naturally wanted him to be in his band. When Armstrong was blowing such horn that he became too great even for the Creole Jazz Band, there is no evidence that any animosity ever occurred at the break; if Joe was loath to lose Louis, it was just the natural reluctance of any band leader to let a good man go if he could persuade him to stay.

But while the two great cornet players were together they played some memorable music. Louis was no less a second cornet than a soloist or ensemble player and some of the two-cornet breaks that electrified dancers and listeners alike were indeed masterpieces of timed accuracy, drive, and polish. When musicians talk to-day of playing by ear they seldom think in terms of the tremendous standard set by Oliver. He and Louis would work out a break or a bridge passage in a matter of seconds, during the playing of the actual number. Jelly Roll Morton has said: 'My God, what a memory that man had. I used to play a piano chorus, something like *King Porter* or *Tomcat*, and Oliver would take the thing and remember every note. You can't find men like that to-day.'

It was while at the Lincoln Gardens that King Oliver and his Creole Jazz Band made their greatest contribution to the appreciation of jazz music. Within the space of eight months in 1923 were waxed thirty-seven titles for four different record labels, Paramount, Gennett, Okeh, and Columbia. These were the first records made in the genuine New Orleans jazz style and nearly all the discs have since become collectors' pieces, valuable not only for their rarity but also for their concise exposition of the style, despite the defects of acoustic recording. They have become so much the criterion of all that is desirable in collective improvisation, hot tone, jazz harmony, and counterpoint, that it has long been the greatest compliment of all to tell a jazz band that it sounds just like the Oliver record.

The band which made these fabulous records consisted of Oliver and Armstrong, cornets; Dutrey, trombone; Johnny Dodds (succeeded by Buster Bailey and Jimmy Noone), clarinets; Lil Hardin, piano; Baby Dodds, drums; and Bill Johnson or Bud Scott on banjo. Fortunately for the English collector, sixteen of these sides are available still; their value for the purpose of studying the 'genuine article' is so great that all are listed below:

J–4

Dippermouth Blues/*Canal Street Blues*   Brunswick 02200
Mandy Lee Blues/*I'm Going Away*   Brunswick 02201
Just Gone/*Weather Bird Rag*   Brunswick 02202
Chimes Blues/*Froggie Moore*   Tempo R.6
Snake Rag   Tempo R.7
Southern Stomps   Jazz Collector L.4.
Krooked Blues/*Alligator Hop*   Tempo R.4
Mabel's Dream/*Riverside Blues*   Brunswick 03575
Zulu's Ball/*Workingman Blues*   Tempo R.29

For the beginner in jazz appreciation at least eight of these currently available sides are recommended as representing the epitome of all that is jazz; seven players welded together by the bond of almost telepathic mutual sensitivity which alone can produce jazz perfection. For the average jazz collector all except the last named coupling are indispensable; while the avid specialist collector will probably accept even the last two sides, which, dubbed as they are from a poor quality record, contain too high a percentage of extraneous noise for pleasant listening. [1]

It would be invidious to select any of these sides to say they are the best in jazz, but some deserve special mention. *Snake Rag* is a wonderful example of well-knit collective improvisation, each instrument taking its correct contrapuntal place in the ensemble. The whole record consists of one ensemble chorus after another, each successive chorus being different from the last and containing what might be test pieces of various aspects of New Orleans style. The lead is taken practically all the way through by the twin cornets of Oliver and Armstrong, Dodds interlaces a high, weaving clarinet part, taking breaks in the second chorus, whilst Dutrey's trombone plays the third bass part by means of wonderfully conceived glissandi. The whole effect, with the rhythm section supplying the rock-steady four beats to the bar, is a musical effect which is at once forceful, yet perfectly relaxed. This relaxation is a feature of all Oliver's records and one which is often overlooked by many an ambitious jazz student. Jazz is nothing if not relaxed; once a sense of strain creeps into the sound of the work then it ceases to be jazz. *Canal Street Blues*, named, of course, after the widest street in the world, in New Orleans, the street which divided 'uptown' from 'downtown', is equally perfect in demonstrating the effect of a driving ensemble possessing this relaxation. Such an atmosphere is created only by musicians

---

1. As a matter of interest only one copy of the original Gennett recording is known to exist.

until midnight at a pool-room for a pittance. In a series of letters reprinted in *Jazzmen*, written by the hand of the man who did more than any other to propagate the Real Jazz and who once commanded the highest salary in Chicago, the following extract summarizes the intense pathos of the situation: ' . . . I got teeth waiting for me at the dentist now . . . I've started a little dime saving bank. Got one dollar sixty in it and won't touch it. I am going to try and save myself a ticket to New York. . . .'

He never got his teeth; he never saved enough dimes for that ticket to New York. Instead high blood pressure caused rapidly failing health and he couldn't afford treatment. He died on 10 April 1938, and his sister could not even raise the money for a headstone for his grave.

*

Having proceeded chronologically to the end of King Oliver's tragic downfall we shall now go back to the early Chicago days and take a look at some of the other musicians who were there all the time pushing King Oliver; when the wealth of talent in the city at that time is seriously considered Oliver's greatness is imprinted on our minds all the more; that he was able to rise head and shoulders above such as Tommy Ladnier, Freddy Keppard, Sugar Johnny, and Manuel Perez is evidence enough of a tremendous talent.

TOMMY LADNIER[1] (*1900–39*) was born at Florenceville near New Orleans and started to play trumpet at a very early age, having to borrow instruments at first. He came to Chicago the same year as King Oliver and did not actually start playing professionally until he was twenty-one, quite an advanced age in these days of precociousness. He quickly rose to the forefront, playing at the Red Mill Café with Roy Palmer, trombone, William Baudraud, clarinet and Teddy Weatherford, piano. During this period he established for himself the title 'King of the Blues' and recorded many titles with a group led by pianist Lovie Austin, providing also the accompaniment to such Blues singers as Edmonia Henderson and Ida Cox. A great admirer of King Oliver, Ladnier displays in these records (most of them now rare, unfortunately), the same sense of control and relaxation which produced the beautiful phrasing which has made his reputation as a jazz trumpet player second only to Armstrong.

Unlike Armstrong, however, Ladnier's career did not follow a spectacular course which would have kept him in America's

1. Once spelt 'Ladinier'.

public eye. In 1925 he toured Europe with Sam Wooding; the next year he was in New York, playing in Billy Fowler's Orchestra, along with Benny Carter and Jimmy Harrison and in Fletcher Henderson's Orchestra with which he recorded. The records by Henderson are not recommended as good examples of New Orleans style; they are performances by a large commercial orchestra which plays, nevertheless, in the jazz idiom, featuring many good jazzmen as soloists. This is the usual feature of Henderson's discs – a string of solos loosely linked by arranged reed passages and supported by a rhythm section which rarely drives the group to great heights. Louis Armstrong's sojourn with this band is dealt with in Chapter Seven and the same remarks apply to Ladnier – his personal style, tone, powerful attack, and simplicity of melodic invention rise above the busyness of the arrangements. It is interesting to compare Ladnier's rougher tone with that of the purer Joe Smith in such records as *Clarinet Marmalade/Fidgety Feet* (Brunswick 02634) where, in company with Buster Bailey, clarinet, and Jimmy Harrison, trombone, he imparts considerable lift to the band.

In 1926 he returned to Europe again with Sam Wooding, playing in several countries and joining Noble Sissle in Paris. When he returned to New York with Sissle he soon left to form a smaller group, the New Orleans Footwarmers, with Sidney Bechet, but their style of playing did not suit the Savoy for very long and Tommy, in disgust, retired to the country for five years. It was not until the autumn of 1938 that he returned to New York again, to record some memorable sides with Bechet and Milton Mesirow. Organized by Hugues Panassié, the French critic, these records demonstrate fully the hot jazz tone, the relaxed simplicity of Ladnier's playing. Every note is hit with a firmness equalled only by Armstrong at his best and a terrific swing and tension is the only result possible. The following records are recommended as containing the best of Ladnier:

Weary Blues/When You and I Were Young, Maggie HMV B.9411
Really The Blues/Ja Da HMV B.9236
Royal Garden Blues/If You See Me Comin' HMV B.9416
Everybody Loves My Baby/Ain't Gonna Give Nobody None of My Jelly Roll HMV B.9447

Another well-conceived solo is to be heard on the Rosetta Crawford record of *Double Crossin' Papa* (Brunswick 03461), a complete chorus of beautiful relaxed jazz.

The records with Mesirow confounded many critics who had

not only forgotten Ladnier but never thought he would be able to 'come back'. On the threshold of a new career his ambition was never realized, for he died within two months of *Double Crossin'* *Papa*, his last record.

*

When King Oliver's Creole Jazz Band finally disintegrated, Papa Joe lost not only the greatest jazz trumpeter, but also the greatest clarinet player, JOHNNY DODDS (*1892–1940*). Another native of New Orleans, he was schooled by Big Eye Louis Nelson, the 'father' of all the great clarinettists. Dodds played with the Ory Brownskin Babies and left to tour with Billy Mack's vaudeville show in 1918. Returning to New Orleans, he was summoned by King Oliver, who wanted a replacement for Jimmie Noone. With the King he supplied just the right attacking style for the Creole Jazz Band, a mobile and fluid counterpoint for the powerful lead of Oliver and Armstrong. His records with Oliver have already been listed and are good examples of his work; in fact, Dodds suffered less from the recording shortcomings than did his leader.

When he left Oliver, presumably wrapping up his clarinet in its usual piece of newspaper, he went on to play at the Chicago night spots, chiefly at Kelly's Stables, and doing a spate of recording. He reached the peak of his abilities when he joined Louis Armstrong for the first Hot Five and Seven Records and even Louis did not overawe him. These records, electrically recorded, bring out the full intense quality of Dodds's vibrato; using a hard reed, there was no subtlety about his attack, whether in the high or low register; nevertheless, there is sheer beauty in his choruses in *Wild Man Blues*, *Potato Head Blues*, *Once In a While*, *Melancholy* and many others. These records will be dealt with more fully in Chapter Seven; at this juncture *Melancholy* is singled out as being one of the most deeply moving passages in jazz recorded history – and one of the most perfect. These solos of Johnny's are not to be considered in the same light as solos from (to quote an extreme), Benny Goodman in 1935; the listener is aware, during a Dodds solo, that this is a vital part of a musical whole; on the other hand the Goodman solo is the end in itself, around which the remainder of the orchestra supplies the mere padding. Excelling in solo work with Louis as he did, Johnny Dodds was no less an integral unit of the ensemble; *Potato Head* and *Weary Blues* are wonderful examples.

Until 1929 Johnny Dodds was continuously active in the jazz life of Chicago, leading his own groups, playing with, and thereby inspiring, dozens of younger clarinet players and, fortunately for posterity, continuing to record examples of the way he felt about music. Throughout his career, if his records are a criterion, he never played with more than the traditional seven-piece New Orleans combination. For many years, except for the BLACK BOTTOM STOMPERS' *Wild Man Blues* (Brunswick 02065) and *Melancholy* (Brunswick 02001), these were unobtainable in this country, but thanks to the co-operation of the recording companies with the National Federation of Jazz Organisations the following were issued during 1950-1: NEW ORLEANS WANDERERS' *Perdido Street Blues/Gatemouth* (Columbia DB.2860), and *Too Tight/Papa Dip* (Columbia DB.2920), DODD'S WASHBOARD BAND'S *Weary City/Bucktown Stomp* (HMV B.10082).

Also, in 1951, the resuscitated Vocalion label came out with two of the 1927 BLACK BOTTOM STOMPERS' titles *Come On And Stomp Stomp Stomp/After You're Gone* (V. 1003), of which the first is infinitely the better. The choice of Gerard Reeve as trombonist was unfortunate, but Dodds more than compensates for this with one of his characteristic solos.

Of this period one example is on the label of one of the small companies who have issued some of the Blythe State Street Rambler sides, *Cootie Stomp/Weary Way Blues* (Tempo R.18) being representative.

The depression of the early thirties hit Johnny Dodds as hard as any jazzman, but he never deserted his principles, still playing in the clubs in Chicago's South Side, the Negro quarter. He did not appear on wax again until 1938, making some sides for Decca, in New York. In spite of an effete accompanying group, Dodds recalls all the early grandeur of his work with Oliver and the Hot Seven on *Blues Galore/29th and Dearborn* (Brunswick 03205). Other titles from this session which were issued in England have, unfortunately, been deleted from the catalogue. The following year, Johnny was seriously ill, only to emerge in 1940 with a grand coupling using hand-picked musicians, *Red Onion Blues/Gravier Street Blues* (Brunswick 03168). But jazz suffered another loss when, a few days later, Johnny Dodds died.

*

When jazz enthusiasts get together and the subject of Dodds is introduced there are always comparisons made with his rival of Chicago days, JIMMIE NOONE (*1895-1944*). He was quite young when he first played with Keppard's Olympia Band and later played with Ory's Band, where he replaced Johnny Dodds. He went to Chicago for the first time to replace George Baquet, of the Original Creole Orchestra, who were just at the end of their triumphant six years' touring, but returned once again to New Orleans. Then he went north again to play in King Oliver's first band, in which history reversed itself and Johnny Dodds replaced Noone. The next few years were spent in Doc Cook's aggregation but in 1927 he realized his ambition to lead his own group and played for a while at the Apex Club, from which he derived the name for his band. He made many records during this time, none of which, unfortunately, has been issued in Great Britain. Noone was always an intense individualist and, while never departing from the true spirit of New Orleans in his ability to play his part in an ensemble, he was never the driving instrumentalist that Dodds was. Johnny really *blew* his clarinet; Noone seems to coax the notes out, deriving the full delicate beauty from the tonal variations of which the instrument is capable. The complete technician, he shows a fluidity and prodigious ability for variation upon the melodic line which has never been equalled, even by Dodds. Where Dodds played with passionate intensity, Noone played with a grace and lightness almost feminine in quality – reminding us forcibly of the clarinet's original role in the three-part counterpoint of the traditional front line, the female voice above the tenor and bass.

His career closely paralleled that of Johnny Dodds in that he too refused to have anything to do with large orchestras. All the records he made with his Apex group and subsequent groups until 1931 or thereabouts were with a small band often without a trumpet. Perhaps he felt that a strong lead would deprive him of the opportunity to give his fund of ideas of melody and harmony full scope; whatever the reason he defied convention and had an alto saxophone, Joe Poston, as his lead. It is more correct to say that he shared the lead with Poston, for first one, then the other would provide the lead and second parts. With Earl Hines playing what was virtually a third part, using the piano almost for the first time in jazz as a melodic instrument, these records are indeed unique and show that New Orleans is adaptable to different instrumental arrangement – but only men of Noone's and Hines' calibre can succeed in such an experiment.

Jimmy Noone achieved what was little short of a miracle when he recorded with a New Orleans group in 1936, right at the peak of the hysterical swing movement, and when the keepers of the tradition were only just earning a precarious living on Chicago's South Side. The following records show the differences between Noone and Dodds and emphasize clearly the incomparable tone he was able to produce, soft and smooth, yet without a trace of sweetness; in the low register it is more apparent but it remains too in the sweeping melodic line of the higher flights of Jimmy Noone's inspiration. With him are Guy Kelly, trumpet (who should have recorded much more), and Preston Jackson, trombone, a tenor saxophone and rhythm; but these are Noone's records.

> *Sweet Georgia Brown/Way Down Yonder in New Orleans* Parlophone R.2281
> *He's a Different Type of Guy/The Blues Jumped a Rabbit* Parlophone R.2303

He made a few more records after this; his beautiful tone is once again exemplified in *Four or Five Times* (Brunswick 03303). He visited his home in New Orleans and was playing with great success with Kid Ory in Los Angeles just before he died.

*

While for sheer beauty of tone as a clarinet player Jimmie Noone cannot be matched, on the recorded evidence he was not such a great jazzman as Dodds; neither was he such a great jazzman as one of his pupils, OMER SIMEON (*born 1902*). Easily the most underrated clarinet player in jazz, Simeon's tone and technique are almost as limpid and delicate in their purity as Noone's; to this he has been able to add much to Dodds's fire and exuberance – to such an extent that Jelly Roll Morton valued his presence on recording sessions and said he was his favourite clarinet player. Morton did not throw compliments about, and when some of the records are spun the mystery of Simeon's comparative obscurity is only more profound. Born in New Orleans, his first work was in Chicago. He had studied under Lorenzo Tio but soon came under the influence of Dodds and Noone. He played with Charlie Elgar's Creole Band and in 1926 made the first discs with Morton. In one of the great discs of jazz, *Doctor Jazz*[1], he teams up with George Mitchell and Kid Ory to produce the Noone tone, the Dodds warmth and a rich feeling for ensemble playing, especially in the last chorus, in which he takes two perfect clarinet breaks. His supple style is heard to advantage on

1. Jelly Roll Morton's Red Hot Peppers, HMV B. 9848.

Morton's *Georgia Swing*,[1] and the hectic *Shreveport*[2], but the moody *Mournful Serenade*[3] in which he fits perfectly into Morton's highly original conception of a front line which fitted his sombre mood, trombone, clarinet, and piano against a simple drum rhythm, is perhaps the best of these.[4]

Omer Simeon's obscurity is partly his own fault; for many years he buried himself in large orchestras, those of Earl Hines and Jimmie Lunceford, mainly. Before his interment in the reed section he played in Chicago with King Oliver, Erskine Tate, and others, but he never seems to have made much impression. But finally he was resurrected and replaced Noone in Kid Ory's successful band in Los Angeles in 1944. No better replacement could have been found and no clarinettist was more suited to write Jimmy's epitaph on wax when the Ory Band recorded *Blues for Jimmy* (Jazzman, J.M.B.22).

Fame is only just around the corner for Omer Simeon; for some reason he does not choose to seek it. He has everything that a New Orleans clarinet player should have and he has it all in abundance; he is still among the living – it only needs a spark to set his instrument afire. Two little-known records are available in this country to supplement the Morton examples. Supported by James P. Johnson and Pops Foster his Blues sense is fully developed; two fast sides show him still a technician if necessary, but *Creole Lullaby* is exquisite.

Lorenzo's Blues/*Harlem Hotcha*   Tempo A.15
Bandanna Days/*Creole Lullaby*   Tempo A.27

These Trio recordings, adequate as they are, only leave the listener with a sense of frustration when the Morton records are recalled. With Dodds and Noone gone, Simeon is the greatest New Orleans clarinet player alive to-day.

*

It has already been mentioned that Picou's *High Society* has always been a test piece for New Orleans clarinet players. In Jelly Roll Morton's version of this title (HMV B.9216) ALBERT NICHOLAS (*born 1900*) passes with honours. Another who came from New Orleans about the same time as Simeon, he, too, came

1. Jelly Roll Morton's Red Hot Peppers, HMV B. 9221.
2. Jelly Roll Morton's Trio, HMV B. 9220.
3. Jelly Roll Morton's Trio, HMV, B. 9221.
4. See also Chapter Seven (Jelly Roll Morton).

under the influence of Lorenzo Tio. He played with Kid Ory and Oak Gaspar, but his greatest thrill was to march with Manuel Perez's Onward Band. In 1922 he was leading his own band, playing at Tom Anderson's reformed cabaret, with a band which included Luis Russell, a pianist from Panama. Arriving inevitably in Chicago to join King Oliver, he later toured the world with Jack Carter's Band, not returning to the U.S.A. until 1929, three years after he left. From this time until the beginning of the Second World War he played almost continuously with Luis Russell's Orchestra in New York, with whom, before the advent of Louis Armstrong, he clung to his New Orleans style of playing. Several excellent records by Russell are still available to demonstrate the quality of Nicholas's style, so often overlooked during many years of jazz appreciation, overshadowed by sheer volume as he was by the forceful solos of Higginbotham, Henry Allen, Jr., and Charlie Holmes. The Russell Band was what must have been the first 'Swing' combination, characterized by arranged passages and strings of 'hot' solos; for such a band it was certainly the best of its kind and Nicholas's work on the recorded examples is most satisfying. Some idea of his agile and fluid style, similar in many ways to Simeon's, can be heard to advantage on *Jersey Lightning*, *Feelin' The Spirit*, *Panama*, and *Saratoga Shout* (Parlophone R.740, R.1882, R.963, R.2225 respectively).

In recent years he has gone back to the small groups. playing with Zutty Singleton before doing a war job in Washington and then, on his return to the jazz world, playing with Kid Ory in Hollywood.

*

It has been a feature of this book to describe the careers and styles and to attempt to evaluate the relative importance of the main characters in the history of New Orleans jazz. In this chapter the musicians dealt with have been King Oliver and Tommy Ladnier, cornets, Johnny Dodds, Jimmy Noone, Omer Simeon, and Albert Nicholas, clarinets. If this were an encyclopaedia of jazz the next 500 pages would consist of potted histories of the many other jazz musicians who left their native city in Louisiana to find a place where they could play the only kind of music they knew. The life stories that have been chosen have been expanded for two reasons: they are considered to be the best New Orleans musicians who have represented their music during the long period following the exodus from the Delta at the close of the First

World War until the Revival in the 1940s; and their lives epitomize the story of jazz as it was spread far and wide to the four corners of the United States, though mainly to that corner 'at the bottom of Lake Michigan'.

Some critics will disagree with the selection; but the intention has not been primarily to categorize or to place in order of merit. Among the trumpeters, ERNEST 'PUNCH' MILLER (*born Raceland, Louisiana, 1897*); LEE COLLINS (*born New Orleans, 1901*); ANATIE 'NATTY' DOMINIQUE (*born 1896*); have all played their part in keeping the music alive in their own hearts. BARNEY BIGARD (*born New Orleans, 1906*); DARNELL HOWARD (*born New Orleans, 1892*) among the clarinettists, ROY PALMER, HONORÉ DUTREY, EDDIE VENSON, trombones, are only the first few names which spring to mind among the dozens of players who fervently blew their music throughout Chicago's South Side during the Roaring Twenties – blew it with such insistence that the echoes are still reverberating.

Neither must those 'backroom boys' of jazz, the men of the New Orleans rhythm section, be forgotten. Those who have heard the drumming of Johnny Dodds's brother, WARREN 'BABY' DODDS (*born New Orleans, 1897*), will know from what source every rhythm section of to-day found its inspiration, either directly, or through his many disciples. All string bass players must recede into insignificance when considered against GEORGE 'POPS' FOSTER (*born McCall, Louisiana, 1892*); as must guitarists (or banjoists) against JOHNNY ST CYR (*New Orleans, 1900*) or BUD SCOTT (*New Orleans, 1900–50*).

The life stories of all these men mentioned so far constitute, in fact, the history of jazz – just as the way they felt about expressing themselves in a musical form *was* jazz. For jazz is an intensely personal music; it is composed and executed simultaneously; spontaneity is its very essence.

How the phrase 'born in New Orleans' has recurred with almost monotonous regularity throughout! It is only transparently correct to speak of a Chicago School or a New York School of jazz musicians; for they were all either weaned in New Orleans, or were directly influenced by musicians of that city. Even in this latter category, there are very few great names which spring to mind, and while the following final biographical sketch is of a musician who acquired the New Orleans style, it must not be taken as typical of many; in fact, GEORGE MITCHELL (*born 1899*) can be regarded as an exception which proves the rule.

He was born in Louisville, Kentucky, birthplace of Meade Lux Lewis, the pianist, Jimmy Harrison, the Henderson trombonist, and Lionel Hampton; an assorted list which should disperse any theories on the possibility of there being a Louisville School of Jazz! Though it has been emphasized already in earlier parts of this book the point is worth reiterating: jazz is a folk music; it is music from the heart not from the mind; therefore jazz movements and jazz performances will come from individuals or groups who have assimilated the same mental approach to the music and not from people who have merely played in the sort of places which are *supposed* to be conducive to the playing of jazz.

George Mitchell, then, of Louisville, had a comparatively academic background and the brass band with which he played in early years was not quite the same sort of thing as the Onward Band of Perez. However, ably instructed by Bobby Williams, one of the early trumpet men who died before recognition, Mitchell, or Little Mitch as he was called, was soon playing amongst the best jazz talent in Chicago. From 1919 onwards he played with Tony Jackson, Carroll Dickerson, Doc Cooke (replacing Keppard), and Earl Hines. Since then he has played no more jazz and his present whereabouts are unknown. Yet in that short time he proved himself equal to the best, and furthermore has recorded several examples of his impeccable style. His fine work with a group known as the New Orleans Wanderers, masterpieces of ensemble jazz, are obtainable in England on Columbia DB.2860 and DB.2920. An interesting comment on Mitchell is supplied by the fact that the trumpeter on these was long thought to be Louis Armstrong until it was discovered that contract difficulties prevented the latter from being present. Yet the styles are dissimilar, as an attentive ear will note.

The essence of Mitchell's style was the essence of the New Orleans trumpet style: simplicity. He never embellished where a plain statement of the theme would suffice, and he achieved his object by skilful selection and timing. His use of the mute was never to gain an effect as such, but to improve upon the open horn in the particular context.

If New Orleans jazz can be played by outsiders the converse is also true. Every hot player from New Orleans did not necessarily turn out to be a New Orleans jazz stylist. Henry Allen, Jr., the same Henry Allen who played the well-known *Patrol Wagon Blues* (HMV B.6377), can be heard to-day, for example, playing riffs and enough flattened fifths to make his father turn in his grave. And for several years now Edmund Hall has been doing his best to emulate Benny Goodman.

*

This period in jazz, lasting for approximately two decades (from 1920 to 1940), has more often than not been dealt with as a 'Chicago' period. Though for the purpose of this book, which is to show how, when, and whence jazz left New Orleans, the geographical scope has been extended a little further. Nevertheless it must be conceded that the jazz music that was played in the Windy City from about 1918 until 1928 represents about nine-tenths of all the jazz that was played between the closing of Storyville and the Renaissance of the Nineteen-Forties. Students and collectors of jazz records should bear in mind that knowledge of jazz has been influenced to a greater extent than is strictly logical by what has been recorded in the studios of the O-Keh, Columbia, Gennett, Paramount, and Victor Companies. There were scores of good jazzmen of the Chicago period who, for various reasons, never left any recorded examples of their work for posterity – and few contemporaries took the trouble of conducting *Metronome* polls. But it is safe to assume that there were as many fish left in the South Side sea as ever came out of it, men such as Junie Cobb, Bobby Schoffner, Joe Sudler, Bobby Williams, Willie Hightower, Ruben Reeves, Chiff Matthews, Sugar Johnny, Johnny Dunn. . . . Jazzmen like these, it can safely be said, kept the torch aflame during the Roaring Twenties as much as did the famous ones. To Johnny Dodds and Jimmy Noone must go the garlands for having repeatedly rekindled the torch when it was virtually reduced to an ember; but the great unknowns should never be forgotten.

G. F. Gray Clarke puts it much better:

. . . in him (Johnny Dunn), because we know enough of him for him to become a definite figure, we can honour the class to which jazz owes more than to any other: the unobtrusive, unselfconscious coloured players who made good jazz for no other reason than that it was in them and had to come out. I respect them as I respect all who remain true to their own artistic instincts. 'A crazy old guy who only knew how to play one way and couldn't or wouldn't learn any other' is a better epitaph than most of us will earn. [1]

---

1. *A Note on Johnny Dunn.* Jazz Appreciation Society Booklet *Jazz.*

CHAPTER SEVEN

The Great Individualists

THIS chapter is devoted to three of the great individualists of jazz: these three being deemed most worthy of that distinction for reasons which will be made clear in each case.

LOUIS ARMSTRONG (*born* 1900)

The first claimant for the honour is one whose name is almost a household word – to such an extent that it has become synonymous with jazz. He has been eulogized as the greatest of all hot musicians and quite possibly the greatest living musician *of any kind.*[1] This sweeping statement is the sort of thing which is calculated to bring jazz and jazz lovers into disrepute, but, on the other hand, the sober verdict of the American composer Virgil Thomson is a reliable opinion which can be accepted as good evidence for Armstrong's right to a place in the sun. Thomson said: 'His style of improvisation would seem to have combined the highest reaches of instrumental virtuosity with the most tensely disciplined melodic structure and the most spontaneous emotional expression.'[2]

*

The first time that Louis Armstrong achieved public attention was at the age of twelve, when his enthusiasm for the new year of 1913 led him into the forbidden joys of letting off a pistol in the streets of New Orleans. Captured by a zealous policeman, he was charged with 'firing firearms within the city limits', and for this piece of juvenile delinquency he was sent to the Waifs' Home, or what we should now term a reform school. The generally accepted story is that his position as the greatest jazz trumpet virtuoso dates

1. My italics.
2. *Modern Music Quarterly.* May–June 1936.

from this occurrence, since it is said that the Captain Jones who was in charge of the Home gave him his first lessons on the bugle, which later led to the cornet and an honoured place in the Home's Brass Band.

The story is neat and tidy, but probably apocryphal, because on Bunk Johnson's evidence the Armstrong boy was:

. . . fooling around with my cornet every chance he could get until he could get a sound out of it. Then I showed him just how to hold it and place it to his mouth and he did so and it wasn't long before he began getting a good tone out of my horn. . . . Now here is the year Louis started in behind me to begin showing him how to play the Blues. It was in the latter part of 1911 as close as I can think. If I am not mistaken Louis was about eleven years old. Now I have said a lot about my boy Louis and just how he started to playing cornet. He started playing it by head, and as for learning to read music he began that after he started playing with Jones' little band.[1]

Certainly Armstrong has always expressed great admiration for Johnson's cornet playing, and has spoken of his boyhood days when he would follow his idol who led the Eagle Band through the streets, adding his own quota to the music by whistling or playing his tin whistle. It is most probable that he *did* attempt several instruments before going to the Home, for he was a boy bred in the heart of a city which was steeped in a musical tradition, jazz or otherwise. The matter, however, though of interest, is of relatively small importance.

What does count is the fact that within a few years of leaving the Home at the age of fourteen, he had mastered the cornet to such good purpose that he was soon playing around the 'district' in the companionship of Sidney Bechet and Joe Lindsay, and in 1918, when Joe Oliver left 'Kid Ory's Brown Skinned Babies', it was Armstrong who was chosen to fill the vacancy.

The following year saw him working the river-boats with Fate Marable (a phase in his career which has already been mentioned in the last chapter), and then, tiring of this, he returned to New Orleans where his fame was already being established.

It was in 1922 that his first big chance came, when Joe 'King' Oliver sent him a telegram from Chicago asking him to join the band where it was playing at the newly opened Lincoln Gardens. Oliver had received enthusiastic reports of the young cornet player from all who came North, which confirmed his own opinion

1. From a letter to William Russell in *Jazzmen*.

of the lad's worth as a first-rate jazzman. He may also, of course, have been influenced by the thought that sooner or later the promising young Armstrong would make his own way to the Windy City, and decided that it would be better to have him as a member of his own band than as a rival.

It was in this band that he met the pianist Lil Hardin, whom he married in 1924, and it was due to her insistence that he should make a name for himself that he eventually left the Oliver Band. [1] Encouraged by her, he was attracted by the bright lights of New York, and in September 1924 he joined Fletcher Henderson (q.v.) at the Roseland. Henderson was an old friend from New Orleans who had at one time conducted a theatre orchestra there, and as early as 1920 had sent word for Armstrong to join him in New York, so with Henderson pulling and Lil Hardin pushing, it is easy to imagine the impatience with which Armstrong awaited the opportunity to visit the 'big city'.

The realization of his dreams, however, did not fulfil the anticipation. He had been used to a small group playing jazz as he had always known it, and the big Henderson Band, with its three-piece trumpet section and its three-piece reed section playing from written scores was a poor exchange for the crisp cleanliness of the Oliver group. He was, of course, given the opportunity to take solos, and some of the recordings of that year with Henderson can be listened to with interest in the same way that a few of the Paul Whiteman records are bearable because of the occasional solo taken by Bix Beiderbecke. Most of the records which were originally issued in 1925 are, naturally, now out of print, but *What-Cha-Call-Em Blues*, *How Come You Do Me?*, *One Of These Days* are still available (Parlophone R.2825, Tempo R.34, Tempo R.28, respectively). They are heavy and plodding apart from the trumpet solos, the one on the second-named title being a wonderfully conceived reminder of Armstrong's greatness.

The chief asset to jazz of his stay with Henderson was that his presence in New York coincided with that of Clarence Williams, Sidney Bechet and many of the great Blues singers. Bessie Smith, Ma Rainey, Clara Smith, Maggie Jones, Trixie Smith; he accompanied them all.

His accompaniment to Bessie Smith's *Cold in Hand Blues* is a model of poignant muted delicacy, while the melodic line of his phrases in *St Louis Blues* (titles are backed on Parlophone

1. The recordings made by the band in 1923 have been covered in Chapter Six.

R.2344) makes up for the more than lugubrious harmonium accompaniment of Fred Longshawe.

Other examples of his accompaniment to Bessie Smith which are available in this country are: *Reckless Blues* (Parlophone R.2476 (backed with *St Louis Blues*)) and *Careless Love Blues* (Parlophone R.2479). It is unfortunate that his recordings with Clarence Williams Blue Five are not generally issued, for in some of these he shows that brilliant attack and jazz style of his to perfection.[1]

His wife returned to Chicago before him, and not only founded her own orchestra to play at the Dreamland, but ensured a place for Louis in it. He did not need much persuasion to get back to the New Orleans style of playing jazz in Chicago, and in the late autumn of 1925 he was soon drawing huge crowds to hear the 'world's greatest jazz cornettist' in Lil's Dreamland Syncopators.

This return to an atmosphere of creative jazz was celebrated by the formation of the first 'Hot Five' group, and recordings in November of that year were followed by more in the following February. The group consisted of New Orleans musicians, with the exception of his Chicago-born wife, but she, too, had absorbed enough of the style to create a strong drumless rhythm section with the assistance of St Cyr's banjo. Kid Ory and Johnny Dodds completed the front line. *Cornet Chop Suey* and *Muskrat Ramble* (backed on Columbia D.B. 2624) are excellent examples of Armstrong's style which had developed considerably by this time. The first title is virtually a showcase for his improvisations with a spot for Lil Hardin's piano, while the second displays a collectively improvised music which does full justice to this composition of Ory's.

Exactly the same group went to the studios in May 1926 to record *Drop That Sack*[2] and *Georgia Bo Bo*,[3] but this time they adopted the title of 'Lil's Hot Shots'. The second title is most reminiscent of *Royal Garden Blues*, but it is the 'Sack' title which deserves full attention. Armstrong's self-possession and flights of melodic invention place this as one of the finest examples of his work on record quite apart from the superb collective improvisation in the last chorus. On that same day, and in the same studio,

1. Virtually the same group, with his wife replacing Williams, comprised the Red Onion Jazz Babies, *Cake Walking Babies* being issued on Tempo R–21.
2. Now labelled 'Louis Armstrong and His Orchestra', Brunswick 02502.
3. Now labelled 'Louis Armstrong and His Orchestra', Brunswick 02065.

he took part in a session for Erskine Tate's Vendome Orchestra, for he had achieved success at the Vendome Theatre as well as at the Dreamland. His natural acting ability was displayed to its full extent when he appeared on the stage there, and it was during this period that he developed that showmanship which he has since used to so marked a degree, and which has caused shallow thinkers to belittle his jazz on that account.

It is true, of course, that there have been periods in his career when he has sacrificed the jazz to the showmanship, but, generally speaking, he has always used it as a natural accompaniment to the jazz which he knew as a child, and which was, without any frills of 'folk music', just plain entertainment – although not so plain at that!

These Vendome Orchestra recordings are interesting in that they enable a comparison to be made with the easy and relaxed music of the Hot Five group. It is not that *Stomp Off* and *Static Strut*[1] are stodgy or musically messy, but apart from Armstrong and the pianist Teddy Weatherford they lack the complete coherence which is such a feature of small group jazz.

It would seem that within certain limits, a good Jazz law could be expressed as: jazz quality varies inversely as the square of the number of musicians taking part.

Be that as it may, Armstrong left Erskine Tate soon afterwards in order to join Carrol Dickerson's Orchestra which was playing at the Sunset Café, and it was here that he met the pianist Earl Hines. This was a period of great recording activity for the Hot Five group, and Armstrong accompanied many other small groups and Chicago singers in the Okeh studios, and when Dickerson himself left the Sunset in 1927, Armstrong stepped in to take his place.

1927 saw the inception of the 'Hot Seven' group, too, when he augmented the rhythm section by a tuba player – Pete Briggs, and drummer Baby Dodds. The atmosphere of the records they made during May of that year captures the full flavour of the period, and Armstrong's own warmth of tone and fantastic execution are sufficient excuse for the listing below of all the titles available. Without analysing each individual title, which would be wearisome for the reader who has not the records to hand, it is enough to say that quite apart from Louis's own drive and jazz feeling, he has the complete sympathy and mutual creative spontaneity from Dodds's clarinet.

1. Brunswick 03594. Wrongly labelled as being recorded in 1927–8.

Willie the Weeper/Weary Blues   Parlophone R.2393
Potato Head Blues/Alligator Blues   Parlophone R.2185
Melancholy Blues/Wild Man Blues   Parlophone R.2162
S.O.L. Blues   Parlophone R.2774
That's When I'll Come Back To You   Parlophone R.2704

Of these, *Potato Head* is a showcase for Armstrong alone, while *Wild Man* shows the exquisite dove-tailing of his cornet with Dodds's clarinet.

It was a busy time for Armstrong, and during this phase the white musicians used to crowd into the clubs where he was playing just to hear the brilliance of his horn. After some changes of *venue*, he settled down for a while with Carroll Dickerson again at the Savoy Ballroom, and perpetuated the name in *Savoy Blues* (Parlophone R.2127), which he recorded in December 1927 with the original Hot Five.

He was the great attraction there until the early part of 1929, and during the summer of 1928 he went to the studios with a newly constituted Hot Five. The men were drawn from Dickerson's Band, and included the pianist Earl Hines, a trombonist with a fluent style which gives the impression of immense latent power, Fred Robinson, the somewhat reedy clarinettist Jimmy Strong, Mancy Cara on banjo, and the newest recruit up from New Orleans – drummer Zutty Singleton.

The records they made, although still regarded as of importance, were not up to the standard of the earlier Hot Five and Hot Seven examples. They lack that *esprit de corps* which was such a feature of those small bands which, it must always be remembered, were almost the Oliver Creole Band in everything but name. It is unnecessary to list in full the titles which they made on their June session, but *West End Blues* (Parlophone R.448) is memorable as being the first of the 'New Rhythm Style Series' which was issued in England by Parlophone in 1934; memorable, too, for the sombre plangency of Armstrong's trumpet solo after the florid introduction. It is true that the piece is hackneyed, but the essential beauty is there just as it is in the case of other good music which loses its appeal through being heard to excess.

This was the time that the big band complex was making its presence felt in the jazz world generally, and the repercussions extended to Armstrong and his Savoy Ballroom Five. The influence can be heard quite clearly in *Basin Street Blues* (Parlophone R.531) and *No* (Parlophone R.1767) which were made in the December of that year. There is an arranged atmosphere about these which presaged the arrival of professional arrangements – and, indeed, later in that month Don Redman and Alex Hill were employed for that purpose when a further series of recordings were made. One is sufficient to quote as an example – *Beau Koo Jack* (Parlophone R.2066), in which Don Redman also plays alto saxophone: the 'riff' obsession in this begins to show quite clearly, and it is equally obvious that Armstrong himself was awkward and ill at ease in the new school of thought which later led to swing. There is a manufactured quality about the music, heightened as it is by the angularity and non-hotness of Earl Hines' piano, which makes a vivid contrast with, say, *Drop That Sack*. This *ersatz* effect is even more marked in the self-consciously morbid version of the old *Gambler's Blues*: the last title made with this group, and issued under the new name of *St James' Infirmary* (Parlophone R.643).

When the Chicago Savoy Ballroom closed down in the early part of 1929, Armstrong and his band migrated eastwards to New York, but they arrived in such a low financial state that they had to split up in order to find work.

Eddie Condon remembers this period very well, and relates the following episode:

Louis Armstrong came on from Chicago that spring for a one-night stand at the Savoy Ballroom in Harlem with Luis Russell's Orchestra. Afterwards an impromptu banquet was staged in his honour. I looked around the table and shook my head; I had never seen so many good musicians, white and coloured, in one place at the same time. 'You ought to make a record while Louis is here,' I said to Tommy Rockwell, Armstrong's adviser at the time.

He looked uneasy. 'I don't know about using a mixed group,' he said. 'If Victor can do it Okeh can do it,' I said. I told him about what we had done with *I'm Gonna Stomp Mr Henry Lee* and *That's a Serious Thing* (coupled on HMV B.4987). 'That's good news,' he said. 'I'm glad to hear it.'

He looked round the table. 'I've got a date at nine this morning with the Luis Russell Band. I'll put it back to this afternoon. Get your boys together and I'll speak to Louis.'

It was then four o'clock. At nine I reported at the Okeh studio with Jack Teagarden and Joe Sullivan. The coloured musicians who joined us were, in addition to Louis, Kaiser Marshall, a drummer, and Happy Caldwell, who played tenor saxophone. Eddie Lang, the guitarist, had been scheduled to play with the Russell Band; no one had been able to reach him[1] and he was on hand. He took my place and the group made *Knockin' A Jug* (Parlophone R.1064) and *I'm Gonna Stomp*. I stayed

1. Condon obviously means 'me'.

for the afternoon date, when Louis and the Russell men made *I Can't Give You Anything but Love* (Parlophone R.753) and *Mahogany Hall Stomp* (Parlophone R.571). Backing up Louis' trumpet were J. C. Higginbotham on trombone, Lonnie Johnson on guitar, Pops Foster on bass, Luis Russell on piano, Paul Barbarin on drums and Charlie Holmes, Albert Nicholas and Teddy Hill on saxophones. They let me sit in a corner and hold my banjo.[1]

It is obvious that by this time Armstrong was already a great figure in the eyes of contemporary jazz musicians, quite apart from his huge following among the general public. It was not long before he was installed with Carroll Dickerson's Band at one of the most fashionable night clubs in Harlem: Connie's Inn. It was virtually Louis Armstrong's Band, however, with many of his Chicago musician friends included, such as Fred Robinson, Jimmy Strong, Manzy Cara, Pete Briggs, and Zutty Singleton. It was a busy time for him, because he was also featured in the revue 'Hot Chocolates' on Broadway – a most successful show in which he introduced his colleague's[2] ever popular *Ain't Misbehavin'* (Parlophone R.462) – a song which Armstrong still regards as his favourite in that class.

After a time 'Hot Chocolates' closed down, and Dickerson's Band left Connie's Inn. Most of the musicians from the band went back to Chicago, but Armstrong arranged to join Luis Russell, and toured with him for some months. Judging by some of the recordings of this period he was more at home in a jazz sense, spurred on by the fire and drive of the Russell rhythm section dominated by the bass player Pops Foster. The influence of European orthodoxy is, however, only too evident in most (see Chapter Nine), and there is a pedestrian quality in the arrangements which does not justify giving a complete list. Pops Foster can be heard in *Dallas Blues* (Parlophone R.973) manfully struggling to lift the musical vehicle out of the rut, whilst Higginbotham's rich and hoarse trombone does much to aid things in *Bessie Couldn't Help It* (Parlophone R.698). Of *St Louis Blues* (Parlophone R.618) the less said the better, for this old traditional tune, which was 'composed' by Handy, sinks towards the end into a pit of repeated riffs which even Armstrong could do nothing to save.

When the tour finished, he went to Hollywood and was booked to appear with Les Hite at Sebastian's Cotton Club, where the band was under his name. It included Lawrence Brown, who joined Duke Ellington's trombone section in 1932, and Lionel

1. *We Called It Music*, by Eddie Condon and Thomas Sugrue.
2. Fats Waller.

Hampton, the Louisville jack-of-all-trades who joined Benny Goodman in 1937. The Hollywood influence of Hawaiian guitar effects and the use of that hybrid instrument which is totally unsuitable for jazz, the vibraphone, can be heard (if desired) in *Confessin'* (Parlophone R.909) and *Memories of You* (Parlophone R.854) respectively.

1931 saw Armstrong back in Chicago forming his own band, and he drew the musicians from among his many old New Orleans associates. He can be heard introducing them by name in *The Lonesome Road* (Parlophone R.2829).

From 1932 to 1935 he was visiting and re-visiting England and the Continent. The consequent world-wide publicity tended to increase his spectacular top note flights for an awe-struck and jazz-misinformed public. 'After all,' they said, 'a man who can play 250 top Cs in succession and then finish on top F *must* be good.' So he gave the public what it wanted, and real jazz was neglected for a long time.

1940, with its revival of interest in basic jazz, showed that he had lost neither the capability nor the desire to express himself fully with a small group of his old colleagues. Claude Jones, Sidney Bechet, Luis Russell, Bernard Addison, Wellman Braud, and Zutty Singleton joined him at a studio in New York to revive their memories of the 'Crescent City'. The results were more than satisfying. Once again he exhibited the fact that, given the opportunity, he was still the world's greatest jazz trumpet man, except for the final phases of *Perdido*, when the effect of many years of playing to the swing gallery is rather evident.

Perdido Street Blues/*2.19 Blues*   Brunswick 03164
Down in Honky Tonk Town/*Coal Cart Blues*   Brunswick 03165

Coal Cart Blues was waxed without the trombone, piano and drums, and is a tribute to Armstrong's career, for he must review his life with satisfaction. It is a long and weary climb from driving a coal cart in the streets of New Orleans after you have been discharged from a reform school to the position of the world's greatest trumpeter, fêted, welcomed, and honoured over the whole world.

To conclude this brief résumé of Armstrong's history, let us hear the opinion of England's greatest jazz trumpet player who was present at Nice on the occasion of the first International Jazz Festival in 1948.

To analyse in any detail Louis's playing at Nice would take a whole article of this length in itself. So I will be content to say here that his performance left no doubt in my mind that he is still the greatest figure in jazz, with a grandeur and majesty of style which no other musician – except perhaps Sidney Bechet – can approach. I was particularly struck at the Festival by the almost puritanical simplicity of his playing; all the old trappings and ornaments which were such familiar characteristics of his earlier phases have been swept away. The long glissandi, the repeated high notes and the rambling codas which we had come to regard as inevitable, all were conspicuously absent; and there was left a music which, with its purity and serenity, brought us perhaps nearer to the fountain-head of his genius than we have ever been before. [1]

Had Walt Whitman been alive to witness this phenomenon, he would have had even more incentive to pen those imaginative words of his:

> I hear the key'd cornet, it glides
> Quickly in through my ears,
> It shakes mad-sweet pangs through
> My belly and breast.

SIDNEY BECHET (born 1897)

Until quite recently it was almost a universal supposition that Sidney Bechet must have been born about the same year as Buddy Bolden and various guesses at his age in recent years have placed him at between sixty and eighty years of age. The main reason for this fallacy was probably the knowledge that in his early days in New Orleans he had played with all the great jazz pioneers, most of whom had died long ago. Sidney was, in fact, born on 14 May 1897, but he was interesting himself in the clarinet as early as 1903! He used to practise surreptitiously on his brother's instrument and eventually, when his mother realized her son's talent, Sidney received it as a gift. Being something of an infant prodigy he soon began to play all round the clubs and cabarets; at the age of ten he was playing with Freddie Keppard.

Bunk Johnson had a high opinion of him and persuaded him away from the little 'Silver Bell' Band, consisting of three Bechet brothers and Sidney Desvigne, to join the Eagle Band during its most famous period, from 1911 to 1914, Bunk says:

I went to Sidney Bechet's mother's house and asked her to let him play clarinet with me in the Eagle Band. She told me yes but here is what I would have to do. 'You'll have to bring Sidney home after he is through playing each and every job, that would be the only way that I can let him go in your care if you promise me that you will do that.' [2]

1. *Lessons of Nice*. Humphrey Lyttelton. *Jazz Music*, Vol. 3, No. 8.
2. Quoted from *Jazzmen*. Fred Ramsey, C. E. Smith.

Bechet was influenced by Big Eye Louis Nelson and was taught by George Baquet, but the latter was unable to teach the creative-minded Sidney anything orthodox. The young clarinettist preferred to go his own way and the fact that his fingering was a little different from the acknowledged way did not worry him in the slightest. For he was a born musician; if there had been no accepted method of fingering at all he would quickly have invented one. He played, in addition to the Eagle Band, and Keppard, with Buddy Petit and Jack Carey, and in 1914 went on tour to Texas with a show in which Clarence Williams was a comedian. Sidney's main contribution to the entertainment was an act in which he progressively took his clarinet to pieces whilst still playing until he was left finally with the mouthpiece! He returned to New Orleans in 1916 with Joe Oliver and was in Chicago in 1918 with Sugar Johnnie and Eddie Venson. During his appearances on Chicago's South Side, Will Marion Cook, who was organizing a band for a European tour, chanced to hear him, and Sidney began the first of his many visits to the Old World.

His love of travel and the long periods he spent overseas are responsible for the fact that, until recently, few players have been influenced by him in the same way as they have been by Johnny Dodds and Jimmie Noone. Yet wherever he went he created a great impression by his rich and powerful tone and, above all, his tremendous technique. Nevertheless it did not pass unnoticed that this technique was only a means to an end; a vehicle for the boundless imagination and fund of ideas which thirty-five years later is still not exhausted. The well-known Swiss conductor, Ernest Ansermet, showed an amazingly clear vision and insight into the then completely unknown music[1] and wrote the following:

... What a moving thing it is to meet this very black, fat boy with white teeth and that narrow forehead, who is very glad one likes what he does, but who can say nothing of his art, save that he follows his 'own way' and when one thinks that 'his own way' is perhaps the highway the whole world will swing along to-morrow.[2]

When the rest of the world was going mad over the tin cans and paper hats of the Original Dixieland Jazz Band it was a tragedy that some publicity was not given then to Ansermet's prophetic words.

1. See Chapter Fourteen.
2. *On a Negro Orchestra*, Revue Romande, 15 October 1919.

It was during his European tour with Cook, incidentally, that Bechet first took a liking for the soprano saxophone, subsequently devoting more and more of his time to it, until to-day he rarely plays the clarinet.

He played also with Benny Peyton in Paris, returning to New York in 1922 where, shortly afterwards, he made his first recordings with Clarence Williams Blue Five. One of these, under the name of the Red Onion Jazz Babies, has been issued here; in company with Louis Armstrong, Charlie Irvis, trombone, Lil Armstrong and Buddy Christian, banjo, he demonstrates how a soprano saxophone can be used as the 'female' voice just as well as the clarinet. Providing the perfect foil for Armstrong's lead he plays in much the same commanding fashion as he does to-day, giving an exhilarating effect throughout the record. *Cake Walking Babies* (Tempo R.21), recorded in 1924, shows that already Bechet was not content to remain just a member of a band; there is the imparted sense of one seeking self-expression in a highly individual way.

This individualism was soon realized; after a spell with Duke Ellington he went to Europe again in 1925 with a Negro Revue, the same, in fact, in which Josephine Baker made her debut. This tour was a wildly successful one for Bechet; billed as the 'Talking Saxophone' he visited Paris, Brussels, Berlin, Turkey, Egypt and distant Moscow, where he met Tommy Ladnier for the first time, beginning a jazz friendship which was to have many happy results in the shape of some fine records. Both Tommy and Sidney joined Noble Sissle's Orchestra in Paris and returned to America with Sissle in 1930. Until they left the band in 1932 a few records were made, one of which, *Basement Blues*, unfortunately not available here, contains some fine solo work by both musicians.

The two friends must have felt musically frustrated with the large orchestra, for they formed their own group, the New Orleans Feetwarmers, playing at the Savoy and recording a memorable session for Victor. All have been issued in England, but *Shag*, the best side, is now not available. Nevertheless, the following discs can be obtained: all show Bechet's capabilities to the full.

Sweetie Dear/*Maple Leaf Rag*   HMV B.9408
I Want You To-night/*Lay Your Racket*   HMV B.9091

Though by no means an example of true ragtime style, in *Maple Leaf* 'Sidney dominates everything, taking chorus after chorus, yet always with new and more vivid ideas, and his tremendous power of execution makes one think more of the trumpet than a saxophone.'[1]

But the Feetwarmers' stay at the Savoy was short-lived; large swing bands were in the ascendant and Ladnier retired to the country in disgust. Bechet, however, rejoined Sissle, and remained with him continuously until 1938. *Polka Dot Rag* (Brunswick 02511) contains a fine Bechet solo (upheld by a good, but comparatively little known rhythm section), but the best records he made during his stay with Sissle are undoubtedly the ones he made under the name of Noble Sissle's Swingsters:

Viper Mad/Sweet Patootie   Brunswick 02652
Blackstick/Southern Sunset   Brunswick 02702

When he left Sissle in 1938 to play in small groups he was, as far as the collector was concerned, one of many clarinet players but one who also played soprano saxophone; five years later he was considered among the best jazzmen; to-day he is acknowledged by many to be, with Armstrong, the greatest of all time and certainly the best exponent of jazz music as far as contemporary performance is concerned. His sudden rise to fame was largely a result of his recordings, which received some extra publicity as a result of the sudden impact of his fierce vibrato upon Goodman-schooled critical ears; but since the end of World War II he has had many opportunities of playing before appreciative audiences everywhere.

Before leading his own rejuvenated New Orleans Feetwarmers, Bechet played some fine accompaniments to Trixie Smith and Coot Grant, which were issued here on the old Vocalion label; there were also a few poor sides with a rather mixed personnel, and then the session supervised by Hugues Panassié in which the Bechet-Ladnier partnership was resumed.[2] He had suddenly achieved recognition and was in demand by almost everyone who was organizing a recording date. The Blue Note Company issued several sides; Jelly Roll Morton included him in the session which produced *High Society* (HMV B.9216), already mentioned for Nicholas's work on it, and which is covered in full in the section of this chapter devoted to Morton himself. Bechet's best solo is, perhaps, on *Winin' Boy Blues* (HMV B.9217), but he is prominent on all four. He also played again with Louis Armstrong, for the first time since the Clarence Williams Blue Five days of 1923, on a session made especially for the Brunswick New Orleans

1. Hugues Panassié.   2. See Chapter Six.

album – these discs are also dealt with elsewhere in this chapter, under Louis Armstrong. It is sufficient in this context to remark that Bechet has never played better than on these records; his well-conceived introduction and the growling solo on *Perdido Street Blues* (Brunswick 03164) are most satisfying, whilst on *Coal Cart Blues* (Brunswick 03165) he provides the perfect harmonic background for Armstrong's simple but effective lead and then leaps away at the end of Louis's vocal to give every indication that he was by now second to none – not even to Louis.

Showing a supremacy over all other players of the soprano saxophone which enabled him not only to excel as a reed player but also as a *lead* player, Bechet led a series of small groups which were unique in that the trumpet played either a secondary or at most, an equal role with the soprano instrument. These New Orleans Feetwarmers groups made many records, the best of which are selected here as being truly representative of Bechet's highly personal and individual style. Max Jones has described this complete supremacy of musicianship:

As a musician, showman and personality, Bechet towers above the run of jazz players. For that reason, perhaps, he fits into the traditional jazz band line-up no better than Louis Armstrong does to-day. Both seem endowed with such creative ability, such musical eloquence, that the essential discipline of small-band ensemble playing irks them. [1]

Whilst later records have shown that Bechet can still fit in with ensembles, it is undoubtedly true that his never-ending inspiration and wealth of ideas are responsible for his domination of the scene in many of them. This narrowness of approach tends to enhance his reputation as a technician; the listener cannot fail to be amazed at the boundless energy with which he drives on and on, note following note in a flood of instrumental brilliance. But on the debit side is the fact that as musical entities, performances like *Swing Parade* (HMV B.9402), *One O'Clock Jump* (HMV B.9340), *Stompy Jones* (HMV B.9329), and *Rip Up the Joint* (HMV B.9474) are not wholly satisfying.

When Bechet turns his attention to the standard jazz tunes, the 'good ol' good ones', the impression is at once much better. Bechet gives a new and enlivened treatment to *Baby Won't You Please Come Home* (HMV B.9385), *I Ain't Gonna Give Nobody None of My Jelly Roll* (HMV B.9368), *Ain't Misbehavin'* (HMV B.9136), and *When It's Sleepy Time Down South* (HMV B.9329). The rendering of the Blues is undoubtedly Bechet's *forte*; and

1. *Jazz Photo Album.*

in this series (on which he plays almost entirely soprano saxophone), he gives of his best. *Wild Man Blues* (HMV B.9086) is a good version of this number, with Bechet contributing to a well-balanced ensemble and interjecting clipped and precise breaks. Throughout all these records this precise attack, every note hit cleanly and surely, as with Louis, is a most impressive feature. And in many cases the other musicians were inspired by this; trumpet players like Sidney de Paris, Rex Stewart, and Henry Allen – each seemed to possess an extra intangible quality when playing with him. Charlie Shavers, noted for his emotionless muted style, plays very well with Bechet in *Texas Moaner* (HMV B.9474), while Henry Allen recalls some of his former taste in the subtle *Egyptian Fantasy* (HMV B.9378), built round an unusual theme, yet lending itself to collective treatment in New Orleans fashion.

The best of all the Bechet Blues is the beautiful *Blues in Thirds* (HMV B.9340) in which he forms a trio with Earl Hines and Baby Dodds. This is Bechet *in excelsis*; not Bechet the New Orleans clarinettist, but Bechet the individualist, saying what he feels about the blues with more expression and depth of emotion contained in his clarinet than could ever be put into words. This is a great jazz record by any standard, building up to a climax with all the attack, tone, and exquisite phrasing of which he was capable.

Bechet is nothing if not versatile; on one session he made two titles (under the name of Sidney Bechet and his One Man Band) in which he played six instruments, each one being recorded separately and superimposed upon the others. This record is not available in England; neither are most of the titles made for the Blue Note Company, though *Bechet's Fantasy/Old Stack-o-Lee Blues* (Jazz Parade E.1) has been issued here.

But some of Bechet's best work, the sides made under the name of the Mezzrow-Bechet Quintet, are available. These sides are all excellent and rank with *Blues in Thirds* as some of the best jazz records, not only by Bechet but by any jazzman in recent years:

Ole Miss/Out of the Gallion   King Jazz 1
Old School/Bowin' the Blues   King Jazz 2
Funky Butt/Where Am I   King Jazz 3

Many other records demonstrate his lyrical imagination:

China Boy/Four or Five Times   Melodisc 8001
That's A Plenty/If I Could Be With You   Melodisc 8002
Ce Mossieu Qui Parle/Buddy Bolden's Story   Esquire 10–057

Bechet's Creole Blues/Anita's Birthday   Esquire 10–058
Ridin' Easy Blues/The Onions   Esquire 10–059
Panther Dance/Blues in Paris   Esquire 10–060

The Esquires were recorded in Paris with Claude Luter's New Orleans style group and the French boys provide some of the happiest accompaniments to Bechet's brilliance that have so far been captured on wax. They were recorded when Sidney was visiting what was almost his second home, in 1949, and during this visit to Europe he was persuaded to come over to England for a short stay, at the invitation of two London promoters of jazz concerts and clubs, Bert and Stan Wilcox.

British jazz enthusiasts owe them an undying debt of gratitude for having made it possible for Bechet to be heard on a London concert stage. During a jazz concert at the Winter Garden Theatre, he was noticed in a box and given a tremendous ovation by the audience, after which the compère asked if he would step down to accompany Humphrey Lyttelton's Band for a few numbers. There followed the greatest single jazz performance ever seen or heard in England. The audience were left spellbound by the classic jazz which surged from Bechet's soprano and clarinet. Critics and reporters alike ran out of adjectives; though Tin Pan Alley was strangely silent.

He taught us many things – a great deal of showmanship – how to keep the tension all the time and the importance of being supremely confident in one's own abilities. Stanley Dance wrote:

His most daring flights may momentarily have made the listener a little nervous, a little doubtful of the outcome, but all were accomplished with confident ease.[1]

He showed us too that the much-despised riff is not solely a substitute for lack of ideas in a twenty-four piece power-house band, but that used intelligently as a support for a solo the repeated phrase does no harm.

Bechet, in fact, proved as no other could to-day how truly magnificent are the great figures in jazz.

As he learned from the great clarinettists of the New Orleans classic period so he is passing on the tradition to the younger generation of jazz players, almost half a century later. His most adept pupil, Bob Wilber, has given us a fitting clue to his genius:

As a listener, Sidney has the intuitive ability to sense the value of any music he hears. I've never heard him say 'That's an awful tune'. He

1. *Jazz Journal*, January 1950. Ed. Sinclair Traill and Tom Cundall.

loves all music because he sees the way to play it. There are some things you cannot realize about Bechet just from a study of his records. For instance, in clubs he plays plenty of 'pop' tunes, and plays them for all he's worth. He plays the melody, and when he improvises it's improvising on the melody. That, in brief, is his theory of jazz. [1]

JELLY ROLL MORTON (Born Ferdinand La Menthe)
(1885–1941)

'Hello, Central! Give me Doctor Jazz.'

If one were to make such a plea to a telephone operator, she could not do better than to connect you, if she could, with Ferdinand Joseph Morton, or 'Jelly Roll' Morton as he was pleased to call himself.

We are already familiar with many of his characteristically colourful observations in the ragtime chapter and elsewhere, but he is such an important figure in the history of recorded jazz that he has been included in this chapter devoted to the great individualists. His qualification for such inclusion, if proof be needed, may be judged by the following opinions expressed by eminent jazz critics:

Max Jones:

. . . Jelly Roll Morton was a musician of consequence, historically and artistically, in addition he was a man of marked individuality. Like many others he witnessed the transitional process from ragtime to the 'swinging music' of ragtime bands, and beyond to the highly integrated jazz of New Orleans during its 'classic' period. Throughout all but the few earliest years he was a participant rather than spectator. To a greater degree perhaps than any other jazzman he absorbed conflicting musical influences; opera, ragtime, Spanish, Blues, New Orleans Brass Band, popular ballad, and folk-song.

Stanley Dance:

. . . There is no more enlightening collection of jazz records to be found under the name of any one man. Not all of the records are good, but they are of great variety and they illustrate remarkably jazz development and tendencies. Through them all, like a golden thread, runs the insistent beat of Jelly Roll's uncompromising, incomparable piano.

Alan Lomax:

. . . Jelly Roll's life story spans the whole of the 'jazz age', from the street bands of New Orleans to the sweet bands of New York. With him we can leave behind the market-places of Hollywood and Tin Pan Alley and return to the moment of germination in New Orleans. In his sorrows and his fantasies we can find the very quality which distinguishes

1. *Jazz Music.* Vol 3, No. 10, Ed. Max Jones.

Jazz from the many other forms of American music rooted in Africa – from the spirituals, from the Work Songs, from the Blues and ragtime.

Rudi Blesh:
. . . His playing is the definitive jazz piano and represents the highest development of and from ragtime in which the set form of the score is subjected to ceaseless and significant variation. He broadened the expressive power of ragtime, infusing it with the hot elements of jazz and the Blues, making ragtime piano tone hotter and bluer, choosing judiciously elements of harmony, rhythm and figuration from barrel-house. He introduced true stomping into the rag.

Hugues Panassié:
. . . His splendidly constructed phrases strikingly recall the phrases of the great New Orleans trumpets. The passion of this great pianist is tempered by his relatively delicate touch and his pronounced feeling for melodic curves gives his playing a delicious freshness and reveals his frank and moving sensitivity. Few jazz pianists are as melodic as Jelly Roll. But because certain traces of ragtime remain in his playing (notably certain cadences in his left hand) modern musicians think he is 'corny'. In reality, these traces of ragtime in no way harm the beauty of his discoveries nor the phrases he swings, though they do give his choruses a slightly archaic effect.

These opinions are but a few culled at random from magazine articles and books; many more could be quoted, but these are sufficient to show in what regard he is held on both sides of the Atlantic.

He has referred to the musical instruments with which he seems to have been surrounded in his home during childhood, and he has also recalled that when he was only eight or nine years of age he was familiar with such Blues tunes as *Isn't It Hard to Love* and *Make Me a Pallet on the Floor*, playing them on his guitar which he is said to have learnt from the age of six. That the street bands and spasm bands intrigued him may be gathered from his own reminiscences:

For instance, when I first started going to school, at different time I would visit some of my relatives per permission, in the Garden district. I used to hear a few of the following Blues players who could play nothing else – Buddy Cantor, Josky Adams, Game Kid, Frank Richards, Sam Henry and many more too numerous to mention – what we called 'ragmen' in New Orleans. They can take a ten cent Xmas horn, take the wooden mouthpiece off, having only the metal for mouthpiece, and play more *Blues* with that instrument than any trumpeter I have ever met through the country imitating the New Orleans trumpeters.

That is probably a piece of typical Jelly Roll Morton hyperbole; the distance of childhood lending enchantment to the view!

His introduction to the glories of the piano came about through visiting, at a surprisingly tender age, parties where he heard the talented pianist and Blues singer Mamie Desdume and others. He insists, however, that Mamie was the one who impressed herself chiefly on his mind:

'My, but she really could play this number:

> Two-Nineteen done took my baby away,
> Two-Nineteen took my baby away.
> Two-Seventeen bring her back some day.'

The piano cast its spell on him to such an extent that he gave up the guitar, especially as BUD SCOTT was making quite a name for himself on that instrument, and Jelly Roll decided that he didn't want to share guitar honours with anybody. He dropped his scruples about the piano being a 'cissy' instrument, and took lessons from a number of teachers, but he soon discovered their limitations. One amusing incident stood out in his memory:

... Mrs Moment was no doubt the biggest ham of a teacher that I've ever heard or seen since or befo'. She fooled me all the time when I'd take these numbers and place them in front of her she would rattle them off like nobody's business and about the third one she rattled off sound like the first one; then I began to get wise and wouldn't take lessons any further. Then I demanded I would either go by myself and learn the best way I knew how, or be placed under an efficient teacher: which I was then placed under a teacher at the Saint Joseph University: a Catholic University in the City of New Orleans, and I become the 'lion' under the Catholic tutorage, which was quite efficient. I then later taken lessons from a known professor, coloured professor, name professor – Nicholson – which is considered very good. I tell you, things was drivin' along then.

Yes – things were driving along well until his parents discovered that he was sometimes deputizing for pianists in the unmentionable Basin Street district, and was familiar with the frank lyrics of such Blues as *See See Rider*:

> I've gotta momma, she live right back o' the jail,
> I've got a sweet momma, she lives right back of the jail:
> She's got out a sign on her window: 'Good Pussy for Sale.'

Not unnaturally, this caused parental wrath, and resulted in his leaving home to make the first step on the long jazz road which he travelled, adopting at that time the title 'Jelly Roll' in place of

Ferdinand. It was imitative and it probably arose from a kind of hero-worship of a Georgian pianist of the name who visited New Orleans. It may have been a gesture of defiance on Morton's part towards his family, because the title (in spite of all the pretty-pretty explanations which have been given describing it as a 'kind of sweetmeat') connoted sexual prowess.

At any rate, he did play around the various spots in the 'district' for a time, and then, before he was nineteen, he travelled around, taking jobs and broadening his outlook by his contact with the ragtime pianists of other towns.

It was at Mobile that he met Porter King, one of the few pianists for whom he had a good word in later life. This pianist must have made a deep impression on Morton, for he said in relation to his own composition *King Porter Stomp*:

This was inspired by a very good friend of mine and a marvellous pianist now in the cold, cold ground, a gentleman from Florida, an educated gentleman with a wonderful education, much better than mine, and this gentleman's name was Mr King – Porter King.

His recollection is that he returned to New Orleans for several years, playing around the various night spots of the South until about 1908, when he returned for a time, only to leave again on the first stage of his journey northwards to Chicago. Memphis was the first stop, and it was here that he met W. C. Handy, and it is from this meeting that their mutual dislike appears to have sprung. Both men in later years claimed to have 'invented' jazz, but whereas Morton himself was a great exponent of jazz and admitted freely the factors which influenced his compositions and his playing, Handy committed to paper and copyrighted old traditional Blues which he had heard since his youth – e.g. *Yellow Dog Blues* and *St Louis Blues*.

The final straw for Morton was in 1938 when Ripley introduced Handy in one of his 'Believe It Or Not' radio programmes as the originator of Blues and Jazz! This produced an acrimonious article from Morton which was published in the American jazz magazine *Down Beat*, in which he said:

Mr Handy cannot prove that he had created any music. He has probably taken advantage of some unprotected material that sometimes floats around. I would like to know how a person could be an originator of anything without being able to do at least some of what they created.

The last phrase refers to the Memphis period of their meeting, when Morton is said to have challenged Handy's violin-laden orchestra to play some real jazz – a challenge which was refused. Hence Morton's ironic:

Of course, Handy played mostly violin when I first arrived in Memphis. Violinists weren't known to play anything illegitimate even in New Orleans.

and Handy's sarcastic reply:

Yes, I remember when Jelly Roll played for Barrasso in Memphis on coloured what we call T.O.A.B. time. But we were too busy to take notice of his great musicianship.

Perhaps it was wrong to say that both men claimed to have *invented* jazz. Morton merely said: 'Man, I discovered jazz' – a very different thing from having *originated* it.

To return to Morton's earlier days. He was attracted inevitably to Chicago, and, although the actual date of his arrival is obscure, he was leading a five-piece band there in 1914 when the Original Creole Band (q.v.) visited that city and caused such a musical sensation, for he has said:

I happened to be there myself with a similar combination to that Freddie Keppard used to have. They turned the town upside down and caused my trumpet player to quit. He couldn't play that kind of trumpet, and I had been teaching him a little bit. He was a little stubborn, and when Freddie played he wanted to hit him with a rack.

Then, after playing at different spots in Chicago, the wanderlust spirit which seems to have permeated his life took him to California, and he formed a small group which was composed of himself, Dink Johnson, Buddy Petit, Wade Waley, and Frank Dusen. He sent word home to New Orleans for these last three in 1917, and relates that when they arrived at Los Angeles station, they had to be rushed off to a tailor so that their tight pants and box coats would not shame the band. This action seems to have affronted their dignity, and then, to crown it all, Morton and Johnson jeered at their ingrained frugal habits of taking their own food to cook when employed in a palatial night club which provided food for the musicians – 'They cooked up red beans and rice in a bucket'. Petit and Dusen thereupon gave in their notice and returned home, which was a blow to Morton, for he has described Petit as one of the greatest hot cornet players he had ever known, and second only to Freddie Keppard.

However, he rallied others to his banner, and formed the 'Black and Tanners' who held together until the early twenties. This was a period of big money for the band, and Morton, always hankering after a business career, lost most of it in unfortunate speculations. This wild groping for security was almost certainly inborn: his ancestors in their heyday of Creole superiority had always been respected and respectable business men, and the downfall of the Creoles coupled with the instability of a jazz musician's life must have induced in him a mild form of schizophrenia.

Be that as it may, during the years 1921–4 he was around and about all over the place: Los Angeles, St Louis, Kansas City, Memphis and New Orleans. He has recalled hearing the great Joe Oliver's Band in Los Angeles in 1922, whilst the evidence of his piano solos made at Richmond, Indiana,[1] in 1923 and 1924 verifies his presence in the vicinity of Chicago.

It was in Chicago that he made his first band recordings, or, at any rate, near enough to that city to prove his presence there in 1923, when he assembled Zue Robertson on trombone, Natty Dominique on cornet, Horance Eubanks on clarinet, and an unknown drummer to record two titles, one of which was his own *London Blues*.[2] In June of that year with an entirely different band, at Port Washington, Wisconsin, he put on wax four titles of which one, *Muddy Water Blues* (Tempo R.7), is available in this country . . . as an example of jazz music, it is not to be recommended to those accustomed to the slick efforts of swing, but is of great academic interest to the student of recorded jazz. On this session he included Floyd Towns (alto saxophone), Roy Palmer (trombone), Jasper Taylor (drums), and an unknown trumpeter and clarinet player. The latter spills out broad sweeping phrases, whilst the trumpet man is concise and forthright.

At this time he was living in the great flowering period of New Orleans jazz in Chicago, listening to Joe Oliver, Clarence Williams (a pianist for whom he had no great regard), Earl Hines, Paul Mares, Rappolo, and the other members of the New Orleans Rhythm Kings. That this group held *him* in high regard is proved by the use of four of his compositions in their recording sessions: *Wolverine Blues*, *Mr Jelly Lord*, *Milenburg Joys*, and *London Blues*.[3]

Somehow or other, he did not manage to get himself into the public eye in the way that Oliver and the New Orleans Rhythm Kings did, and there followed a series of tours until he suddenly

1. Example: *New Orleans Joys/Perfect Rag*. Tempo R.5.
2. American issue Okeh 8105. N O R K version Brunswick 02210.
3. Morton himself played piano on some of the sides recorded at this session.

came into prominence with a touring band which he first called the 'Incomparables' and later the 'Red Hot Peppers'.

This was in 1926, the year in which he made those famous piano solos including *King Porter Stomp* and *The Pearls* (Brunswick 03564), and had also accompanied the singer Edmonia Henderson in company with Joe Oliver. The title of 'Red Hot Peppers' must have appealed to the public taste, for he kept the name for both his touring and recording bands until his eclipse in 1930. The separation of 'touring' and 'recording' is used advisedly, for except upon very rare occasions he was most careful to pick his recording groups from musicians outside his touring band.

How well he picked them and how magnificently they interpreted his ideas is jazz history, for that first group of Red Hot Peppers which met in a studio in Chicago on 15 September 1926, by the fire and intensity of their playing; their instinctive feeling for jazz; and their individual performances, whether playing solo or collectively, created one of the outstanding sides in jazz (HMV B.10048). *Black Bottom Stomp* displays the fine use of 'breaks', upon which Morton laid such stress, while *The Chant* (MVH B.5164), which at the moment of writing is still deleted from the catalogue, has been cited by Rudi Blesh[1] as a well-nigh perfect example of pure New Orleans style. . . .

Incredible *tour de force* – *The Chant* – incredible masterpiece, too! Here is all that New Orleans polyphony means. . . . As clearly as if Morton introduced them by name, each instrument shows what it can – and should – do in jazz: the bold, clear driving trumpet, the sharply sweet and fervent clarinet, the Blues shouting trombone, the plangent banjo, the swift-striding stringed bass, the light, elastic, but firm piano, the rolling parade drums. Thus Morton takes his bow as composer and organizing genius while the order of his appearance indicates, as clearly as his band playing always does, that he recognizes the somewhat minor position of the piano itself in the band.

Who were these paragons that managed to integrate the music of Morton so exquisitely and so rightly? George Mitchell, the trumpet man, was from Louisville, Kentucky, but all the others were from New Orleans and its environs: Kid Ory for trombone, Omer Simeon, whose clarinet playing exactly suited Morton's conceptions, John St Cyr, banjo, John Lindsay, string bass, and Andrew Hilaire on drums.

A few days later, another session was arranged, with the addition of Darnell Howard and Barney Bigard, when they made the

1. *Shining Trumpets.*

semi-jazz, semi-comedy number which may still be found occasionally in second-hand record shops, *Sidewalk Blues* (HMV B.5212). and the now reissued fine *Steamboat Stomp* (HMV B.9979).

16 December of that year saw the same group reassembled in the recording studio to make five titles, including one of Joe Oliver's compositions, and one to which we must pay tribute and attention. It was *Doctor Jazz* (HMV B.9848), a demonstration of jazz both in conception and performance, and it would be difficult to find another example which shows all the ingredients so deftly interwoven. Apart from its appeal to the jazz student, it has a spontaneous gaiety which reaches out over the intervening quarter of a century to transmit itself to the listener. That an arrangement was 'roughed out' beforehand is obvious – a procedure which was known as a 'Head' arrangement, and upon this framework is built a complicated pattern of collective and solo improvisation, breaks, suspensions and releases, and an exciting tension which is typified by the long-held clarinet notes.

The vocal chorus, which is taken by Morton himself, has a lyric which is a refreshingly clear and concise statement of what the singer wants. It is a far cry from the modern type of song which Constant Lambert[1] decries:

In modern songs it is taken for granted that one is poor, unsuccessful, and either sex-starved or unable to hold the affections of such partner as one may have had the luck to pick up.

He also says:[2]

The most irritating quality about the Vododeo, poo poop-a-doop school of jazz song is its hysterical emphasis on the fact that the singer is a jazz baby going crazy about jazz rhythms.

There is no hysteria present in *Doctor Jazz:* just a straightforward statement full of *joie de vivre.*

> Aaaah, Hello, Central! Give me Doctor Jazz.
> He's got what I need; I'll say he has.
> When the world goes wrong
> And I got those blues,
> He's the man that make me get
> Out both my dancin' shoes!
>
> Ooh, the more I get, the more I want, it seems.
> I page old Doctor Jazz in ma dreams.

1. *Music Ho!* Pelican 195, Penguin Books. 1948.
2. *Ibid.*

When I'm trouble-bound and mixed
He's the guy that get me fixed –
Hallo, Central! Give me Doctor Jazz.

The backing, *Jelly Roll Blues*, shows a strong Spanish tinge in Morton's piano work, while *Grandpa's Spells* (HMV B.10048) and *Cannon Ball Blues* (HMV B.9979) are both examples of skilful integration and spontaneous performance.

*

This period in Morton's life was most successful, both musically and financially, and he branched out into the music publishing business, but when times got bad for him, and the general trend of jazz seemed to be turning towards New York, he went there with a band, and again we are able to hear him through the medium of the recordings which he made. The line-up of the Red Peppers had changed, and it was with Ward Pinkett on trumpet, Geechy Fields (trombone), still the same Omer Simeon on clarinet, Lee Blair (guitar), Bill Benford (tuba) and Tommy Benford (drums) – all of them Harlem musicians except Simeon — that he visited the Victor studios to make a series of full band, trio and quartet recordings, some of which are available in this country.

The first title made, and the one to which we shall first turn our attention, was *Georgia Swing* (HMV B.9221). The change of musicians is obvious, the lithe buoyancy of John Lindsay's string bass being replaced by the stodgier tuba, while neither Pinkett's trumpet nor Fields' trombone have anything like the facile fluency of Mitchell and Ory. This is not to say that the performance is poor; far from it. It is simply that it fails to achieve the heights of *Doctor Jazz*. In its favour can be put the agile clarinet phrasing of Simeon, and the sixteen bar Morton piano chorus. Morton stressed the importance of the riff in jazz, and it is developed extensively towards the end of the performance.

The reverse, *Mournful Serenade* (HMV B.9221), is a twelve bar Blues by Simeon, Fields, Tommy Benford and Morton, that has a haunting nostalgic quality. Apart from the savage growling trombone chorus, there is a settled peace about the whole atmosphere which is given emphasis by the nuances of lament in the clarinet solos and again in the chorus which plays subdued organ harmonies behind Morton's piano.

Very much in contrast is the gay, high-riding trio side, *Shreve-*

port Stomp (HMV B.9220), from which the trombone was omitted. The symbiosis between Morton and Simeon is revealed very strongly, and explains the reason for Morton's use of this clarinet player in so much of his recorded work. He once described Simeon as the greatest clarinettist alive, and there can be no doubt that he meant it; Simeon deserves half the credit for this stomp interpretation of the ragtime composition by Morton.

The clarinet arabesques flowering against Bill Benford's forthright tuba passages in *Shoe Shiner's Drag* and Lee Blair's banjolike guitar which rides a steady rhythm section in the gay if somewhat rough *Kansas City Stomps* (titles backed on HMV B.10151) should not be missed.

Deep Creek Blues (HMV B.9220) was the product of a session six months later, in December 1928, at a time of perhaps his greatest affluence. Joe Garland has recalled the memory of those days:

When I worked with him (Morton) as a kid back in 28, Jelly Roll wore a big diamond stick-pin and always carried a thousand-dollar bill around on him. If you accused Jelly of being broke, he would flash that G-note and laugh in your face.[1]

This was the time when bands were getting bigger, but not necessarily better. The influence extended to Morton, for at this session the personnel included three trumpets and three reed instruments.

It is a thoughtful development of the twelve-bar Blues, and induces a melancholy throughout which is very reminiscent of an Ellington treatment of that old jazz stand-by; not musically, but in the sombre mood evoked.

1929 was the last year which saw Morton leading his own regular band, for, although he had temporary bookings, both for dances and recordings, after this year he had to assemble musicians when and where he could to form a Red Hot Pepper group. He was touring New Jersey that year, and it has already been recalled that a happy chance brought George Baquet into the Camden studios. Eight titles were made, but only one was ever issued here, and that is now deleted.[2]

From 1930 until 1938 he was in eclipse. The big sweet bands which arose about that time edged him out of public fancy, and

1. *Downbeat.*
2. *Tank Town Bump*, HMV JF. 56.

he took part in several business ventures which were not very successful, but the publicity which arose from *l'affaire Handy* resulted in his visit to Alan Lomax and the now historical recordings of his music and reminiscences for the Congress Library Archives of Folk Song. As has been mentioned elsewhere, these were eventually issued by *Circle Records* as a limited edition of twelve albums containing ninety twelve-inch sides in all.

They are, of course, extremely rare, very few of these editions of *The Saga of Mr Jelly Lord* as they are called having found their way into this country. However, the revived interest in jazz and Jelly Roll Morton during 1938 and 39 spurred the Victor Company to approach him in 1939 with a view to making some new sides with a pick-up group. He assembled the best musicians available in New York, and on 19 June they recorded four titles which might be styled 'Memories of New Orleans'. The instrumentation was not strictly New Orleans style, and the choice of Sidney de Paris was a little unfortunate, since the swing influence is all too audible in his trumpet work, but on the whole jazz lovers should hear every one of these sides, which, since they are all available, are listed below.

JELLY ROLL MORTON'S NEW ORLEANS JAZZMEN
New York 19/6/1939

Sidney de Paris	Trumpet
Claude Jones	Trombone
Albert Nicholas	Clarinet
Sidney Bechet	Soprano Saxophone
Happy Caldwell	Tenor Saxophone
Jelly Roll Morton	Piano and Vocal
Lawrence Lucie	Guitar
Wellman Braud	Bass
Zutty Singleton	Drums

Didn't He Ramble/Winin' Boy Blues   HMV B.9217
High Society/I Thought I Heard Buddy Bolden Say   HMV B.9216

Then, on 28 September of that same year, they returned to the studios for another session, but Bechet was absent, and the trombonist was changed to Fred Robinson. This time Morton concentrated more on the ragtime style, particularly in *Climax Rag* and *Ballin' the Jack*.

Climax Rag/West End Blues   HMV B.9219
Don't You Leave Me Here/Ballin' the Jack   HMV B.9218

On the strength of these recordings, and the general interest in his music which was accorded by various jazz personalities in America, Morton felt that he was well on the way to re-establishing his name, particularly when the General Record Company asked him to record some of his early piano rags and Blues. These were issued with an accompanying booklet by Charles E. Smith. [1] Other records were made also, and he appeared on the radio and made various appearances in public, but he embarked on a series of lawsuits which failed, and this, coupled with increasingly poor health, turned him into an embittered and prematurely old man. He died in Los Angeles County Hospital in July 1941.

*

I could sit right here and think a thousand miles away,
I could sit right here and think a thousand miles away;
Since I had the blues this bad, I can't remember the day.

1. American issue.

CHAPTER EIGHT

Piano Jazz

THERE are those who would view this chapter heading as a contradiction in terms, since they argue that the piano's arrival in the development of jazz was so late in the day that it should be classified according to its true origins, and termed 'Piano Ragtime'. As long ago as 1927 R. W. S. Mendl said: 'You cannot play jazz music as a pianoforte solo: if you perform syncopated dance music on the pianoforte it is ragtime, not jazz. It only becomes jazz when it is played on a jazz orchestra.'[1]

There must be considered, however, a school of piano playing which developed from the guitar style of wandering musicians in the Southern States, and which has been given the unfortunately puerile label of 'Boogie-Woogie'.

Furthermore, there is another style which has been based on the pianistics of Earl Hines, whose attempts to translate Armstrong's trumpet phrasing into an instrument ill-suited for the idiom resulted in its being christened 'Trumpet-style'. Hines and his followers have sacrificed the jazz for the sake of ornament *generally speaking*.

Ragtime has been dealt with in Chapter Four, so it is to the Blues in its specialized form of boogie that we shall devote our attention.

The first time that the word 'boogie' appears to have been used on record was in 1928 by the Chicago pianist Pine Top Smith (q.v.); but Chicago was not the birthplace of boogie-woogie, although it was fostered in that city to such an extent that its prior claim to existence is sometimes overlooked. Bunk Johnson has said that he heard the style used by pianists in the logging towns of Mississippi and Louisiana long before the twenties, and that insistent repetition of the bass patterns with the left hand which is such a feature of piano boogie quite obviously derives from an imitation of the guitar chording used by strolling singers.

1 *The Appeal of Jazz.*

The style was taken into the little dives and clubs of New Orleans, up the river to St Louis, Chicago and Kansas City – but Chicago had the conditions and environment which brought it to its peak of development during the period which followed Prohibition (1920).

Simply speaking, boogie-woogie consists of *piano* versions of the twelve-bar Blues where the left hand plays a percussive 'walking bass' while the right explores variations of the twelve-bar chords in a rhythmic manner: the whole effect being to create an exciting music full of cross-rhythms. It is essentially a piano style, and the many attempts to convert it into a big band style have resulted in a hybrid result filled with swing riffs and boredom.

Although only a handful of its exponents have achieved fame, there were many who practised it in Chicago before its recognition – ROMEO NELSON, whose *Head Hop Rag*[1] was re-issued by the Hot Record Society in 1938, WILL EZELL whose *Pitchin' Boogie* (Tempo R.31) recaptures the smoky atmosphere of its breeding ground in the little back-street dives of the Windy City, complete with accompanying cornet and guitar; MONTANA TAYLOR who disappeared from sight until the mid-forties, and whose 1929 *Detroit Rocks* (backing of HRS 8) illustrates bass figures which became known as 'the rocks'.

Then there was the pianist from Alabama, CHARLIE 'COW COW' DAVENPORT (*born 1894*),[2] who went to Chicago as early as 1920, and derived his nickname from the words of his *Cow Cow Blues* which related to the cowcatcher on a train. There were CRIPPLE CLARENCE LOFTON, LEMUEL FOWLER, CHARLIE SPAND[3] and SPECKLED RED: there was a legion of pianists playing around in clubs and at rent parties, where their contribution to this economic drive on the part of the host was limited to giving their services while the other 'guests' brought money and/or gin. This was known colloquially as 'pitchin' boogie' – hence the term as applied to the jazz piano style.

1. Incorrectly labelled *Head Rag Hop* on HRS 8 (American).
2. Davenport also claims the invention of the term 'boogie' when quite young: it was derived, he said, from the music's connexions with low life, hence the devil, who was called the 'boogie man'. He also claims to have inspired Pine Top Smith (q.v.).
3. His *Hastings Street* accompanied by Blind Blake, issued on Amer. Col. 37336, illustrates the sympathy between piano and guitar. The reverse is Meade Lux Lewis's 1929 *Honky Tonk Train Blues*. Two titles on Jazz Collector L.18, *She's Got Good Stuff/Big Fat Mamma Blues*.

JIMMY YANCEY (1898–1951) made the inevitable claim to fame in a broadcast of 'We, The People' in the late thirties. He said: 'I invented boogie-woogie', thus adding to the growing throng of old jazz musicians who make sweeping statements when plunged into the limelight of publicity. What he intended to infer, no doubt, was that in the early twenties, after he had toured America, and had made a trip to London, appearing before King George V and the Royal Family, he returned to Chicago and was influential in spreading the fame of his boogie style which he had developed to a marked degree. He was certainly one of the most famous pioneers of the subject, and was fêted and welcomed at most of the house parties where a pianist was wanted – and that was most of them.

Of his own early recordings none is available, although the 'Fives', one of his original favourites, was made by him in October 1939, after his rediscovery, and re-titled *Five O'Clock Blues*.[1] This, together with the others issued[2] from this session, show by their vitality and individuality that his method of learning piano by teaching himself to finger out the Blues was no mechanical process. In Yancey's music there is always interest and colour, and he plays with a delicate touch full of mournful expression. This is to be heard most markedly in his accompaniment to Faber Smith, the Blues singer, in *I Received A Letter* (both titles backed on Parlophone R.2959) and *East St Louis Blues*. In both of these, as well as in the other titles mentioned, it will be noticed on hearing them that he uses his own peculiar trade-mark – a change of key for the last two bars.

Three other pianists derived much of their style from Yancey, and received publicity for many years whilst he was a forgotten figure. One was MEADE LUX LEWIS (*born 1905*) whose *Honky Tonk Train Blues* (Parlophone R.2187) (made in 1936 after a long search for him by the American jazz collector John Hammond) was perhaps the first introduction of the style and the word 'boogie' into this country. In the heyday of Chicago pianists he had recorded it for the Paramount Company, but with the years of the depression which followed the Wall Street crash, he had fallen into obscurity, and was found only after more than two years' search, this fine pianist having been reduced to earning a living by washing cars. Having been brought up in a district where

1. Backed by *Yancey Stomp*, HMV B. 9366.
2. *State Street Special/Tell 'em About Me*, HMV B. 9381. *Slow and Easy Blues/The Mellow Blues*, HMV B. 9374.

the trains thundered by every few minutes of the day and night, it was natural that his music should have been influenced by the rattle of wheels in their ever-varying rhythms over the rails. It would be interesting to have Honegger's reaction to this piece of music which was possibly only subconsciously affected by the railway, when he himself composed *Pacific* 231 to demonstrate his passion for locomotives.

Lewis's style has more energy than Yancey's, and his variations change repeatedly, producing kaleidoscopic patterns which shift and alter before the ear has time to accustom itself to the shape.

His *Yancey Special* (Brunswick 02243) was a tribute to the man who inspired him to give up the violin and take to the piano when he was seventeen years old, while his *Whistling Blues* (HMV B.5879) and *Celeste Blues* (Brunswick 02243) show a versatility almost akin to that of Cripple Clarence Lofton, who accompanies his own piano playing by whistling, singing, snapping his fingers, and stomping his feet. The modern 'chee chee' board of Rose Murphy was a device used many years before she was born!

The soft, careful bass figures which stamp much of Lewis's playing, as exemplified in *Yancey Special* and *Bear Cat Crawl* (Parlophone R.2909), are in marked contrast to those displayed by another of Yancey's admirers – ALBERT AMMONS (*1903–49*). Ammons and Lewis played around together a good deal, since they found themselves working in the same taxi-service in the early twenties, when they would park their cabs and get into some little spot where they could enjoy themselves while playing the Blues. Although he travelled around with a small band, even taking them to New Orleans, he did not record at all until 1936, when he took the band which had currently been playing with him at the Club de Lisa into the Decca Studios in Chicago and made four titles [1], of which *Boogie-Woogie Stomp* is sufficient to hear in order to realize the powerful drive and rhythm which he imparts to his playing. It is regrettable that these sides should have been made with the accompanying band, which reverts to riffing towards the end of this title. However, towards the end of 1938 he went to New York, where he recorded for several companies, and amongst his solos which are available, and which show his forceful style, is *Shout For Joy*. [2]

It was these two pianists, Mead Lux Lewis and Albert Ammons,

1. *B–W Stomp/Nagasaki*, Brunswick 02187. *Early Mornin' Blues/Mile or Mo' Bird Rag*, Brunswick 02336.
2. Parlophone R. 2909 (reverse of M. L. Lewis, *Bear Cat Crawl*).

who shared lodgings with CLARENCE PINE TOP SMITH (*1900–28*). He was an eccentric character who slept all day and mooched around the clubs at night, travelling, when finances permitted, to St Louis and other cities where boogie pianists were popular. His version of the music which he helped to make known was the one which first put the word 'Boogie-Woogie' on record, and consists of an excellent example of the style on piano, and is accompanied by his instructions to dancers just what to do as they danced to it.

> I want all o' you oughta to know
> This is 'Pine Top's boogie-woogie'
> I want everybody to dance just like I tell ya
> And when I say: 'Hold yerself'
> I want all of yer git ready to stop.
> An' when I say 'stop' – Don't move
> An' when I say 'git it':
> I want all of you to do a boogie-woogie.

This *Pine Top's Boogie-Woogie* (Brunswick 03600) has been copied by many of the boogie and pseudo-boogie pianists and also by full bands. Not one recaptures the simplicity and charm of the original version. *Pine Top's Blues* (Brunswick 03600), still in the boogie idiom, has a lyric which is worth quoting in full, if only as a warning to weak men who allow themselves to be bossed by their wives.

In the usual twelve-bar form, the first line is, of course, repeated in each couplet.

Now, my woman's got a heart like a rock cast down in the sea;
She 'magines she can love everybody and mistreat poor me.

Now I cook her breakfas', even carry it to her bed:
Now she's taken one bite and threw her teacup at poor Pine Top's head.

Gonna spend my money till her bank account done got low,
An' she had the nerve to tell me: 'Pine Top, you gotta go.'

Now I combed her hair, even manicured her fingernails:
Every time I git in trouble she let me go to jail.

I'm gonna buy myself a graveyard of my own –
I'm gonna bury that woman ef she don't let me alone.

I can't use no woman ef she don't help me rob an' steal:
Wake up early in the mornin' – can't eat a decent meal.

I'm goin' down on State Street jes' to buy a gallon o' booze,
Cos my bes' gal done lef' me with these Pine Top Blues.

His opening to *Jump Steady Blues* (Brunswick 04426) is a delightful 'dig' at the other pianists who were getting recordings right and left while many of the best boogie men were not. He says, in answer to the question: 'Why, hallo there, Pine Top, what are you doin' sittin' 'round here lookin' so sad with yo' head hung down?' . . . 'I jes' thinkin' 'bout all these piano players goin' 'round here makin' big money playin' on these here records.' 'Why don't you play on some of these records?' 'Boy, that's a good idee, I b'lieve I start rehearsin' right now.' He then plays one of his best examples of thoughtful and restrained boogie. His friend's comment at the end is an epitome of praise. He just says: 'Boy, that ought to get it.'

Pine Top Smith might have achieved fame in the public eye had he not been unlucky enough to be shot in a dance hall. The accounts vary: some say he was an unfortunate onlooker, others that he was involved in a dispute about a girl. The details are of no importance: the fact of his death was a definite loss to jazz piano playing in Chicago.

St Louis was not silent in the matter of boogie pianists, for it will be remembered that this city fostered the growth of ragtime at an earlier date, and had a reputation for breeding jazz pianists especially. Wesley Wallace, Jabo Williams, Henry Brown, and Doug Suggs were practising boogie where their forerunners such as Turpin and Charles Thompson had carried the ragtime torch.

In Kansas City, too, PETE JOHNSON (*born 1904*) was bitten by the fever in 1922, and teamed up with Joe Turner, a bartender and Blues singer. They played and sang at various Kansas City night clubs, where the impatient crowds would shout: '*Roll 'Em, Pete*' (Parlophone R.2672), thus giving him a ready-made title when he was due for a recording in 1938 after the midnight closing law had sent him searching for work and fame in New York. The relentless full pressure style of his had developed fully by this time, as shown by his version of *Boogie-Woogie* (American Columbia 37334) which he recorded in Chicago in October of 1939, a year after he had teamed up with Meade Lux Lewis and Albert Ammons for their famous piano trio in the boogie medium – *Boogie-Woogie Prayer* (Parlophone R.2649). This is a hard-hitting power-house style from start to finish: a much better result was obtained when Ammons and Johnson took advantage of the popular craze for their music in New York in 1941, when they went to the Victor Studios to make eight duets, two of which are available here.[1]

Having made this brief review of the outstanding boogie pianists,

1. HMV B. 9251, *Barrel House Boogie/Cuttin' the Boogie*.

it would be as well to stress that the style is self-sufficient. It has no developmental future: it is essentially a piano style which crystallized out of certain influences, and the only thing which can be done with it is to do it again, with variations.

We have reached New York in the early forties, when jazz and boogie piano music had made its reappearance after a satiety of swing, but it must not be imagined that New York was devoid of any jazz piano music in the earlier days. There were pianists there before the arrival of the small New Orleans and Dixieland groups in the early twenties; young and aspiring musicians from the main cities which had fostered the growth of solo pianists in their small clubs and cabarets. Their names are now mostly forgotten, but among them were Lucky Roberts, Jack the Bear, and One Leg Willie; ragtime players who supplied the incentive for a small boy of twelve who moved into town from the outskirts with his parents. His name was JAMES P. JOHNSON (*born 1891*).

*

Now affectionately known as the 'Grandfather of Hot Piano', James P. Johnson had studied music at home and under capable teachers before he was taken into the heart of New York, and under the influence of the many pianists he heard there, he soon became a professional around the clubs – even running a small band of his own in Harlem by the time he was twenty-five. He had spent the intervening years in the formation of a Blues style which, without exaggeration, places him in the forefront of all Blues pianists. It is unfortunate that his early work, which was recorded for player-piano rolls, one of which has been transcribed on to a record,[1] is not available in this country. It demonstrates his freedom of approach, the flavour of ragtime, clean execution, and breadth of conception all of which were far ahead of their time.

His training in classical harmony and composition led him into the field of revue, and in 1920 he accompanied the Jim Europe group for a six months' tour of England and the Continent with their show 'Plantation Days', for which he had written some of the numbers. Upon his return, he devoted much time to similar ventures, writing the music for 'The Great Ziegfeld', and composing melodies which are still popular. *I Can't Give You Anything but Love* and *Runnin' Wild* are but two examples.

1. *Make Me a Pallet on the Floor*, Century 4001. Same title issued on Jazz Collector L.60.

Although he recorded several piano solos during these years, it is profitless to discuss them, since they have never been re-issued here, but some of his work as an accompanist to the great Blues singers who were in New York is available; one outstanding is the restrained and sympathetic treatment which he used in *Back Water Blues* (Parlophone R.2481) by Bessie Smith. These two had much in common, and his contribution to the success of the 'Empress of the Blues' must not be overlooked, for he first met her when he was touring Atlantic City as a solo act, and found her as a member of a singing trio. He aided her career, and accompanied her on tour as well as on record.

Other singers during this period which he accompanied for recordings were Trixie Smith, Clara Smith, Ethel Waters, and Lavina Turner. He also took part in some recordings for McKinney Cotton Pickers and the Louisiana Sugar Babies. The latter group included his pupil Fats Waller (q.v.) on organ.

Before his retirement in 1930, when he went to Jamaica to concentrate on serious composition for eight years, he waxed a title which is the one of the few piano solos of his available in this country at the time of writing. It was an exploration in the 'riff' field, in which he demonstrated the variations which could be made in a simple phrase; it was called, simply: *Riffs*. [1]

His return to the jazz fold in 1938 was celebrated by a session in which he accompanied Rosetta Crawford, together with Mezz Mezzrow and Tommy Ladnier. These discs [2] have already been mentioned in Chapter Six, and if his position as the doyen of Blues pianists were to be questioned, these alone would confirm it.

His work with the Mezzrow Orchestra under the *aegis* of Hugues Panassié in November 1938 is by no means representative, and the reason for this is to be found in the following rather lengthy quotation from the book *Really the Blues:* [3]

When we hit upon Sidney de Paris for the second trumpet on this date, I noticed Tommy Ladnier screw his face up and frown, because he was afraid Sidney played in a too modern idiom.... Things had gone along fair for about the first nine choruses, but then Sidney's suppressed 'modern' instincts got the better of him and he got evil and began to growl on his horn. The riff he growled was a discordant one that went

1. Parlophone R. 1072. Note that 'Jimmy' Johnson and James P. Johnson are one and the same person.
2. *I'm Tired of Fattenin' Frogs/Double Crossin' Papa*, Brunswick 03461. *Stop It Joe/My Man Jumped Salty on Me*, Vocalion V.1002.
3. Milton Mezz Mezzrow and Bernard Wolfe. 1946.

way tangent to the whole spirit of the music, and it made Tommy furious. Then Sidney wound up the first ending of the tenth chorus with a real modern swing riff that's a terrible cliché. That made Tommy say '*Merde*' real loud on his horn, and it scared everybody in the band so bad that we didn't have our bearings to start the eleventh chorus.[1] . . . On that same date we made *Revolutionary Blues* (HMV B.9470), a type of Blues that comes from the real old school and has been almost completely forgotten. It has thirty-two bars, but differs from the standard thirty-two bar chorus that Tin Pan Alley uses, because it isn't divided into first eight bars, second eight bars, then the release for eight, and then back to the first eight. It starts with sixteen bars, then resolves back to them with no release, and the last eight bars have a definite resolution that was invented by the real New Orleans jazz school. . . . I'm afraid not many people got the point.

Well, we never did get to finish our fourth side on this date, although we started one. Tommy and James P. Johnson were so fed up with the way things were going, and Tommy resented Sidney's modern style so much, that both he and James P. got real juiced. In the middle of the next record Tommy yelled '*Vive la France*' and James P. fell off the piano stool.

The very commercial sides made under the name of Frankie Newton and His Orchestra are no indication of the fine work which James P. Johnson created after his return to the jazz field. His version of *Frankie and Johnny* under the title of *A Flat Dream* (American Columbia 37333) is an excursion into the boogie field which shows versatility and an exercise in right-hand technique which is flavoured with ragtime and Czerny. It would be a great service to jazz if his *Snowy Morning Blues* (Asch 350-3 (American) could be issued here, in addition to the 1938 Pee Wee Russell Rhythmaker[2] and Trio discs.[3]

James P. Johnson is a great Blues pianist, and it is to him that the myriad admirers of Fats Waller have to give a certain amount of their credit, for he it was who helped foster and mould the style of that great entertainer.

THOMAS 'FATS' WALLER (1904–43)

Fats Waller was unique, and for this reason it will be useless to try and trace any future developments of his style. It can be copied, of course, with varying success, but the imitation is usually so poor a carbon copy that it is pointless.

1. *Comin' on with the Come On. Part* 2. HMV B. 9468.
2. *Baby Won't You Please Come Home*/*Dinah*, Melodisc 1137.
3. *I've Found a New Baby*/*Everybody Loves My Baby*, Melodisc 1144.

His uniqueness lies in the fact that he achieved world fame in both the popular sense of the word and in the jazz field, an extremely difficult feat, for in most cases excursions into the realm of 'what the public likes' result in an adulteration of artistic integrity. An artist may produce drivel for public consumption and create things that really matter for his own benefit, or for the benefit of a few friends to appreciate. The drivel he may serve up with his tongue in his cheek, carefully turned away from his audience.

Fats Waller managed to take some of the rubbish which he knew the public enjoyed, and, by his own legerdemain, transmuted it into an enjoyable guying of its own worst aspects. Not only that, he managed to take the public into his confidence, as if he were saying: 'Now look, you know this is tripe, and I know it's tripe, but let's see what we can do with it to make it palatable, and, at the same time, see if we can have some jazz and get a little fun out of it!'

This must not be taken to imply that he was always the lovably satirical entertainer. His piano solos, and his work as a rhythm section painist with many jazz groups, point to a jazz feeling and interpretation which is unequalled in many respects, and that inborn sense led him to make the classic reply to a lady who asked him what rhythm was. He replied simply and in perfect good faith: 'Lady, if you has to ask, you ain't got it.'

He has no history of knocking around the dives of New Orleans or Chicago, listening with bated breath to the legendary jazz 'greats', no marching in the second line of a street parade, for he was born in Harlem and his father, Pastor Waller, intended him to follow in his footsteps, perhaps in time to preach at the Abyssinian Baptist Chapel. To prepare him for this, he was given piano and organ lessons, and, as a boy, used to play the harmonium at open-air prayer meetings.

One can well imagine the grief and chagrin which greeted his first attempts at ragtime on the family harmonium, and the even greater opposition which must have been raised when he announced his intention of taking up the new 'jass' music as a career. But take it up he did, and in his teens was playing in Harlem theatres and picture houses.

It was this medium which gave Waller his greatest impetus, for it was here that he met James P Johnson, who coached him in music and became his life-long friend. That he quickly profited by the excellent tuition may be judged by the fact that the pupil won a piano-playing contest at the Roosevelt Theatre in 1919 against many much older contestants. Between this date and 1924 he was engaged around New York as a solo pianist and accompanist, and for occasional spots with different bands. After a year with Erskine Tate's Orchestra in Chicago, he returned to New York and took part in several recordings with Fletcher Henderson's Band, playing organ, one title which they made in 1927 still remaining in catalogue – *I'm Comin' Virginia* (Parlophone R.2540).

Although he had recorded this year with a group which was known as Morris's Hot Babies, the first jazz waxed under his own name was made in such colourful circumstances that it is well worth hearing Eddie Condon's account:[1]

... The Southern Music Company had an interest and an investment in Fats: Fats, who was having alimony trouble, had become indifferent to his Victor recording dates – he didn't get what he earned so he didn't care. Either he didn't keep the appointments or he arrived with a band which was unrehearsed. The Southern Music Company was disturbed, Mr Adams said. It had advanced Fats some money ... 'We would like you to undertake the task of finding Waller and delivering him to the studio on time and with a well-rehearsed band.' It sounded difficult. I hadn't yet met Waller; why should he let me discipline him for the sake of the Southern Music Company? 'We'll pay you seventy-five dollars if you can do it,' Mr Adams said. At the moment I would have attempted to produce Herbert Hoover in a soft collar. 'I'll try.' I said. ... At the end of the first day I was not overly worried except in the matter of my capacity for gin. Obviously it was suicide to match Fats drink for drink. I began to duck and sidestep. All during the second day and the second night I kept trying. 'Fine! Wonderful! Perfect!' Fats said whenever I mentioned the recording date. 'Now let's have a little gin and talk about it.' The third day I was desperate; as night came on I kept talking and Fats kept handing me drinks. There was still no band. 'After we get the band together what shall we play?' I asked. 'Why, we'll play music,' Fats said. 'Now let's have a little drink and talk about it.'

Things grew faint and finally dark. When I awoke I was lying on the wall cushions at Connie's Inn, fully dressed. It was half past ten in the morning. On another cushion Fats was curled up, also fully dressed, asleep. I staggered over to him. He opened his eyes and smiled. 'It's half past ten,' I croaked. 'We're due at the studio at noon.'

He sat up, stretched and yawned. 'That's fine! That's wonderful! That's perfect!' he said. 'Now we've got to see about that band. Look around for some nickels so I can make that telephone go.' He went to the phone booth and made three calls. By the time we finished washing

1. *We Called It Music.* Eddie Condon and Thomas Sugrue.

and straightening our clothes three musicians had arrived: Charlie
Gains, a trumpet player: Charlie Irvis, a trombonist: and Arville
Harris, who played clarinet and alto saxophone.

'What are you going to play?' I asked, though by now I figured it
didn't matter. Mr Adams would throw me out after the first note. 'You
mean what are we going to play?' Fats said. 'Man, you're with us.
Where's your banjo?' 'But I'm not supposed to play with you,' I said.
'I only came to make the date and help you to get the band together.'

Fats looked hurt. 'You mean you don't want to play with us?' he
said. 'I would love to play with you', I said. 'My banjo is at the Riverside Towers.' 'We'll stop and get it,' Fats said. 'Charlie, get a taxi.'

We piled into a taxi and headed down Seventh Avenue. 'Now here is
what we are going to play,' Fats said suddenly. He hummed a simple,
basic pattern of rhythm and melody, a Blues in a minor key. When we
had it memorized, he explained what each of us was to do. 'You got
that, Charlie?' he said.

Both Charlies said yes. They had it.

... 'Well Mr Adams,' Fats said, 'this morning I think we'll start with a
little thing called *The Minor Drag* (titles backed on HMV X.6252, but
reversed). It's a slow number. Then we got a little ol' thing for the other
side we call' – he hesitated – '*Harlem Fuss*' (titles backed on HMV
X.6252, but *reversed*).... We set up our instruments and Fats repeated
his instructions. He played the theme for us; as soon as I heard him I
knew why we didn't need drums – his left hand would take care of the
bass ... we listened to the playback. I had a difficult time believing
what I heard because it sounded so wonderful. I looked at Mr Adams.
He was smiling. 'You see,' he said to me, 'what careful rehearsal will
do? You have performed your job excellently.' ... 'I wonder, Mr
Waller,' he said, 'if we could have some piano solos now?'

'Wonderful!' Fats said. 'Perfect! we'll have some piano solos.' Without moving from the bench he made *Handful of Keys* and *Numb
Fumblin'* (titles backed on HMV B.4347). *Handful of Keys* turned out
to be the most popular of all his recorded piano solos.

'We must have some more of these dates,' Mr Adams said. 'This is
an excellent example of the wisdom of planning and preparation.'

After that the Southern Music Company, with careful planning and
preparation, brought out the record on a Victor label with the titles
reversed: *Harlem Fuss* was called *The Minor Drag* and *The Minor Drag*
was called *Harlem Fuss*. I got my seventy-five dollars.

Waller became a prolific recorder, and sat in with many different bands, and to them all he brought that spontaneous gaiety
which characterizes his work, and which was such a feature of his
playing and singing. That powerful left hand which was such a
support to the rhythm section is heard to advantage in a later
session of his 'Buddies', an entirely different group. There are no

solos in the titles issued,[1] but they are well worth hearing for the integration of the rhythm section alone.

In 1931 his presence with Ted Lewis made one or two of that leader's records bearable, especially when it is remembered that Muggsy Spanier and Georg Brunis were also fellow musicians. *Dallas Blues* and *Royal Garden Blues* (titles backed on Columbia CB.446) are suggested as an example of his playing and singing before the formation of his 'Rhythm' group in 1934. Also, before that time, he had taken part in the Billy Banks' Rhythmakers' sessions in New York City in July 1932, of which *Yellow Dog Blues* (Parlophone R.2810) might be taken as representative.

Needless to say, the singing on this record is not by Waller. It has been cited to show the style of his piano work with the pick-up group.

In 1934 he got together a small group of jazzmen and the title which he chose lasted with him until his last appearance in 1943. It was aptly chosen, for 'Fats Waller and His Rhythm' describes most of the music which he created under that name. The driving force and the dynamic energy which comes bursting through those nine years of playing and recording carries the Waller hall-mark in every link, whether it be the early *You're Not the Only Oyster* (HMV JF.11) or *Original E Flat Blues* (HMV BD.906) of later years.

It would be pointless and exhausting to list his recordings during those years. Reference to HMV catalogues will show which are still available, and it is the greatest tribute which can be paid him to say that it does not matter much which is chosen. They are all good entertainment, and most of them are filled with the jazz spirit and interpretation.

Writing of Waller in 1950, Ed Kirkeby (who was his personal manager and almost constant companion for six years) said:

I remember one critic who said, 'He is a volcano that erupts laughter and music' . . . and that is exactly right. His great skill at the keyboard was equalled only by his effervescent and lovable nature. What an audience regarded as an exhibition of rare piano artistry, was just 'Fats' enjoying himself at the piano. He lived for music, and would stay up all night and day if he could play, or just be where music was.[2]

It was wrong, perhaps, to infer that his particular piano style ended when he died of heart failure on 15 December 1943. Cer-

1. *Ridin' But Walkin'/Won't You Get Off It Please*, HMV B. 4971.
2. *The Music of Thomas 'Fats' Waller*. John R. T. Davies. J. J. Publications.

tainly there is none to take his place, no one to radiate all the facets of his inimitable playing and singing. But Una Mae Carlise, Joe Sullivan and Art Hodes are still with us, and when any of those pianists play the Blues, that powerful left-hand phrasing and rhythm which comes through their music comes to us by courtesy of Fats Waller – and they would be the first ones to admit it.

It has been a fad among some jazz purists to sneer at much of Waller's work as being too commercial. That is a fallacy. He had the gift of taking commercial popular tunes and turning them into jazz in a manner which has never been equalled.

Perhaps his best epitaph is the modest little phrase used about him by Panassié in 1936:[1]

When Fats Waller, the pianist, sings, he exhibits great spirit and an exquisite sense of humour.

1. *Hot Jazz.*

CHAPTER NINE

The Influence of European Orthodoxy in Arrangement

In Chapters Six and Seven it has been indicated how, after the era of the Chicago Roaring Twenties, jazz was kept alive by the great individualists like Armstrong and by many true jazzmen who were engulfed by the commercialism of the 1930s. Many readers will wonder if bands like Fletcher Henderson and Duke Ellington have been forgotten – for these names were for many years synonymous with jazz to the average layman with a mild interest in all types of music. They have not been forgotten, but they are being by-passed, as it were. This book takes what will inevitably be termed in derogatory fashion a 'purist' outlook.

During a broadcast in which he was being questioned about his outlook on jazz, Humphrey Lyttelton stated that 'if being broad-minded means saying I like something when inwardly I know I detest it then I'm narrow-minded and proud of it'. This book takes a similar attitude. If being catholic in its outlook on jazz means accepting as jazz forms of music which are utterly divorced from the real thing then this is a purist book, 'and proud of it'.

Nevertheless the outlook is not the extreme one of condemning all other forms of 'hot' music as being completely worthless; much of Henderson, Redman and Lunceford is good music of its kind; most of Ellington is unique as an original musical form; but it is not jazz in the strict sense.

Jazz – the traditional jazz – still very much alive *as long as it was played by men steeped in the virile tradition of New Orleans* (even outside of that city and after the classic period), was weakened as soon as the influence of European classic orthodoxy was felt. This is not to say that it was a direct influence; but centuries of appreciation of classical music in schools, concert halls, and salons had created a hide-bound convention, a convention that the only music of any stature was music which was written down. Implicit in that essential was the convention that music was a product of the mind, sometimes romantic, sometimes severe, analytical or lyrical, but always the expression of thought methodically transposed into a written form. The conventional outlook has always been careful to ignore the basic fact that music, an aural sensation, cannot logically be represented visually; Toscanini may do his utmost with Beethoven's Fifth but neither he nor anybody else can ever know what was in Beethoven's mind when he wrote it; neither can they ever know exactly how Beethoven himself wished it to be played. The nearest approximation is the extent to which Beethoven was able to produce visually what he felt *within the limitations of the written conventions.*

All the arrangers and leaders of orchestras who employed arrangers played from the mind; the leaders of the eleven- to fourteen-piece bands were confronted with jazz having already approached music as a whole from the normal orthodox direction, that of learning to 'read the dots' and absorbing the structural conventions which produced these dots. Jazz, on the other hand, like all folk music, is emotional in outlook. It is 'playin' from the heart'. Improvisational in form, it is highly individual in so far as complete freedom of expression is allowed, limited only by the boundaries of three-part counterpoint and rhythmic foundation. Inspiration, spontaneity, exuberance, absence of inhibition, all these qualities are axiomatic in jazz. Once the ideal number of six or seven musicians is increased by an extra melodic instrument; once a single clarinet is replaced by a section of three or more reed instruments, scored passages, stereotyped arrangements become indispensable (if sanity is to be preserved); spontaneity and the opportunity for improvisation disappears – and the jazz spirit is lost.

Conscious arrangement, therefore, when it reaches the stage in which the structure of the performance is controlled in its entirety by a preconceived design, can only be detrimental to genuine jazz.

In the light of this dictum the value of the so-called jazz arrangers will be discussed if only to discount any impression that arranged jazz has ever had any 'progressive' effect, or indeed any influence at all on the traditions of Perez, Ory, and Oliver.

The men responsible for this divergence from the path of New Orleans jazz were, in the first place, Negroes who were educated in the North and who had already experienced other forms of music before coming into contact with jazz. They had been brought up with a social background which was advanced beyond the standards of the Vieux Carré of New Orleans to a point of sophistication. Jazz, to them, was almost as much a novelty as it was to the white students of the Austin High School in Chicago. FLETCHER HENDERSON (*born 1898, in Georgia*) is the best (and chronologically the first) example of a musician who drew upon the jazz idiom just sufficiently to suit his own end; which was to produce a music which at once satisfied his own musical tendencies and at the same time satisfied the customers at the Roseland Ballroom, New York.

He is remembered by the historians of jazz mainly for the incredible number of first-class instrumentalists who played with him at one time or another and for the incredibly small proportion of worthwhile records out of the many hundreds he produced. He played every winter season at the Roseland from 1920 or thereabouts until 1936, which, considering he was an indifferent business man, was quite an achievement and an indication that, if he did not play pure jazz, at least he played a good deal of what the public wanted. He played very little more than dozens of the larger bands of the period, in content that is; but what he did was generally much better, more polished; the arrangements were neater and, an important factor, they were not too complicated either for musician to play or average audience to follow. The trite clichés, the standard contrast of reed against brass, the repeated riff – all the hall-marks of the swing era some ten years later, are to be found in almost any Henderson record of the mid-twenties. What is of interest to the jazz enthusiast is the occasional gem of a solo from a gifted jazzman who had found his way into the aggregation; listening to some of these early discs (some of them are appalling) it is difficult to understand how Armstrong and Ladnier were able to derive any inspiration at all in such an atmosphere. For the appreciation of jazz, therefore, no records are recommended in addition to those which have already been mentioned in connexion with Ladnier or Armstrong.

Of the many virtuosi who played with Henderson at one time or another and who followed the same school of thought in providing a glossy arranged background for a limited amount of solo work was DON REDMAN (*born 1900*). He stayed with Henderson from 1925 until 1926, when he left to join an orchestra from Detroit known as the McKinney Cotton Pickers, which had been formed as a show band as early as 1920. With the addition of Redman as alto saxophone player and arranger the band improved quickly and from 1928 to 1931 were as popular as Henderson; in the Greystone Ballroom in Detroit it was reported that the Cotton Pickers won a 'battle of bands' with Henderson before 7500 people. Redman was a good arranger and could be quite ambitious with such men to support him as Joe Smith, Rex Stewart, Sidney de Paris, Benny Carter, John Nesbitt, and occasionally Fats Waller, Coleman Hawkins, and Lonnie Johnson. Much of the McKinney output around the end of the 1920's would not disgrace, stylistically, many bands of to-day in the field of arranged and ordered eleven- or twelve-piece orchestra music.

Redman was highly thought of in Negro musical circles. During his spell with the Cotton Pickers, he had also taken part in some recordings with Louis Armstrong's Savoy Ballroom Five. Later on, in 1931, he formed his own orchestra, which had a run of success and made a series of records with arrangements either by its leader or by Horace Henderson, with a high percentage of vocal choruses by the whimsical Redman himself or by Harlan Lattimore, a sentimental crooner. Recorded examples are good – of their kind; *Chant of the Weed* (Brunswick 01244) suggests that Redman had real talent in a field outside the scope of jazz.

Mention has been made of BENNY CARTER (*born 1907*), one of the leading musicians of the McKinney Cotton Pickers. He had also played with Billy Fowler (the Chicago Orchestra which included Ladnier), Charlie Johnson, Horace Henderson, and Fletcher Henderson and was responsible for organizing the well-known recording group, the Chocolate Dandies. Carter is an astonishingly versatile instrumentalist, playing clarinet, trumpet, and saxophone, excelling as an alto saxophonist. Most of his solo and arranged work warrants the same comment as Redman – that as a musician he possesses tremendous talent. His powers of invention, technique, tone, all are of the highest order, yet, lacking the essential warmth and drive of the true jazzman, he never entirely satisfies. Listening to Benny Carter is listening to a *demonstration* of beauty; it is self-conscious, never completely relaxed; and it never imparts that sense of urgency which is an essential to jazz performance. The records by the Chocolate Dandies and later orchestras, including some composed of English musicians, have an atmosphere about them which is coldly beautiful, refined, delicate and *studied*. Jazz is none of these things.

It is not without interest to imagine what would have been the position if, when with Billy Fowler's Band in the rough and ready days of the early twenties in Chicago, Carter had not had the advantage of a university education. Possessing an inherent musical instinct as he did he might well have joined forces with Ladnier and sought self-expression in the same way as did that fine jazz trumpet man – from the heart rather than from the mind, the orthodox musical world of crochets and quavers. . . .

Carter will be remembered as a wonderful technician, the possessor of unrivalled melodic inventive powers; yet the comparatively uncultured Ladnier will remain with posterity as a jazz immortal. Orthodoxy versus instinct, the brain versus the heart.[1]

A closely similar career to that of Carter was traced by JIMMIE LUNCEFORD (1902–48); similar in that, like Carter, Lunceford learned his music in an academic way, had a university education, and later developed a form of orchestral swing which used intensive arrangement as its basis. Unlike Carter, however, Lunceford left the arranging to others, such as Sy Oliver, Edwin Wilcox, and Willy Smith. His orchestra was formed as early as 1926, though it was not until he succeeded Cab Calloway at the Cotton Club in 1934 that he became well-known and made records. The keynote of the Lunceford Band was arrangement; the results of the work of Sy Oliver – the foremost of the arranging 'team' – are remarkable for their originality and for the way in which scoring for a fourteen- to sixteen-piece orchestra was brought to perfection. The band was extremely efficient and polished: a criterion of technical discipline; and as the records became known the Lunceford Band acquired an enviable reputation as being second only to Duke Ellington as a large orchestra playing in the jazz idiom. If it is ever accepted that arranged precision is the life-blood of jazz, then Jimmie Lunceford's Orchestra would be amongst the blue-bloods.

In the matter of blue-blooded arrangement the aristocrat of them all is, of course, EDWARD 'DUKE' ELLINGTON (born Washington, 1899). Many and varied have been the arguments for and against Ellington as a jazzman – and no decision has yet been reached by the majority of critics. But to start at the beginning; Ellington studied at the Fine Art School of Pratt Institute in Washington and later turned his full attention to the study of the contemporary popular music. Unlike all the others, however, he

1. The tenor-saxophonist Coleman Hawkins possessed great powers of improvisation which, had they been canalized into a different medium of expression, e.g. the clarinet, might well have secured him a permanent place in jazz.

set out from the start to create his own music out of the basic structure of jazz. At first the Ellington innovations were not particularly revolutionary or distinctive, neither was his band very successful. His first small group was formed in 1918, yet his first records were not made until 1926 – and these had, in the beginning, little to distinguish them from the work of other orchestras.

But this was not for long and with the recording of his signature tune *East St Louis Toodle-Oo* (Brunswick 01681), he began a series of original and individual orchestrations which were to be the first of hundreds and which were to be acclaimed by critics in the field of classical music as the work of a composer of considerable importance. From the start it quickly became obvious that improvisation and freedom of expression were to play little part in Ellingtonian jazz. Much has been made of the fact that many of the players in the band contributed to various compositions, and, in fact, were often given credit for them; but this in no way invalidates the point that there was little freedom for original ideas. Ellington's men (for the most part) thought like their leader; they fitted in with his moods in much the same way as the sections of a symphony orchestra fit in with their conductor's moods. The greater similarity there was between the musicians' moods and Ellington's the better the performance, *as Ellington music*. True jazz feeling was entirely absent; collective improvisation non-existent; the little jazz contained in the earlier performances from 1928 to the mid-thirties is by musicians who, in another element, would have produced some fine jazz; even so, the many solos by trumpeter JAMES 'BUBBER' MILEY (*1903–32*) and JOE 'TRICKY SAM' NANTON (*1900–46*) both of whom played mostly with muted effects, including the highly vocal 'wah-wah' sound, and by ALBANY 'BARNEY' BIGARD (*born 1906*) stand out against the stylized backgrounds like the proverbial sore thumb. Bigard, it will be remembered, was originally with King Oliver and has since left Ellington to join Louis Armstrong's modern version of the Hot Five, where his warm New Orleans clarinet tone and technique is put to better purpose.

While at the Kentucky Club in 1927 Duke Ellington had been noticed by that astute agent and promoter, Irving Mills, who at once took over the band as manager. This fact is probably the reason for Ellington's great success commercially as well as musically. He soon had the most talked-of band in Harlem (where competition is always fierce); in 1928 he appeared in the *Blackbird Review* on Broadway and in 1930 he opened at the

Cotton Club. In 1933 he toured Europe, appearing at the Palladium in London, where he created such an impression on representatives from all musical schools of thought that his visit is still the subject of conversation from Archer Street to the Athenaeum. If Ellington's Famous Orchestra did not show us pure traditional jazz it did prove how far superior were Negro jazz musicians to their white imitators. The hack writers in the musical journals who had tried to convince the Great British Public that English dance musicians were the equal of the American were forced to have second thoughts. Mercifully for mediocre British music circles, London has not heard an orchestra like Ellington's since.

From 1935 until 1940 few examples of the Duke's music reached England in the shape of gramophone records, but soon after the beginning of World War II a series of HMV issues indicated that, basically, Ellington had changed little, though his approach had matured considerably. Far less scope was given to musicians to show their individuality and the best assessment that can be made is that the 1940 band was easily the most original swing band of all time.

Before proceeding further with an analysis of Ellington's influence on jazz and his position in the field of music as a whole and in order to dispense with innumerable footnotes the following records are listed as being representative of the various periods of his development:

1926	*Lil' Farina* Tempo R.17
1927	*East St Louis Toodle-Oo* Brunswick 02308
	Birmingham Breakdown Brunswick 02299
1928	*Creole Love Call* HMV B.4895
	Black and Tan Fantasy HMV B.6356
	Blues I Love To Sing HMV B.4966
	Jubilee Stomp HMV B.4869
	Tishomingo Blues Brunswick 02503
	Hot and Bothered Parlophone R.582
	The Mooche HMV B.4920
1929	*Saturday Night Function* HMV B.4956
	Stevedore Stomp HMV B.6106
	Saratoga Swing HMV B.8828
1930	*Double Check Stomp* HMV BD.5759
	Big House Blues Parlophone R.1044
	Mood Indigo Brunswick 01068
1931	*Rockin' In Rhythm* HMV B.9253
	Limehouse Blues HMV BD.5756
	Echoes of the Jungle HMV BD.5756

1932   *Lazy Rhapsody*   Parlophone R.2890
1933   *Drop Me Off at Harlem*   Parlophone R.2876
       Delta Serenade   HMV B.9345
       Solitude   HMV B.8410
1934   *Saddest Tale*   Parlophone R.2880
1935   *Margie*   Parlophone R.2884
1936   *Clarinet Lament*   Parlophone R.2876
       Echoes of Harlem   Parlophone R.2904
1937   *Caravan*   Parlophone R.3041
1938   *Riding on a Blue Note*   Parlophone R.3062
1940   *Dusk*   HMV B.9115
       Blue Goose   HMV B.9115
       Portrait of Bert Williams   HMV B.9085
1941   *Chelsea Bridge*   HMV B.9309

All these records and hundreds more like them have the Ellington mark stamped indelibly on them. Were it not for the skill of the orchestration and the individual inspiration of the fine jazz musicians employed by Ellington they might well be dismissed on the grounds that 'once you've heard one or two, you've heard the lot'. Ellington has produced a music which is so highly individual that it cannot be pigeon-holed into any category except one marked 'Ellington'.

The records listed give examples of his various approaches; the 'hot' theme – *Hot and Bothered* or *Portrait of Bert Williams;* the mood piece like *Black and Tan Fantasy;* the Blues interpretation as in *Tishomingo Blues* or the concerto style as in *Clarinet Lament.* The examples have been chosen quite at random. Ellington was a prolific composer and several different lists could be compiled equally as representative.

Max Jones neatly summed up Ellington's progress:

At first Ellington was content to contribute modestly to each performance although, even then, his modicum of stylized arrangement served to stamp the piece unmistakably. With the years, he scored more and more precise parts for his men so that there was less freedom for individual variations. The progress of his musical ideas can be charted from the records, which show him toying with jazz, then on to a super swing music, and now transcending the jazz and swing idioms with *tempo*-less tone poems couched in near-jazz phraseology. [1]

Ellington's attempted fusion of jazz with a classical format has, of course, left a deep impression upon many straight musicians and 'serious' critics, who have made many false conclusions. Constant Lambert, for example, talked of Ellington as being the

1. *Jazz Photo Album.* British Yearbooks.

'first jazz composer of distinction'. On a general musical basis, forgetting the strict interpretation of the meaning of the word 'jazz' as used in this book, this is true. Lambert speaks of tone colour: '. . . amazingly skilful proportions in which the colour is used . . . as compared with so-called high-brow composers. I know nothing in Ravel so dexterous in treatment as the varied solos in *Hot and Bothered* and nothing more dynamic than the final section.' And of the slow compositions: '. . . palpably from the same hand. How well we know those composers whose slow movements seem to be written by someone else – who change in the course of the same section from slow Vaughan Williams to quick Stravinsky and from quick Hindemith to slow César Franck. The ability to maintain the same style in totally different moods is one of the hall-marks of the genuine composer, whether major or minor.'[1]

No musical illustration to support the title of this chapter is better suited than Ellington's suite entitled *Black, Brown and Beige*, recorded on four twelve-inch sides (HMV C.3504–5). In this work the movements are divided as follows:

1. *Work Song.*
2. *Come Sunday* (Spiritual).
3. *The Blues.*
4. *West Indian Dance: Emancipation Celebration: Sugar Hill Penthouse.*

It is an attempt to recapitulate the history of jazz in the Ellington orchestral style and shows the latest stage of his musical development, having become more and more influenced by classical composers, notably Frederick Delius. The music shows that either Ellington was a man nurtured on jazz history or that he had primed himself well. The latter is the logical assumption, but while this is transparently a serious piece of composition, the third movement alone, *The Blues* (which should have been so important in a work of this nature), is so steeped in pretentiousness that it belies the genuine character of the composer's background, and the weakness of his jazz instincts.

Much protest has been voiced and penned on the sacrilege of 'jazzing the classics'. There should be an equal protest lodged against classicizing jazz.[2] Ellington has, through the years, produced a music which at the beginning was close to jazz; which, on the strength of his musicians' jazz instincts, was considered

1. *Music Ho!* Constant Lambert. Pelican 195, Penguin Books. 1948.
2. *Tiger Rag*, by the Boston Promenade Orchestra, is a shocking example.

jazz even when he drifted away from it; and which, because of his reputation, is still connected with jazz when only remotely related to it.

When the true meaning for the word 'jazz' is more generally accepted and when the ingratiating radio voices cease to refer to any music played with a saxophone as 'jazz' then perhaps will Ellington be recognized for his full musical worth. But as long as he continues to be identified with jazz, both Ellington and Jazz are the losers.

Another whose musical aspirations reflected many shades of popular music was clarinettist ARTIE SHAW (*born 1911*). He is known mainly for his success with a swing band and his capacity for headline notoriety. Nevertheless, for the student of popular music, as opposed to pure jazz, there is much of interest in the many varieties of Shaw's experiment: for the student of jazz his work provides, like Ellington's *Black, Brown and Beige*, a perfect example of the influence of the European orthodox school.

While Ellington was intensely interested in the effect of contrasted combinations of reed instruments, Shaw was enamoured of stringed instruments. Equipped with this revolutionary idea – strings not having been previously used in the swing world – he plunged into the fray with only a limited experience of band work. His cellos and violins caused quite a stir and were welcomed as a change from the four-brass, four-reed swing convention. From his 1936 *Sugar Foot Stomp* (Parlophone R.2940) in which the strings are used to accentuate the contrasting 'hot' theme, to the delightful *Adios Mariquita Linda* (HMV B.9079) (1940) and the peerless display of virtuosity in *Concerto for Clarinet* (HMV C.3231), Shaw has been obsessed by the possibilities of strings and their use in jazz instrumentation; he has even experimented with a harpsichord and French horns. From time to time he dispensed with the use of strings, occasionally producing such titles as *The Blues* (Parlophone R.2790), which, though excellent swing, is a far cry from jazz, containing as it does not a vestige of collective improvisation.

Shaw's concentration on a parade of virtuosity is, perhaps, the reason why, like all the other protégés of the Swing Era, he could never express the uninhibited style of New Orleans music.

One result of the impact of European orthodoxy on jazz music was the formation in Paris of a small group, the 'Quintette du Hot Club de France' in 1934.

This quintet was formed to play at the Hot Club of France

when Freddy Johnson's Harlemites left, and was due to the fore-sight of Pierre Nourry, who, having heard the talented improvisa-tions of both STEPHANE GRAPPELLY (*born 1910*) on violin and DJANGO REINHARDT (*born Belgium 1910*) on guitar, pro-pounded to them a scheme for an all-string group: two guitars and a string bass to form the rhythm section, with violin and featured guitar to provide the melody. This particular use of a plectrum-played guitar would have been fatal except in the case of a master of the instrument such as Reinhardt, but his fluent phrasing and amazing technique, despite the handicap of a muti-lated left hand, enabled him to create single-string solos of great beauty. Grappelly's mastery of the violin, an innate jazz sense, coupled with the influence of Eddie South, the Negro violinist, and a sympathetic artistic feeling for Reinhardt's work, made the Quintet a success from its début in November 1934 until its dis-bandment in May of 1939.

Their recordings made them internationally famous and, although their earliest ones on the Oriole label have long been out of print, their later work can be heard to advantage in *Limehouse Blues* (HMV B.8463), *After You've Gone* (HMV B.8479), and *I've Found a New Baby* (Decca F.5943).

It was a strange partnership which formed the basis of the Quintet's music. Grappelly: suave, a brilliant pianist in the classical tradition, and an ardent listener to the best in jazz. Rein-hardt: restless, unable to read music, brought up in a gypsy-like existence and wedded to his guitar. The partnership yielded one of the more original offshoots from the jazz stem.

When dealing with large orchestras and the influence of ortho-dox musical convention there must be a certain overlapping with swing music which will be dealt with in the next chapter. Hender-son, Ellington, the McKinney Cotton Pickers, and Lunceford were, in fact, the first swing orchestras. The difference was that they explored the new paths of orchestration (banal though they were) and did not merely follow. Another important feature was that they did not serve as vehicles for exhibitions of technique and virtuosity, which was a feature of the swing bands of the later 1930s.

At least they were possessed of something of greater substance than the shapeless results of muddled thought that produced *Rhapsody in Blue*.

CHAPTER TEN

American Commercial Exploitation

THE success of the early large orchestras did not escape the attention of the big business interests of the United States, in particular the busy organizations of Manhattan which existed solely by the unrelenting exploitation of popular music. As has been noted, men like Henderson, [1] Ellington [1] and Luis Russell [2] were seeking a form of expression which, compared with traditional jazz, was limited in musical content. Further dissemination of this mechanical music was intensified in the early 1930s – the time of the economic depression and when jazz musicians no longer enjoyed the lucrative employment offered by the dozens of clubs in Chicago. The outlet for the big orchestras became the big ballrooms of cities like New York, theatre and cinema circuits; spectacle was the object in view and, to this end, bands grew bigger; the public were suitably impressed by the wild publicity accompanying the careers of the 'Swing' orchestras, as they came to be called, and very soon there was no demand for anything but the highly-disciplined aggregations who could churn out one arranged piece after another, each one meticulously rehearsed down to the last cymbal crash. Managers, agents, high-powered publicity, adulatory public, incessant repetition on radio and juke-box – a combination of these factors ushered in the Swing Era of 1934 onwards.

This movement was not distinguished by colour; there were separate movements by both white and Negro commercial interests and these separate interests often influenced and sometimes merged with each other. This was not the folk music of a section of people; it was the stereotyped music of a section of the commercial world. And the Negro population of the part of New

1 See Chapter Nine.
2 See Chapter Six.

York called Harlem contained a commercial element as did 52nd Street, off Broadway.

The land on which Harlem was built was given to emancipated slaves of the West India Company by the original Dutch settlers [1] as early as 1643, and influxes of other Negro populations combined as time went on to make the district into an exclusively Negro yet nevertheless cosmopolitan community, more distinct and autonomous from the remainder of modern New York than, for example, is Chinatown in London's dockland. Possessing no traditions of their own the inhabitants acquired the sophistication of their immediate neighbours and with it the same musical conventions. There were legitimate musical conservatories which were sympathetic to Western classical form; and, being Negro, fiercely resented the only sample of the music of the Southern Negro, the bastardized 'coon' song. Purer forms of New Orleans never received much attention either, because of the coon song prejudice. Harlem, in fact, has never produced a jazz band, but the superficial swing of the white commercial world was echoed in the Cotton Club and the dance halls of the New York Negroes.

LUIS RUSSELL (*born Panama, 1903*) has already been referred to as the first swing band. To be exact, Russell's type of hot music was not the same as that of any of the other coloured orchestras; it was a smaller band and the accent was on the solo technique of the accomplished musicians. But there were arranged passages and the solos themselves were all carefully prepared; the records Russell made succeed because of the vitality and exuberance of men like Higginbotham and Holmes and the fact that the arrangements are not blatant and repetitive.

Two Harlem bands who were playing at the same time as Russell were Cab Calloway and Chick Webb. Calloway made hundreds of records, most of which are mostly vehicles for the leader's ostentatious vocals, full of exhibitionistic 'scat-singing' which brought him the name of the Hi-De-Ho Man. Occasionally an odd solo [2] on the records suggest that Calloway could perhaps have done something more worthwhile with his band, but to-day he is playing the same tunes as he was in 1930 – and in the same style. CHICK WEBB (*1909–39*) was a better representative of the good things that made up Harlem Swing. He was born in Baltimore, a hunchback, and his life is one of the most remarkable success stories in musical history. Webb had guts – no euphemism

1. New York was once called New Amsterdam.
2. Notably by Ruben Reeves, trumpet.

will otherwise describe the way in which, by his own efforts, he rose from selling papers at the age of nine to leading his own band, mainly composed of non-reading musicians, with himself on drums, at the age of seventeen. This band, by 1931, had attracted to it such musicians as Benny Carter, Jimmy Harrison, and Louis Bacon, and three years later, with the usual 'power-house' instrumental formation, he played at the Savoy Ballroom almost continuously, featuring as his female vocalist Ella Fitz-gerald, whose personality and swing singing helped bring fame to Webb. There is an atmosphere about this band which places it in a class above the rank and file of the Swing Thirties; it has an incisive attack and relaxed precision which is found only occasion-ally – the band of Count Basie is another example. Undoubtedly Chick Webb could have been a fine jazz drummer; truth to tell he was but was a square peg in a self-made round hole; in his life-time he would have starved had he tried to play with small jazz groups. Gene Krupa, the most famous of swing drummers, de-clared: 'When he felt like it, he could cut down any of us, and he sure did a thorough job on me that night his band battled Benny Goodman's at the Savoy!' The Negro population of Harlem felt much the same about Chick; his funeral procession was reported to have stretched over a mile long.

In addition to developing inside Harlem, injections were made from other directions. In the early days, the music of New Orleans pushed its way up the Mississippi and left its trade-mark in the dance halls of the big river cities. The combination of the hot element of New Orleans and the orthodox approach resulted in the formation of almost a separate style of music in St Louis, with Charlie Creath as the chief exponent. [1]

Kansas City, on the Missouri River, was influenced in a similar way, BENNY MOTEN (*1896–1934*) being the best known band. Moten's Kansas City Orchestra recorded (with a six-piece tradi-tional personnel) as early as 1923, and in 1926 was recording quite regularly. A few years later, the riff, i.e. the emphasis on the repeated phrase as a means of building up tension, had become so much a feature of the band that the style became identified with Kansas City. Since many other large bands, particularly Henderson, also employed the riff all too frequently, Moten was not unique; but when, in 1936, the Chicago critic John Hammond discovered Moten's second pianist, WILLIAM 'COUNT' BASIE (*born 1906*), leading a polished band, still riffing, a false con-

1. See Chapter Six.

nexion was made with the consequent false assumption that this was part of a Kansas City Style. All that happened was that, of all the Middle West cities to produce a good swing band, Kansas City happened to be the one; it might as well have been Omaha, or Louisville, or Minneapolis, in which case we should now be familiar with the term Omaha Style, and so on.

But Count Basie undoubtedly had the necessary equipment to make a great success of swing, even in the highly competitive field of that style. Like Chick Webb, the brass and reed teams played with a biting attack and, at times, depth of feeling, which has drawn praise from many serious jazz critics, notably Hugues Panassié. Webb had an enormous influence upon other swing bands, an influence which, compared with that exerted by Fletcher Henderson, was probably the lesser of two evils. Basie, good and bad, can be heard on the same record, *Blue and Sentimental/Doggin' Around* (Brunswick 02644); the former title contains some pleasant, if not exciting, music of a dreamy kind, whilst the reverse is the riff *ad nauseam*. Basie was a good pianist, if not an original one, and his *How Long Blues* (Brunswick 02762), exemplifying his strict economy of notes, would not disgrace any record collection.

Since this is not a discourse on swing, but a contributory chapter in a book on jazz, further space will not be given to the coloured bands of, for example, Andy Kirk, Earl Hines, and Claude Hopkins. These bands had a certain individuality but, compared with the gamut of the rest of the power-house battalions, little to make them worthy of special note.

*

The history of swing followed the same trend as jazz in so far that the white musicians followed the Negroes. Fletcher Henderson was playing in 1920; Ellington, Moten, and Chick Webb were all famous in their own localities during the twenties; yet none reached the heights of national popularity as did the man who was crowned 'King of Swing' almost as soon as the term was invented.[1]

BENNY GOODMAN (*born 1909*) came from a Chicago musical family, several of them being band leaders. Benny, however, was the prodigy of them all and at the age of sixteen was already sitting in as clarinettist with the groups at white 'jam sessions'.

1. Ellington recorded *It Don't Mean a Thing If It Ain't Got That Swing* in 1932 and the term came into general use about 1934–5.

From 1926 until 1931 he was a regular member of Ben Pollack's Chicago Band, which was then playing at various clubs, and he also joined several record sessions, especially with Red Nichols' Five Pennies in New York. In the early days he played with a warm, liquid tone, with a recognizable, though not exaggerated, roughness. [1] But when he formed his large swing band in 1934 he began to concentrate on purity of tone and technique; dexterity is, perhaps, the operative word, for the ability to do anything that was with the pure mechanics of fingering and within the range of the clarinet was Goodman's objective.

He worked very hard, as he had always done, and combined his extensive musical talent with a good judgement of the type of men needed to fit in with his requirements, not only instrumentalists but also arrangers, a necessary adjunct to any swing band. Fletcher Henderson was responsible for many of the Goodman arrangements: *King Porter Stomp* (HMV B.8374) and *When Buddha Smiles* (HMV B.8461) being good examples of the sort of thing that this combination of stereotyped arrangement plus flawless execution by orchestra sections could produce. Above it all there was Goodman's complete mastery over his instrument which drew praise from the critics and adulation from the dancing crowds. The band set the style for several years after 1934, not only in the music but in the presentation – the sleek uniforms, the 'B.G.' initials on the music stands, the showman drummer, all were small details which were set to a standard of perfection just as were Goodman's clarinet solos.

The King of Swing was purely a solo swing musician; he has never been able to play in a collectively improvising group; this fact alone disqualifies him from the description of being a true jazzman. But as a swing man he has no equal, both in the 'tear-ups' like *Bugle Call Rag* (HMV B.8569) and the chamber music quartet style of *Body and Soul* (HMV B.8381). Unlike many swing players who degenerated into nauseating sentimentality or meaningless exhibitionism, Benny has always shown excellent taste within his medium and much imagination in his solo work. He is also to be congratulated for his influence towards the breaking of the colour prejudice in the 'business'. When he engaged Teddy Wilson and Lionel Hampton as members of his quartet – the 'band within a band' – he met considerable opposition from film companies and Southern booking agents, but nevertheless remained firm to his principles. To-day white and Negro

1. Good examples: Decca F. 5883, 5884, by Venuti-Lang Allstars.

musicians are reaping the benefit of some of Goodman's pioneer work in this direction.

The many accomplished swing men who joined Goodman included BUNNY BERIGAN (*1908–39*), whose *I Can't Get Started* (HMV C.2939 (12 in.)) is one of the best-known swing concertos, in which the full range of his tone and technique are demonstrated. He was much admired by other jazzmen and, in other circumstances, and with different opportunities, he could have become the greatest of white trumpet players. Rudi Blesh assesses Berigan rather neatly:

The late Bunny Berigan played in a style modelled eclectically on that of Louis Armstrong. His tone was pure and clear, his high notes impeccable, but the accents of the romantic Irish tenor crept in very subtly and Louis's hot, clipped, commanding phrases crept out.[1]

Wittingly or unwittingly, unconsciously or deliberately, scores of musicians were caught up in the whirl of American commercialism, to churn out the same arrangements incessantly, the only yardstick of success being the ability to play louder, faster, or crazier than the next. Taste in music became an uncommercial proposition: the only taste that mattered was the adulation of the mobs who crowded round the bandstand, shrieking for higher and longer notes on the golden trumpet. HARRY JAMES (*born 1915*) is typical; capable of real jazz feeling, especially in the Blues, he was a great admirer of Armstrong. He could contribute tasteful music, almost jazz, like *Blue Mood* (Parlophone R.2741), yet could descend to the syrup style of *Sleepy Lagoon* (Parlophone R.2859) or the *Flight of the Bumble Bee* (Parlophone R.2848), which is downright exhibitionism.

James was playing this sort of thing at the beginning of the Second World War; by this time, jazz was at a very low ebb; almost every band, white or coloured, was just a flattering backcloth for the soloist leader. GENE KRUPA (*born 1909*), for example, capitalized on his drum technique – which, amongst the small groups of Chicago jazzmen, had been put to some good use in the old days and which had subsequently been one of the foundations of the Goodman Band – to lead a successful swing band which was merely an accompaniment to interminable drum solos. Whole armies of adolescent supporters followed the swing bands either personally or through the pages of the magazines – or the newspapers. Incidents in the life of a swing band, cultivated by

1. *Shining Trumpets*. Knopf.

the publicity department, often reached the front pages of the national dailies. Woody Herman, Tommy Dorsey, Charlie Barnet, Glenn Miller, Lionel Hampton, even Louis Armstrong during his commercial period, all became names as well-known to the American teen-ager as that of the President himself.

From the long viewpoint, Swing's own publicity agents have produced its worst advertisement. The fatal mistake was made of trying to prove that Swing was Jazz or at least a development of it. Many musical journalists went to great pains (and on occasion suffered physical hardship) to prove that Jazz was out-of-date and that Swing was the Thing. The more monotonous the music became the more hysterical were the extravagant claims. Eventually the wild publicity defeated its own object. Those interested in rhythmic music, whatever its label, found the more modest arguments in favour of traditional jazz or traditional dance music more logical and well-founded. These people swelled the ranks of the hard core of genuine jazz enthusiasts who had clung to their Oliver records in preference to buying *Woodchopper's Ball*. Bob Crosby's Bobcats pointed the direction of the coming revival of interest in the pure counterpointed ensemble style and in 1939–40 Muggsy Spanier's Ragtime Band helped pave the way for a complete rejuvenation of jazz appreciation. [1]

The publicity agents should have known better. In attempting to show that swing was progressive music they forgot that eventually some other mongrel music would take its place. Had they attempted to understand what swing really was and tried to assess it on its merits a great deal of untold harm would have remained undone to many musicians who only played swing because it was the music of the day – and who would otherwise have been able to play jazz without the onus of being regarded as old-fashioned. For swing music, in a limited way, had much to recommend it. A test of any recorded piece of music is whether it can be played half a dozen times consecutively without annoyance; and many swing records can stand this test. It still places them well below any reasonable jazz record which can be played scores of times but it also ranks it well above the drivel of the sentimental 'rippling rhythm' or 'sweet strings' or whatever the purveyors of strict *tempo* music called themselves. Swing was a music in the European tradition and as such, to quote once again Rudi Blesh (whose approach to jazz is even purer than that of this book), it had 'considerable beauty'. But that did not make it jazz.

1. See Chapter Eleven.

In recent years the gullible public have been well primed with the propaganda that not only is jazz old-fashioned but that swing is also outdated. The new music, rebop, bebop, or just plain bop, was hailed by the full spate of New York publicity – which the London counterpart meekly followed. The radio and the juke-boxes joined in the fray and before swing could turn round everybody was demanding bop, without anyone knowing in the slightest degree what it was all about. Characterized by meaningless displays of grotesque technique and mathematical chord and harmonic progressions, it appeals only to the analytical musical mind and evokes about the same amount of emotional pleasure as a Euclid theorem. Without melody, without any logical thematic development, it has been supported only by those who allow the musical journalists to do their thinking for them. Musicians have been intrigued by the outrageous approach of bop – and, while not admitting it, have perhaps been a little deceived. But now that bop is dying and the 'progressive' music is wondering which way to progress, the New Orleans Revival is in full flood, as we shall see in Chapter Thirteen.

CHAPTER ELEVEN

The White School

THERE were so many youngsters gathered round the bandstands at Lincoln Gardens and Dreamland in the early twenties listening avidly to the jazz music which had been brought from New Orleans that it is difficult to narrow the field and say: 'This one or that was responsible for absorbing the tradition and carrying it on to produce what has become known as Chicago Style jazz.'

It is not only difficult, it is impossible. So many of these contributed to the trend that it will be necessary to concentrate on those whose music most nearly approximated to that of the Negroes, and consequently are of greatest importance.

One of these, who had already served his apprenticeship with Peavey's Jazz Bandits on river-boats and around the country generally was the banjo player ALBERT EDWIN (EDDIE) CONDON (*born 1905*), whose family moved to Chicago Heights when he was ten years old.

His story of an audition given to the Peavey Jazz Bandits is well worth recounting, showing, as it does, the resistance which had to be broken down in the days before jazz was considered anything but trashy stuff:

We drove to St Paul and at nine o'clock on a Sunday morning stopped the Cadillac in front of Lane's house. Peavey rapped on the door and was admitted. We piled in after him. Lane looked as if the last thing he wanted to hear was a jazz band.

We set our instruments in the living room; the drum spurs fitted nicely into the Oriental rug. The whole street was as quiet as a tomb. Then Peavey nodded and we broke into a jazz version of *Meet Me To-night in Dreamland*. Nobody played the melody, of course, and the time was four-four. Right in the middle of Sunday morning it sounded as if thirty people were getting their throats cut in Lane's front room. He sat in a chair and hung on, rocking softly with the pain. When it was over he whispered to Peavey, 'Could you try something soft and slow, something like *Meet Me To-night in Dreamland?*' 'Certainly,' Peavey said, 'we play that number often.' He gave us the wink and we turned on the maple sugar; even the drums played the melody. We left with a seven-months' contract and an opening date two weeks away. [1]

Before he started that contract, he returned to Chicago, visiting the College Inn, where Louis Panico was playing trumpet in Isham Jones' Band, and, and, what was one of the greatest thrills of his life, he met Bix Beiderbecke.

Condon, as well as dozens of other contemporary musicians, have testified to the enormous prestige which Beiderbecke gained even as a youngster, both for his cornet and piano music, and we must therefore turn our attention to him for a space.

LEON BISMARCK (BIX) BEIDERBECKE (*1903-31*) born in Davenport, Iowa, on the Mississippi, has achieved posthumous fame as the greatest of all white jazzmen, and many are the anecdotes relating to his life and career . . . of how he picked out the air of the second Hungarian Rhapsody on the piano at the age of three; of how he used to listen to the first records of the Original Dixieland Jazz Band and taught himself to play cornet by accompanying their tunes. By the time he was eighteen he was playing in the school band of the Lake Forest Academy in Chicago, and the following year his time was occupied in taking jobs in and around that city and even further afield.

At the age of twenty he was a member of the Wolverines' Band, which was made up of a group of youngsters from schools and Universities in and around Indiana. These boys had arrived in Chicago and had steeped themselves in the music of King Oliver and the New Orleans Rhythm Kings. They were, of course, a younger generation, and as George Johnson said:

. . . they came to the Friar's Inn to listen and learn, and to wait long hours until, late at night when the regular members of the band were tired, we were permitted to sit in with the orchestra to give a member a few moments' relief. This was a privilege, of course, since the Kings were all Kings and we all less than that, excepting Bix.

Despite George Johnson's modesty, the Wolverines can be placed second to the New Orleans Rhythm Kings in the annals of white jazz in the early twenties. One thing alone spoilt their efforts to emulate the music of New Orleans, and that was the inclusion of a tenor saxophone in their instrumentation, thus adding a fourth voice to the traditional three-part melodic line. The effect of this addition is to give a muddy colour to ensemble passages and also to create confusion in collective improvisation.

1. *We Called it Music.*

The introduction of the saxophone to jazz was an unfortunate step, to say the least, for it has been the cause of much blame being laid at that music's doorstep, and, as Percy Scholes has so adequately said:

... the members of the (saxophone) family were often made to perform feats for which providence had not intended them, and the tone quality that resulted was often trying to sensitive ears. [1]

Be that as it may, the Wolverines played on Lake-boats and at various University dates, at one of which a young law student named Hoagy Carmichael was so impressed by Beiderbecke's jazz interpretation that he formed a friendship with him, and eventually gave up law in order to concentrate on music and the composition of popular songs.

In 1924 the band was booked for a series of recordings in Richmond, Indiana, for the now defunct Gennett Company. Students who wish to acquaint themselves with the type of music they played and to hear the earliest examples of Beiderbecke's clear bell-like cornet tones and precise phrasing can benefit by the Brunswick re-issue of some of the titles made.

The musicians taking part were: Bix Beiderbecke (cornet), Al Gande (trombone), Jimmy Hartwell (clarinet), George Johnson (tenor saxophone), Dick Voynow (piano), Bob Gillette (banjo), Min Leibrook (bass) and Vic Moore (drums).

Fidgety Feet/Royal Garden Blues   Brunswick 02204
Jazz Me Blues/Big Boy   Brunswick 02203
Oh, Baby   Brunswick 02501
Copenhagen/Tiger Rag   Brunswick 02205
Note: Bix Beiderbecke plays piano in *Big Boy.*

The band had plenty of engagements, but the constant travelling did not suit Beiderbecke and late in 1924 he left the Wolverines and returned to Chicago to play in Charlie Straight's Band, chiefly because it gave him time to spare to visit the great jazzmen of the time – King Oliver, Louis Armstrong, Jimmy Noone, or the amazing Blues singer, Bessie Smith. He is said to have given her every cent he had on him one night, just to keep her singing.

He tired of Chicago, and in 1925 struck up a friendship with FRANKIE TRUMBAUER, joining his band at the Arcadia Ballroom in St Louis. Money poured in, a hundred dollars a week and more, but it was a case of easy come, easy go. There were bills of two or three hundred dollars owing at bars, and stories of him

1. *Oxford Companion to Music.* Saxophone Family.

mounting the bandstand with his cornet held behind him to hide the evidence of frayed trousers, but the music of this period is preserved for us in such records as *River-boat Shuffle* (Parlophone R.2492), *I'm Comin' Virginia* (Parlophone R.2687), and *Singin' the Blues* (Parlophone R.1838): all of them examples of the changing face of white jazz.

Yes – the face of jazz was changing, and the metamorphosis was not to Beiderbecke's liking. The Trumbauer Band broke up and they both joined the Jean Goldkette Orchestra. By many standards it was not a great band, but it came nearest to their ideals and, in spite of sweetly arranged concert introductions, Bix was given an opportunity to travel his own road at times, as can be heard in *Clementine* (HMV B.9237). It was a high-priced band, however, and there were no bookings after the autumn of 1927. They had made comparatively few records, but – and this is the most important contribution which this band made to white jazz – it was drawn upon for special sessions under the name of 'Bix Beiderbecke's Gang', with whom he created some of his finest recorded work. He was aided by BILL RANK on trombone, DON MURRAY (clarinet), ADRIAN ROLLINI (bass saxophone), SIG-NORELLI (piano), HOWDY QUICKSELL (banjo), and CHAUNCEY MOREHOUSE (drums).

Coming through these records is the vitality stamped into them by Beiderbecke and the others who helped him, and who were already groping for the something in jazz which they knew was being lost by its canalization into a mass-produced pattern.

At the Jazzband Ball/Sorry   Parlophone R.2711
Jazz Me Blues/Royal Garden Blues   Parlophone R.2580
Goose Pimples   Parlophone R.2465
Since My Best Gal Turned Me Down   Parlophone R.2054

Any one of the above is sufficient to show Beiderbecke's fault-less ease of execution, his genius for perfect phrasing and that clean bell-like quality of his tone.

Then he joined Paul Whiteman's Band, although he wrote to his mother, telling her how scared he was of playing in such a big and commercially famous band. Paul Whiteman himself must have been a little scared of having him, because the band had to play the way the public wanted it – and the public had been side-tracked away from jazz.

However, Bill Challis, the arranger, realized the popularity of this young cornet player, and allowed him to take a chorus in the way he would like, but afterwards made him lead the brass section in a conventional manner. Many of the Whiteman records of that period indicate the way in which his tiny solo stands out like a bright colour in a welter of 'busy' noise. This is how it must have appeared to him, although it was his financial peak and a time when idol-worshipping crowds surrounded the stand shouting: 'We want Bix – we want Bix.'

He paid visits to Chicago, too, sitting in at sessions with Jimmy and Tommy Dorsey, Teschemacher, Bud Freeman, and Joe Sullivan until dawn. He was in demand wherever he went, but always haunting him was the bondage of a straight band with stereotyped parts to play. 1929 brought commercial radio, and this was the beginning of his last phase.

He is said to have read 'Wild West' novels propped up on the stand in front of the score when he was with Charlie Straight's Orchestra, but his outlet with the Whiteman Band took the form of too much drink. He became more and more unreliable, and his frequent absences from the stand naturally enough annoyed Whiteman, and so, in 1930, when the band was due for Hollywood and the much publicized 'King of Jazz' picture, he arranged for Beiderbecke to go home for a cure.

The next year he was back in New York looking for a job. One hour with the Camel Radio Hour was enough, and four nights of the ground-out mechanical arrangements of the Casa Loma Orchestra more than enough. He just left.

Although the end was approaching, he did make one last contribution to piano music. He put on paper a number of the piano improvisations which he had been engrossed with for so many years: compositions like *In a Mist* (Parlophone R.1838) – far removed from jazz, but representing the side of his nature which was devoted to classical music and the themes of Debussy.

But he was still drinking too much, and by July 1931 the end was in sight. He formed a plan to bring an all-white band to England, but it never materialized. His health grew worse, and a persistent cough was not improved by long drinking bouts. Then one night, some of the boys had an offer of a one night stand.... 'No Bix, no job' they said. He went.

Pneumonia developed, and on 7 August 1931 he died.

*

Now we must retrace our steps to 1922, when another group of youngsters played together – boys from the Austin High School in Chicago. They were JIMMY LANNIGAN (piano and at a later date, bass), BUD FREEMAN (C Melody sax, and later tenor saxophone), Dick MacPartland (banjo and guitar), his young brother Jimmy MacPartland (cornet), and Frank Teschemacher (clarinet). Here again, the New Orleans Rhythm Kings were their criterion – indeed, it is said that they were more influenced by *Tin Roof Blues* than any other piece of music they heard. This may be a piece of legendary exaggeration, but it is true that they had such a reverence for the Friars' Society Orchestra that the Austin High School Gang, as they originally termed themselves, changed its name to that of the 'Blue Friars'.

When the Wolverines lost Bix Beiderbecke in 1924, they tried to replace him with a trumpet player from New Orleans, SHARKEY BONANO (*born 1904*), but finally decided on JIMMY MACPARTLAND (*born 1907*). As time went along, every member of the Austin High School Gang replaced the personnel of the Wolverines.

MacPartland's style has a similarity to that of Beiderbecke's, under whose influence he came a great deal. There is a less polished tone, but the phrasing is similar in many ways – a statement that can be verified by listening to his work in *Liza* (Parlophone R.2379), which was a sample of the Austin High School Gang's music in 1927, when they recorded under the name of the McKenzie and Condon Chicagoans.

Condon has already been mentioned, but RED MCKENZIE (*1903–48*), was a young jockey who used to hang around the river-boats at St Louis organizing small groups of singers. Finding himself the leader of but one of many similar groups, he hit upon the idea of developing the comb and paper technique to a fine art, and eventually landed recording contracts for his 'Blue Blowers' as they were called. They actually visited England in 1924, but were received with indifference. He was a good business man, however, and it was largely due to his help that many of the Chicago groups went to the recording studios.

Another member of the Austin Gang who helped to mound Chicago jazz was the clarinet and alto saxophone player FRANK TESCHEMACHER (*1906–32*). He was noted for the peculiarly personal tone which he imparted to his clarinet playing which varied from the bold to the delicate; it was a sour tonality which may have been due to his playing off pitch or it may have been due to a deliberate use of quarter tones. His apologists insist that it was a logical development from his early training in violin music, but whatever the cause, it stamped his solos with an individuality which is unmistakable, and to him must go very largely the credit for the atmosphere of the McKenzie Condon Chicagoan records and also the other sessions in which he took part – perhaps the Red McKenzie Chicago Rhythm Kings' *There'll Be Some Changes Made* and *I've Found a New Baby* (Brunswick 03413) being the best illustration of his very personal clarinet technique. It exhibits that tough hard-boiled spirit which is such a feature of the white jazz from 1922 to 1932 (judging it from recordings of the period) and which was a reflexion of the tenacity of purpose which drove them on to try to keep jazz alive in the midst of opposition and, even worse, apathy. It has become fashionable to belittle the efforts of the Chicagoan jazz school: a reaction to the esteem in which it was held until 1939, an esteem which was pardonable in that there was very little New Orleans real jazz music to be heard on recordings. The consequent elevation of the pupil into the master's chair was not surprising in the circumstances. Undoubtedly men like those who formed the New Orleans Rhythm Kings, the Wolverines, and the Austin High School Gang acted to the best of their ability in the interests of keeping the jazz flag flying, and they are to be congratulated. It is we, the listeners, who accepted the shadow for the substance, and in raising it to an unnecessarily high peak, must blame ourselves rather than the Chicagoans for wrongly assessing their contribution to jazz. It is equally wrong, however, for us to let the pendulum swing too far the other way, as some are doing, and dismiss the white music of those years as of little or no importance.

Certainly Teschemacher's death in a car accident in 1932 spelt the end of an era. Many of the musicians drifted away from Chicago, many of them to New York, where ERNEST LORING 'RED' NICHOLS (*born 1905*) had already established a name for himself and his 'Five Pennies'.

It must not be imagined that all the white musicians of that period hailed from Chicago. Many of them were New Orleans born and bred, and their first introduction to music was by way of the jazz they heard in their infancy. Such a one was JOSEPH 'WINGY' MANONE (*born 1904*), who struggled with the difficulties of playing cornet using only one arm, having lost the other in a street-car accident at the age of ten. He mastered the handicap, and after working with a number of bands in New Orleans, he played in Chicago with Teschemacher and others, recording with several groups, of which the Benny Goodman Boys' *After Awhile*

(Brunswick 01264) and *Muskrat Ramble* show his warm tone and jazz feeling to perfection.

Later, when in New York, and after he had formed his own band, he made some recordings for Decca, but, since he was under contract to Brunswick, they had to invent a name for themselves. The name they chose was a compliment to a band which he heard in his early visit to Chicago. It was 'The New Orleans Rhythm Kings', and the tunes they played were mostly those of the old days. It was a tentative start to try to get back to the basic music of jazz, and it was succesful, as it should be, considering that the musicians taking part included Georg Brunis, Sidney Arodin, and Terry Shand. All eight titles are still in catalogue. [1]

The following year, in 1935, he used musicians from Ben Pollack's Band – an aggregation which in that same year formed the nucleus of the Bob Crosby Orchestra, and the general trend of music at that time is exemplified in his version of *Swing Brother, Swing* (Parlophone R.2126). Then came the recording which really put him in the public eye, and of it he says:

> Then I got a chance to make the record that really made a big man out of me, *Isle of Capri*. [2] I have to admit now, however, that when I waxed 'Ol' Capra', I had no idea it would be so popular. When I loused up the lyrics I was just doing it for laughs. But, man, that record sold over a drillion copies. [3]

To BOB CROSBY (*born 1913*), younger brother of Bing Crosby, must go much of the credit for reviving the Dixieland style, whose wide patterns and staccato rhythms came like a breath of clean air through the unhealthy corridors of a music which had begun by this time to rely on the physical attractions of feminine crooners to bolster up its empty repetition. It needed courage to launch *South Rampart Street Parade* (Decca K.876) into waters cluttered with hundreds of sentimental little tunes and high powered swing cruisers, but he did it in 1937, and followed it up immediately by assembling a small group from his orchestra, which he called Bob Crosby's Bob Cats, giving them their first airing in Los Angeles, where they made several recordings, of which *Fidgety Feet* (Decca F.6704) is typical. Later examples in the Dixieland vein are:

1. *Tin Roof Blues/Panama*, Brunswick 01910. *Ostrich Walk/Orig. Dixieland One-Step*, Brunswick 01988. *San Antonio Shout/Jazz It Blues*, Brunswick 02040. *Bluin' the Blues/Sensation*, Brunswick 02337.
2. Issued in England as *Capri, What You Done To Me*, Brunswick RL. 254.
3. *Trumpet on the Wing*, by Mannone and Paul Vandervoort II.

Jazz Me Blues/Washington and Lee Swing (Decca F.7596), *High Society* (Decca F.7594), in which IRVING FAZOLA (*born New Orleans, 1913–49*) takes the tradiuonal clarinet solo, and *Hindustan* (Decca F.7155).

Nor did Bob Crosby neglect the Blues, of which *Five Point Blues* (Decca F.7152) deserves special mention, if only for Yank Lawson's warm tone and interpretation of the Blues spirit.

TO FRANCIS 'MUGGSY' SPANIER (*born 1906*) must go the palm for his unremitting efforts on behalf of jazz. As a boy he was around Chicago with Beiderbecke and George Wettling, and during the ensuing years with such bands as Sig Meyer's, Joe Kayser's, Ray Miller's, Ted Lewis's, and Ben Pollack's he retained his integrity of purpose. Most of the recordings in which he appeared during his early days are now out of print, but his tightly muted and very personal style can be heard in the 1931 Red McKenzie's Celestrial Beings disc of *Darktown Strutters Ball* (Parlophone R.1004); a record which also serves as a show-case for McKenzie's 'blue-blowing' which was mentioned earlier in this chapter, and for Coleman Hawkins's 'hot' tenor saxophone solo which precedes Spanier's chorus.

Like Wingy Manone, he also organized a session in New York, which he called the New Orleans Rhythm Kings, and his 1935 group included some of the musicians which Manone had used – Brunis, Shand, and Pottle. The titles recorded, however, were not from the original Rhythm Kings' repertoire, but were some of the popular tunes of the time. [1]

His ambition to record jazz the way he liked it came in 1939, when he assembled a group of the old-timers including Georg Brunis and ROD CLESS (*1907–44*), the clarinet player who had been his great friend since 1927, and who had studied and based his style on that of Johnny Dodds. Cless is one of the lesser known names in the jazz world, but his work with Spanier at this time reveals him as one of the few white clarinettists who had so steeped himself in Negro jazz that every phrase, every note, and every inflection showed the origins of his music. His feeling for the music is best expressed in his own words: 'It seemed that before we were on the stand we were off it again and the next thing you knew it was time to go home. We hated to leave the place.' [2]

No better trombonist could have been chosen than GEORG

1. Example: *No Lovers Allowed*, Brunswick 02610.
2. *The Jazz Record*. 'Remembering Rod Cless,' by James McGraw, January 1945.

BRUNIS (born New Orleans, 1900), a pioneer of the white jazz
trombone school. These three, Spanier, Cless, and Brunis, created
an integrated music which paved the way for the New Orleans
Revival – a music which even the addition of a tenor saxophone
did not mar. The sixteen sides recorded are so important, and
played such a rôle in reviving an interest in jazz proper, that they
are listed below in full together with the slight changes of personnel on the various record dates.

MUGGSY SPANIER AND HIS RAGTIME BAND

Personnel:

Muggsy Spanier	cornet	
Georg Brunis	trombone	
Rod Cless	clarinet	First Session
Ray McKinstry	tenor sax.	Chicago
George Zack	piano	7/7/39
Bob Casey	guitar	
Pat Pattison	bass	
Marty Greenberg	drums	

As above, except

Bernie Billings	tenor sax.	Second Session
Joe Bushkin	piano	New York
Don Carter	drums	10/11/39

As in Second Session, except

Nick Caiazza	tenor sax.	Third Session
		New York
		22/11/39

As in 3rd Session, except

Al Seidel	drums	Fourth Session
		New York
		12/12/39

TITLES MADE

The number in parenthesis indicates the session at which the title
was made.

That Da Da Strain (1)/*Someday Sweetheart* (1)   HMV B.9028
Big Butter and Egg Man (1)/*Dippermouth Blues* (2)   HMV B.9033
Livery Stable Blues (2)/*At The Jazz Band Ball* (2)   H.M.V. B.9042
Eccentric (1)/*Sister Kate* (2)   HMV B.9047
Dinah (4)/*Black and Blue* (4)   B.9067
At Sundown (3)/*Bluin' the Blues* (3)   HMV B.9092
Mandy, Make Up Your Mind (4)/*Lonesome Road* (4)   B.9103
Relaxin' at the Touro (3)/*River-boat Shuffle* (3)   HMV B.9145

Any of these records is a vindication of Spanier's apt retort to a swing-minded band leader who was constantly pestering him to play top notes – 'Aw, get yourself a piccolo player!'

*

When America went swing mad, and jazz musicians, if they wanted to live, had to play screaming high notes or flashy drum solos to crowds of frenzied jitterbugs, many said: 'Jazz is dead or dying.' But a folk music cannot be killed so easily, especially one as vital as jazz, by dolling it up in dress clothes and trying to smarm the kinks out of its hair with Brilliantine arrangements. Jazz went on behind the scenes, as has already been shown, and New York was the scene of many 'jam sessions' arranged by the old Chicagoans at the Commodore Music Shop and Studios. The Hot Record Society re-issued old discs and waxed new ones, and later a number of private recording companies sprang up, among them being Blue Note, General, Signature, and Collectors Item. Their importance in the jazz field was not only in their own distribution of good music, but the fact that they stimulated the public demand for it with the result that the major companies fell into line by issuing many of the titles which had been neglected on their shelves for years. In addition to this, sessions were arranged where jazzmen like Condon, Kaminsky, Pee Wee Russell, Floyd O'Brien, MacPartland, Wettling, and many others were allowed to play the sort of music they wanted instead of the music the recording companies thought the public wanted.

The results, such as MacPartland's *Jazz Me Blues* (Brunswick 03057), Bud Freeman's *I've Found a New Baby* (HMV B.9029), George Wettling's *Bugle Call Rag* (Brunswick 03059), and Eddie Condon's *Nobody's Sweetheart* (Brunswick 03055) were an indication of the shape of things to come, and was a prelude to the era of the great New Orleans Revival, which will be dealt with in Chapter Thirteen.

CHAPTER TWELVE

Jazz in England

AT best, during the quarter-century which followed the visit to this country of the Original Dixieland Jazz Band, the progress of jazz performance and appreciation has been spasmodic. At worst, it could easily be termed an abuse of the true Folk Music of New Orleans, for it was smitten for a long period with anaemia and was devoid of ideas. This is not to suggest that the fault lay entirely with the English musician, or enthusiast, or critic – each could be excused on the grounds that only false impressions were given in the first place; but the fact remains that not until 1943, when George Webb assembled the Bexleyheath pioneers, did the jazz movement in England assume any semblance of authenticity and consequent dignity.

When Nick la Rocca and the O.D.J.B. visited the English shores in 1921, jazz-inspired though they were, they had, nevertheless, commercialized their music to a great extent; they came to the Hammersmith Palais ready to play what the public wanted, within the confines of their idiom. And this, remember, was the post-war flapper era. What musical purity the O.D.J.B. possessed was lost in a wild helter-skelter of trombones played with the feet, funny hats, and saucepan-lid drum-kits. The inevitable result was that when that age gave way to the more sober years of depression in the later 1920s, people were inclined to look back upon the comedy jazz band as representative of a wild, irresponsible age of which they were ashamed and the name 'jazz' was linked with anything suggesting debauchery or loose living of any kind. The sad part of this turn of events is that the travesty of the truth prevails to-day and the blind prejudice felt by many towards *what they think* is jazz can be traced straight back to the Original Dixieland Jazz Band's comic hats.

It took several years before a further step was made towards the clarification of the jazz idiom in this country. In 1926, a

Spaniard named Fred Elizalde came here from America to study at Cambridge University. He was an excellent pianist who had come to appreciate the kind of jazz played by the New York 'Golden Age' set, they who strove to mould European technical orthodoxy against a jazz backcloth – a cul-de-sac road, but one which Elizalde naturally found acceptable to him and even a source of inspiration. He it was who first acquainted a half-impressed, half-amused group of undergraduates with the legend of Bix and with tales of the greatness of many a white American musician of the Golden Age school. Not only did he guide the taste in this country by articles in the *Melody Maker* but he showed the courage of his convictions in a practical way; he per-suaded some Americans, Adrian Rollini, Bobby Davis, and Chelsea Quealey to join his band of British musicians; with the later addition of Fud Livingston, it was not surprising that the general sound was like the California Ramblers or the Goofus Five, but, nevertheless, Elizalde's music was well ahead of its time until it broke up in 1930.

After this Elizalde himself became disgusted at the general apathy towards his 'Hot Music' and from then onwards devoted himself to classical music, becoming a pupil of Manuel de Falla and achieving no little success as a composer and pianist. It is easy to be cynical in the light of to-day's advance in English jazz appreciation, but it must be remembered that, for its time, the 'Hot Music' of Fred Elizalde *was* hot. He had been influenced by his immediate contacts in the States – the New Yorkers, who were hardly themselves preserving the true strain of jazz lineage, but this was ten times better than anything else in England at the time, as was the group which Spike Hughes led for a while in the early 1930s. Spike took over some of the remnants of Elizalde's Band, added musicians, introduced arrangements, tried the suicidal fusing of jazz and classics, and retired from the jazz field, having made some successful recordings with a Negro band in America.

Throughout the middle thirties what little jazz content existed was to be found in little oases of inspiration in a desert of moribund commercialism, concentrated mainly in the large bands of Bert Ambrose and Lew Stone, who had the good sense to real-ize that the best musicians were the 'hot' musicians. There were too, other groups of enthusiasts, George Scott-Wood's Six Swing-ers, Nat Gonella, Joe Daniels, Freddy Gardner and Duncan Whyte, all of whom, while hardly reaching great creative heights, did at least save the English follower of hot music from complete saturation with the mediocre dance orchestras.

A considerable influence was felt by Benny Carter's visit to this country in 1936, to arrange Henry Hall's BBC Dance Orchestra. Carter sought the local talent and promptly brought out the best in them when he made records under his own name. He introduced to the forefront of English hot music circles Buddy Featherstonhaugh, Tommy McQuater and George Chisholm. Spurred on by the incentive of trying to emulate their versatile leader (who could outplay them on their own instruments) these musicians made a notable advance upon the hitherto stereotyped standard and George Chisholm in particular gave evidence of being able to hold his own among the best. Carter was impressed by Chisholm – enough to take him on a three-month tour of Holland where they played with Hawkins and Freddy Johnson, and, later on, Chisholm made some fine recordings with Danny Polo, the corner-stone of Ambrose's Band, and also under his own name. In these 'Jive Five' discs is to be found strong evidence of an English musician with original ideas, a faultless execution, a good tone and a sense of jazz feeling, a combination of qualities rarely found even to-day. George Chisholm is still one of the better influences on the credit side of English jazz.

Just at the outbreak of war there were signs of a decided improvement in the standard of musicianship in England, a trend due mainly to a West Indian, Ken 'Snakehips' Johnson, who was playing at the Café de Paris, leading a band consisting mainly of coloured musicians. Unfortunately no records of his adequately express the spirit of this band, but several of his men continued his line of thought after the tragedy of the 1941 air raid. Dave Wilkins, Leslie Hutchinson, Carl Barriteau, Joe Deniz – these men paid tribute to their late leader in the best way they could, by playing as Johnson would have wished them to do, in the true spirit of jazz. Somehow they have never quite reached the highest flight, but their attempts to 'pep up' English dance music have had a definite effect. The only other group of musicians apart from the West Indians who seemed to know which way they were going were those who grouped round the nucleus of Carter-coached Chisholm and McQuater to form the R.A.F. Unit 'The Squadronaires'. Modelling themselves on the Bob Crosby Band they brought a crispness of attack into dance music and persuaded the public to accept some of the Dixieland tunes.

But all these groups, whilst showing initial promise, only became engulfed in the maw of commercialism. The odd ray of light filtered through the cobwebs of Archer Street occasionally; Harry Parry formed his Radio Rhythm Club Sextet and other small groups came and went; but, based as they were on American counterparts and with the performance of a set routine for each number as their maxim, the creative inspiration which is the essence of jazz was lacking.

The fact of the matter was that English jazz, schooled in orthodoxy and tongue-tied by mediocre commercialism, had, in 1942, progressed no further than had Elizalde in 1928.

And then came one of those occurrences which can truthfully be described as extraordinary. In 1943, Bexleyheath, Kent, saw the formation of a band which played in the New Orleans style, since when England has rapidly swept to the forefront, both in performance and appreciation. The repercussions of the impact of George Webb's Dixielanders on English jazz are dealt with in Chapter Thirteen.

Renaissance

It has been fashionable, indeed expedient, to indicate with a geographical label the development of jazz from the earliest days. Beginning with New Orleans (or even West Africa, to go further back), it is quite in accordance with the facts to say that jazz spread to the rest of the United States, up the Mississippi to St Louis and Chicago and thence to New York. If the method is to be continued to cover the New Orleans Revival movement, the most accurate description would be West Coast or California Jazz; it is not strictly true, of course, for the Revival rapidly spread to the four corners of the earth, but to certain diehard enthusiasts living in the cities of San Francisco and Los Angeles must go the main credit of putting the resurgence of jazz awareness firmly on its feet.

Chronologically the New Orleans Revival may be divided into three stages: first the great pioneering literary work, the book *Jazzmen*, published by Harcourt, Brace and Company in New York in 1939. Edited by Frederic Ramsey, Jr., and Charles Edward Smith, it was a deeply sincere attempt to resurrect jazz history mainly from statements and letters of musicians before it was too late – for most jazzmen of the pioneering days were getting old. In this book the assistance of the 'faithful' – the collectors and enthusiasts who had scorned swing, sweet, and the various hybrids – was requested and willingly given. Chapters were contributed by Bill Russell, Edward Nichols, E. Simms Campbell, Steve Smith, Wilder Hobson, and Roger Pryor Dodge, the whole being edited in such a way as to put down for permanent record the history of jazz from the days of New Orleans onward *for the first time*. Previous books on jazz had approached jazz in a general way, had been more in the nature of enlarged essays, and had often concentrated on stating the writer's particular prejudices and preferences. Having due regard for the inclusion of certain legends which might be taken with the proverbial grain of salt, *Jazzmen* was a landmark in the history of jazz appreciation.

The second stage followed naturally from the publication of a book which laid such emphasis on the jazz of New Orleans. If this kind of jazz was so immortal, so superior to the power-house swing and the solo-swamped jam session, then the proof of the pudding was in the playing. New Orleans Jazz ought to be played as well as heard on the gramophone. And heard it was, for the first time since Oliver and Louis's Hot Five, strangely enough by a white band. There is nothing particularly remarkable about this apparent paradox; jazz had already reached a final and definitive form; it was open to any band, white or coloured, to play it providing that the fundamental rules were observed and provided that the players were equipped with the necessary flair for improvisation and feeling for rhythm, harmony, and counterpoint. Negroes possess an innate sense of rhythm which gives them something of an advantage, but the results over the past few years have done much to show that, with the right approach, white men can play jazz. Many of the best recordings by leading revivalists cannot be identified aurally as being by a white or coloured group.

The third phase was an unusual one. It took place two or three years after the end of the Second World War when many 'modern' kinds of music were trying to supersede swing in popular esteem. In their attempt to popularize these the critics condemned traditional forms of jazz as outmoded and a solid reactionary movement was formed to combat the attack upon time-honoured principles. Starting imperceptibly in various cities in the U.S.A., it soon spread all over the world, and to-day jazz is vieing for popularity among the lay public with other forms of dance and 'hot' music. The reactionary movement reinforced the efforts of individuals who were beginning to feel the strain of being lone voices in the wilderness of commercialism and the New Orleans Revival became a Renaissance.

This 'phasing' of the New Orleans Renaissance is quite arbitrary and is perhaps an over-simplification, but it will serve as a basis for the conclusion of this story of jazz.

*

The flame of jazz, which had been dying since the depression years, had flickered occasionally during the empty thirties and then suddenly flared up in San Francisco just at the beginning of the War in 1939. LU WATTERS (*born 1915*) had played with dance bands for several years and was a skilled arranger; nevertheless he wanted to play like Oliver or Armstrong, and out of his twelve-piece band which was playing in Sweet's Ballroom across San Francisco Bay, in Oakland, he formed a small jazz group. Encouraged by a small nucleus of jazz supporters Watters's group gained in experience, some of them playing at the Golden Gate International Exposition. Then late in 1940 the Hot Music Society of San Francisco asked the band to play at their monthly jam sessions, held at the Dawn Club. Though Lu Watters's Yerba Buena Jazz Band[1] was not an immediate success among the members of the Society, who preferred the riffs and 'every man for himself' style of jam music, a start had been made by a band in which the individual was subservient to the needs of a group. Soon after this the Watters group came to an arrangement with the manager of the Dawn Club and they started playing one night per week regularly. Again they were not successful and Lu Watters needed all his stubborn powers of perseverance to keep going. With spasmodic changes the personnel settled down to Watters and Bob Scobey, cornets, Turk Murphy, trombone, Ellis Horne or Bab Helm, clarinet, Wally Rose, piano, Clarence Hayes and Russ Bennett, banjos, Dick Lammi, bass, and Bill Dart, drums. The men played as a team, the instrumental line-up being close to that of Oliver's Creole Band. Still the attendances at the Dawn Club showed little improvement and it was reported that Watters was making up losses out of his own pocket. The attitude of the local Musicians' Union was cynical; they thought Lu was wasting his time playing 'nigger' music when he could be earning good money playing commercially.

Finally, however, the run of adverse reception came to an end. Students from the University had been swelling the audiences and even swing-fed people found they could listen to this style of jazz; furthermore a local radio announcer named Hal McIntyre did his best to publicize the band over the air. The Yerba Buenas started broadcasting and made their first records for Dave Stuart's *Jazzman* label. This session, one of the most important in jazz history, is listed in full:

Maple Leaf Rag/*Black and White Rag*[2]   Jazzman 1
Memphis Blues/*Irish Black Bottom*   Jazzman 2

1. Named after the island in San Francisco Bay where they first played.
2. Piano solo only by Rose.

Muskrat Ramble/Smokey Mokes   Jazzman 3
Original Jelly Roll Blues/At A Georgia Camp Meeting   Jazzman 4

Many sessions have since followed, for Lu Watters and his pioneers of the New Orleans Renaissance had finally moved into the bigger money. They had felt from the beginning that everyone was out of step except themselves; and everyone in San Francisco finally had to change step.

Papa Mutt Carey himself came up from Los Angeles especially to hear the Y.B.J.B. and declared that playing with them brought back memories of the old days in New Orleans. He sat in with the band and said he hadn't enjoyed himself so much for many years. In short, the band was wildly successful until the demands of the American armed forces forced the band to break up, though BENNY STRICKLER (*1915–46*) held the trumpet chair for a while until T.B. took its toll. Strickler had spent most of his time with Bob Wills's Texas Playboys but always wanted to go his own way, the jazz way. That he was going in the right direction is proved by the fact that Bunk Johnson mistook a recorded transcription of his for the work of King Oliver!

If the claims of popularity made above seem to have been exaggerated, additional evidence is provided by the fact that, when the Yerba Buena Jazz Band reopened at the Dawn Club after Uncle Sam had finished with the members of the band, nearly ten thousand patrons heard them during the first month. Playing better than ever, they just carried on where they left off in 1942, Watters and Scobey played an unfaltering lead, Watters the more powerful of the two, but with Scobey alternating in the lead part. A perfect team, they sounded as much like Armstrong and Oliver as any two trumpet men have ever done. Bob Helm, the clarinettist, was inclined to be erratic at times, but a steadying influence was that of TURK MURPHY (*born 1915*), the trombone player. One of the best 'tailgate' men of recent years, he holds the doubtful honour of being 13th in the *Down Beat* poll of 1941, and has recently left Watters to form his own group with most of the original band.

Murphy takes few solos, concentrating on ensembles, and the most impressive member of Murphy's Band, which recorded for the *Good Time Jazz* [1] label in Hollywood, is Bob Scobey, who had previously shared the lead in the Yerba Buena Band with Watters. Another interesting feature of this band is the absence of a drummer; the three-piece rhythm section nevertheless provides an

1. Available in England on Tempo. A.74, 75, 80, 81, 82, and 92.

admirable object lesson for the type of drummer who believes he is the most important member of a jazz band.

This brief account of the San Francisco Revivalist School has brought us up to the present day, and to view the other equally important movement which paralleled the Watters groups, is to shift the focus of attention further south, though still in the State of California – Los Angeles, to be exact. There resided Kid Ory who, during the lean thirties, had despaired of playing jazz for a living and had retired from the field. In 1942, however, Barney Bigard, who had recently left Duke Ellington's Orchestra, persuaded Ory to start again, and, rather surprisingly, they were able to hold their own in the small clubs in the vicinity of Sunset Boulevard. In 1943, Rudi Blesh asked Ory's Band to the Geary Theatre for a concert in his *This is Jazz* series, featuring veteran Bunk Johnson; booklets were printed about the theme of New Orleans jazz; recordings of the concert were made and it was broadcast. From then onwards Kid Ory's Creole Jazz Band was the talk of the jazz fraternity of Hollywood. He was recommended to Orson Welles for a radio programme, which, although short-lived, paved the way for further successes. Ory played a regular jazz programme for schools, recorded for the *Crescent* and *Exner* jazz record companies and later for Decca and Columbia; he provided short but welcome fragments of soundtrack for the films *New Orleans* and *Crossfire*. His reputation is now at its highest and his position such that he can command his own price; the sudden success of this, his *second* career in jazz music, is indicative of the way in which jazz has been reborn. The fine virile music he recorded for *Crescent*, with Mutt Carey, trumpet, Omer Simeon, on clarinet, Bud Scott, guitar, Ed Garland, bass, Minor Hall, drums, and Buster Wilson, piano, is now available in England on Jazzman label: *South/Creole Song* (J.M.B.21) and *Blues For Jimmy/Get Out of Here* (J.M.B.22). The delightful *Blanche Touquatoux* with its flavouring of Creole patois should also be heard, as well as its backing *The Girls Go Crazy 'Bout The Way I Walk* (Vocalion, V.1001). In these last-named sides, Omer Simeon is replaced by Joe Darensbourg.

Mention above of the *This is Jazz* concert with Bunk Johnson brings this chronicle to its most romantic phase. In Chapter Five was told the story of Bunk's early life until he retired to the rice fields of Louisiana. It is continued here when, in 1939, Bunk was located by the editors of *Jazzmen*, in their quest for authentic narrative. A letter addressed c/o the Postmaster, New Iberia,

Louisiana, elicited a reply from Bunk himself who, it appeared, was engaged in the not overpaid occupation of driving a truck. Several collectors, notably Dave Stuart, Bill Russell, Gene Williams, Bill Colburn, and Hal McIntyre, among others, contributed to buy Bunk a new set of teeth and a new trumpet. Thus equipped, Bunk practised and was soon confident enough to claim he could play with the best of them, even at his age, sixty-four. And very soon he was able to prove that, while he was obviously unable at his age to emulate the like of Eldridge and Stewart in power and technique, he was nevertheless more conscious of the correct New Orleans style than any pseudo jazzman earning big money in Greenwich Village, New York City. His early records leave much to be desired; the series of sides made for *Jazzman* and *Jazz Information* are poorly recorded, by portable apparatus in New Orleans; yet the spirit is there and they constitute some of the most valuable contributions to recorded jazz history.

In 1943 Rudi Blesh, who had built his audience of his *This is Jazz* series of lectures up from seventy at the first to 700 at the second, fulfilled his ambition and put on a concert featuring Bunk Johnson. Though Bunk arrived only a few hours before the start he was able to relate an amazingly concise and graphic picture of New Orleans jazz, both by narration and by playing; the occasion was a wonderful event; successful beyond Blesh's wildest dreams, it was written up in the New York *Herald-Tribune*, and the magazine *Time* described Bunk as the 'genius of the horn'.

He stayed in San Francisco for a while, playing with Lu Watters, and, by all accounts, producing some wonderful music. The Musicians' Union, however, had other ideas; a Negro playing with a white group was offensive to their 'principles' and back went Bunk to New Iberia. By this time, though, he was too great a figure to remain buried once again for twenty years. During the rest of 1944 he remained in the South, where Bill Russell visited him to record his best work. Destined for the *American Music* label, as yet unreleased in this country, the host of recordings made (Russell recorded everything, even the practices) represent the finest jazz ever preserved from the hearts of the original pioneer jazzmen. For the men whom Bunk gathered around him were pioneers: George Lewis, clarinet, JIM ROBINSON (*born 1892*), trombone, Lawrence Marrero, banjo, Alcide Pavageau, string bass, and Baby Dodds, drums. In the spring of 1945, with the addition of Kid Shots Madison, trumpet, Adolphe Alexander, baritone horn, Isidore Barbarin, baritone horn, and Joseph Clark, tuba; and with Baby Dodds playing snare drums only and Marrero on bass drum, Russell recorded Bunk's Brass Band, to give the student of jazz music the only examples of the New Orleans marching bands. These records are not jazz in its strictest sense, for they represent one of the many musical influences which amalgamated into jazz; but such sides as *In Gloryland* and *Didn't He Ramble* should ultimately be in every collection.

Soon after these historical records, however, Bunk moved to the North again and before long he was with Sidney Bechet in Boston and then in New York where he was able to demonstrate in the quarter where it was most needed how jazz should be played:

His conception of the correct role which a trumpet player should fill – cuts through that carefully worked up cult of 'great soloist' exposing it for what it is: a publicity man's creation aimed at enhanced box office returns. There is no doubt that the trend towards soloist in front of a band as opposed to musician within a band, is one which is essentially inimical to the production of Jazz. [1]

On 28 September 1945, Bunk Johnson's New Orleans Band opened at the Stuyvesant Casino, on New York's lower east side. Here Bunk, his lip harder, his old mastery regained with two years' practice, led his band with a *verve* which, eye-witnesses claim, has never been equalled on record. Reporting on the phenomenon of a New Orleans Band in New York, Ralph Sturges describes Bunk's style:

Where Louis melts your heart with his magnetic personality, overpowering strength, and his vast flights of inventiveness, Bunk substitutes a subtle mastery of melodic 'know how', an endless play of searching understatement which relentlessly guides the other instruments along a secure path. [2]

The over-enthusiasm of the first Bunk Johnson enthusiasts had led to a certain exaggeration of his abilities which had been eagerly seized upon by the critics of the real jazz; at that time, 1942, Bunk's lip and lack of practice were not conducive to faultless technique and earsplitting volume, qualities which were essential to gain favour in the eyes of the modern critics. At the Stuyvesant, however, Bunk amply demonstrated that, if he cared

1. Max Jones's Foreword to *This Is Jazz*, Rudi Blesh, Jazz Music Books.
2. *Jazz Music*, Vol. 3, No. 9. Ed. Max Jones.

to use it, he had technique right enough; but he reserved items like *Carnival in Venice* for his practices.[1]

In this club, Bunk had returned with jazz to its original role, the functional one of providing music for dancing. He showed that jazz does not rely on the rendering of a few 'standard' jazz tunes; like Bechet he believed that jazz is defined not by *what* is played but by *how* it is played. Consequently popular tunes of the most trite kind were featured in his repertoire; he has recorded *You Always Hurt the One You Love* and *I'll Take You Home Again Kathleen*, reminding us that, forty years ago, the jazz 'classics' were then only popular tunes of the day.

Though the best of his recordings are not issued in England Bunk's importance is such that every record available is listed:

Panama/Down By The River   Jazzman J.M.B.8

Moose March/Weary Blues   Jazzman J.M.B.9

When the Saints Go Marching In/Darktown Strutters Ball   HMV B.9511

Sister Kate/One Sweet Letter From You   HMV B.9517

Does Jesus Care/The Lord Will Make a Way Somehow   Melodisc 1102

Where Could I Go But To the Lord?/God's Amazing Grace   Melodisc 1101[2]

Tishomingo Blues/Alexander's Ragtime Band   Brunswick 04437

When a man reaches the age of sixty-nine and still plays jazz for a living it is not a pessimistic assumption that he won't be around playing jazz for very much longer. Yet when Bunk died on 7 July 1949, at his home in New Iberia, where he had retired in 1948, the whole of the jazz world was profoundly moved; the impact of such a personality across the years from New Orleans in 1900 to New York in 1945 was one which had a greater effect upon the consciousness of the musical world than any number of young revivalist groups, however authentic and sincere they may have been. Bunk *was* New Orleans Jazz, he was not just a trumpet player; he represented the music itself – as Derrick Stewart-Baxter has written concerning his records:

In such men as Johnson, Lewis and Robinson we have the perfect team. Each has been born and bred in the Crescent City and each has lived and worked under the same social conditions. Their outlook is identical and they have the same passionate love of their idiom. In consequence there is a complete absence of self-consciousness. There is no

1. Don Ewell corroborates that when his lip was in, Bunk hit G above high C.

2. The Melodiscs are accompaniments to Sister Ernestine Washington.

striving for the unobtainable. There is a logical development of the theme, from its calm and ordered beginning to the always exciting climax. And every number the band plays bears the unmistakable touch of its leader.[1]

Of the musician friends of Bunk Johnson who remain, GEORGE LEWIS (*born 1900*) remains to carry on the tradition. Though he has always been associated with the older pioneer New Orleans men he is actually of the later generation, the one which produced Louis Armstrong. At the early age of nine he had persuaded his mother to buy him a toy flute and when he was sixteen he paid four hard-earned dollars to a pawn-shop for his first clarinet. In the early twenties he played with many of the great New Orleans trumpet men who had not gone north to Chicago, notably Buddy Petit, who Lewis claims (and he is not alone among the veterans to make the claim) to be yet another of the great unrecognized jazzmen. Not until 1942, however, was anything heard of George Lewis outside New Orleans; in that year Bunk named him as his clarinettist for the epoch-making *Jazzmen* records and as a result of his work on these, where he sustained the ensembles when Bunk's lip failed him, the name of another New Orleans clarinet player[2] reached the reference books. Since then he has been able to mix some profitable jazz with his stevedoring – for that was his only source of income during the lean years – and he has appeared on every Bunk record, apart from some discs made under his own name and with the Original Zenith Brass Band.[3] Best of all has been his Trio record *Burgundy Street Blues*, with Marrero, banjo,

*

1. *Jazz Notes*, May 1949. John Rippin, Adelaide, South Australia.
2. Lewis preferred an E-Flat clarinet, 'an old metal clarinet, full of rubbers and things', so that it could be heard better above the heavy brass of the marching bands.
3. Recently a number of George Lewis records have become available in this country, and are listed here:

GEORGE LEWIS AND HIS NEW ORLEANS STOMPERS
   Climax Raf/*Deep Bayou Blues*   Vogue V.2051
   Milenberg Joys/*Two Jim Blues*   Vogue V.2052
   Justa Closer Walk/*Just a Little While*   Vogue V.2053
   Fidgety Feet/*Dauphine Street Blues*   Vogue V.2054
   Don't Go 'Way Nobody/*Careless Love Blues*   Vogue V.2055
THE ORIGINAL ZENITH BRASS BAND
   Salutation March/*If I Ever Cease To Love*   Esquire 10–101
   Bugle Boy March/*'Taint Nobody's Biz-hess*   Esquire 10–102
GEORGE LEWIS AND HIS NEW ORLEANS MUSIC
   Mama Don' Allow/*Willie The Weeper*   Tempo A.94
   Yaaka Hula Hicky Dula/*Burgundy Street Blues*   Tempo A.95

and Alcide Pavageau, bass, two versions of which have been made. So far in this chapter the focus has been upon the three main figures of the Renaissance; the three, in fact, who combined with promoter Rudi Blesh on that memorable day at the Geary Theatre, 9 May 1943, to bring New Orleans jazz into the public eye. Lu Watters, Kid Ory, and Bunk Johnson, with their successors, initiated a movement which was to resurrect and rejuvenate a music which had for so long been pronounced dead by the critics that the fallacy had been accepted. To them must be conceded the lasting credit for rescuing jazz from an abyss of oblivion.

Let us turn now, however, to the remainder of the United States and the rest of the world. The romantic discovery of one of the early pioneers in the rice-fields of Louisiana and the amazing resurrection of King Oliver's music in the Dawn Club in San Francisco had not escaped notice among jazz enthusiasts throughout the globe; Lu Watters and Bunk Johnson supplied the incentive for the formation of dozens of jazz bands; here at last, for the first time, was jazz in an authentic form, a solid foundation for creative energy. The bubble of the rhythm club 'hot jam sessions' was burst; and New Orleans jazz came into its own.

In America the end of World War II saw several groups formed with the traditional approach. BOB WILBER (born 1926) led a group of teen-agers into Jimmy Ryan's Club on 52nd Street, New York, one afternoon late in 1946 and immediately created a sensation by playing standard New Orleans tunes like the veterans. So refreshingly new was the sound of this band playing as a group and not as a collection of soloists that they were signed immediately for a recording session with Commodore. Wilber was taught to play clarinet by Sidney Bechet, while the trumpet men Johnny Glasel and Jerry Blumberg might have been taught by Bunk himself, to judge from their style. Several records made for the Rampart label have been released here, *Trouble In Mind*/*When You Wore a Tulip* (Tempo A.52) being recommended as representative.

Meanwhile, over on the Pacific coast again, but over the border from California, in Portland, Oregon, Monte Ballou had formed in 1944 a group which somehow managed to obtain dates in the local clubs, one of which gave rise to the band's name, the 'Castle Jazz Band'. This group is inclined to stray from the four-four time of New Orleans but nevertheless produces an infectious and, at times, driving beat. *Georgia Camp Meeting* (Tempo A.46), one of their earliest records, is also one of their finest. Quite a number of their discs have been released here, the later ones revealing a whimsical sense of humour which reminds the listener that jazz is not to be worn with a frown.

Leslie Hurlebath has observed[1] that, as the Mississippi river-boats took jazz out of New Orleans to other parts of the U.S.A., so the humble freighter, carrying gramophone records, spread the music to the four corners of the earth; a neat comparison and a very true one. Unfortunately only a very small percentage of the shellac was of the New Orleans vintage, but even this tiny proportion found avid ears in Britain, France and Holland, to name only European countries. PETER SCHILPEROORT (*born 1918*) was one of the early record students and as early as 1939 he had formed the Swing Papas in The Hague to put into practice what he had learned from Johnny Dodds and Cecil Scott – and from Benny Goodman. The combination of tone and technique gleaned from these masters has given to Schilperoort a highly individual style, which has been enlivened by a certain attractive stridency to make his playing immediately recognizable. The Chicago-style Swing Papas disbanded hastily when the Nazis invaded Holland and forbade all Negro non-Aryan music, but after the war, the 'Orchestra of the Dutch Swing College', to translate its imposing Dutch title, continued the development of good jazz in the Low Countries. A co-operative group formed by students at Delft University, they are insistent that their style is not merely a copy of Oliver; and indeed there is something about this band which marks them apart from the other revival bands. They are not too tightly enmeshed with the close-knit New Orleans ensemble; they use two clarinets and Kees van Dorsser, the trumpeter, stems from Spanier rather than Oliver; but with a rocking rhythm section which includes an excellent drummer in Arie Merkt the output of this band is always interesting. The following selection from the limited number of their records available in England are excellently recorded and indicate the leader's absorption of the tone quality of Jimmy Noone.

Absent Minded Blues/*Original Dixieland One-Step* Tempo A.21
Alexander's Ragtime Band/*Birthday Blues* Tempo A.32
Black Bottom Stomp/*Everything's Wrong* Decca C.16144
Tin Roof Blues/*That's A Plenty* Decca C.16164

*

France has always been in the forefront of all artistic development, especially any school of thought which tends towards the

1. *Playback*, July 1949. Ed. Orin Blackstone, New Orleans.

revolutionary. The impact of jazz, therefore, has never met with such bitter opposition in Paris as it has done in London or Berlin. The New Orleans movement found its adherents soon after the War and in 1945, the year in which so many of our present-day bands were born, CLAUDE LUTER (*born 1927*) formed the band which, in spite of the date, the place and the environment, immediately gained the reputation of being the purest New Orleans-style band in the world. There was no subtlety about clarinettist Luter, or any of his henchmen; they just knew what they wanted to play and how to play it – and they were indefatigable. They owe much to Henri Bernard, the French collector, who played them his wonderful collection of New Orleans records, but they owe more to their own enthusiasm and clarity of vision whereby they accepted no compromise with later, weaker styles of jazz. They became quite well known in the Quartier Latin and were enabled to present their music to a regular public at Le Club du Lorientais. His admirers even made a collection so that the band could make their own records, but it was not long before record companies were seeking them. The greatest honour fell to them to be chosen to represent France at the Festival of Jazz, held at Nice in 1948. The choice met with much opposition from the Paris musical world, but Luter's Band was the success of the Festival. Baby Dodds, who was present, thought he could hear his brother playing when he heard Luter; a selection from the following records, available in England, will confirm that Johnny Dodds's music is not dead yet:

Panama/Weary Way Blues Esquire 10-023
Gatemouth/Sweet Lovin' Man Esquire 10-024
Tiger Rag/Wild Cat Blues Tempo A.11

Another Frenchman who has absorbed the style of a New Orleans jazzman is PIERRE BRASLAVSKY (*born 1930*), whose ability on the soprano saxophone shows a faith in Bechet bordering on adulation. Like Bechet he prefers to lead the group and he has gone so far as to continue to dispense with a trumpet or cornet player. With the front line consisting of Braslavsky, Réné Franc, clarinet, and Bernard Zacharias, trombone, the band has a peculiarly French flavour, with a strong orthodox influence. The uninhibited spirit of Luter is replaced by a thoughtful, carefully developed logic, which, though far from the purity of the Crescent City, has much to recommend it.[1]

Before leaving France, mention should be made of CLAUDE

1. Three records have been released on the *Tempo* label.

BOLLING (*born 1930*), a pianist who was leading his own New-Orleans-style group in Paris at the age of fifteen. The Bolling Band is composed of good musicians who can play anything musical, from New Orleans to Ellington; the effect is somewhat similar to that of Braslavsky – excellently played yet lacking the sparkle of Luter. Nevertheless, like all the European revivalist bands, youth is on their side and much may yet develop. [1]

*

Almost since the first notice was taken of jazz, back in 1920, when Ernest Ansermet showed his appreciation of Sidney Bechet, Europe has always regarded England, from a jazz point of view, as something of a wet blanket; a rather soggy blanket which occasionally oozed some fragment worthy of scant attention, no more. During the past five or six years, however, the position has entirely changed; with Gallic enthusiasm and eagerness to accept new creeds, France, the centre of fashion trends in all European art, has tried everything, so that now Paris is inclined to be Jean of all Trades. London is now the centre of jazz in Europe and its rise to this position can be attributed to one man – pianist GEORGE WEBB (*born 1917*).

Unlike the musicians of Paris, English jazz enthusiasts had no opportunity of gaining inspiration from the visiting American stars who descended upon France as soon as World War II was ended. George did not even wait for that; as early as 1943 the few gramophone records which had filtered across the Atlantic on the ocean-going counterpart of the Mississippi paddle-wheeler were sufficient inspiration for him. Whatever advantage the Continent may have had through greater tolerance and vision on the part of their Trades Unions has been more than counteracted by the fact that, the only free country left in Europe during the war, Great Britain was in a position to absorb new influences from the U.S.A. Lu Watters cast some long-forgotten seed; it fell upon no more fertile soil than that of Bexleyheath, Kent.

In a pub called the 'Red Barn' George Webb gathered around him a group of amateurs who, being natural musicians, held collective improvisation as practised by Lu Watters and the jazz veterans to be far more important than the endless riffing of *China Boy*. The music of Louis's Hot Five and King Oliver was, they felt, the only kind of hot music which could satisfy their creative

1. Records available on *Esquire*.

needs; if, by some coincidence, the public liked what they heard, so much the better.

Jazz listeners on the Continent refused to believe their ears when the BBC broadcast George Webb's Dixielanders one night in 1945. They were prepared to swear that they were listening to some carefully processed discs of King Oliver himself, but enquiring letters to England elicited the information that the line-up was, apart from George on piano, Owen Bryce and Reg Rigden, cornets, Wally Fawkes, clarinet, Eddie Harvey, trombone, Buddy Vallis, banjo, Art Streatfield, tuba, and Roy Wykes, drums. It had taken twenty-one years to begin to undo the harm done to jazz appreciation in this country by the comic hats of the Original Dixieland Jazz Band.

There is some good permanent evidence of the sort of music that the Webb Dixielanders turned out. Some sides were cut for a private label, *Jazz*, who were pioneering the field in recording amateur jazz talent, and the Decca company also issued two couplings. The historic importance of this short-lived group is such that all their records are listed:

New Orleans Hop Scop Blues/Come Back Sweet Papa Jazz 0001
Riverside Blues/Dippermouth Blues Jazz 0002
South/London Blues Decca F.8735
Muskrat Ramble/Jenny's Ball Decca F.9385

By 1946 they had played before an audience numbering 2000 at the Birmingham Town Hall, and in 1947 the personnel reverted to the Hot Seven line-up rather than the King Oliver Creole Jazz Band by the substitution of one cornet instead of two. At that time I commented: 'Humphrey Lyttelton's work is a definite contribution on the credit side.'[1] Before enlarging upon this masterpiece of understatement, however, it is necessary to retrace our steps chronologically once again – by some three or four years – to 1943, and to transfer our attention geographically by some 13,000 miles – to Melbourne, Australia. For it is from 'down under' that the English jazz revival movement received its greatest single stimulus – in the shape of GRAEME BELL (*born 1914*) and his 'Australian Jazz Band'. The early story of this band follows much the same lines as many a band story and it is hard to pinpoint the factor which has given them the little extra something which has brought laudatory adjectives to the lips of the purest of critics. They used much the same approach; their capa-

1. *Sound*. June 1947.

bilities were by and large no more than average; they had had what might have been the deadening experience of dance-band work; why, then, the tremendous success of Graeme Bell and his band and why, then, the tremendous influence?

In a few words the success was due to courage and the influence was the result of personality and faith in an ideal, as the following narrative will help to show.

The Bell Band came together in 1943, after playing in and around Melbourne for perhaps a decade, in various degrees of heat, from frenzied jam sessions to cool tea-dances. However, they did not allow these experiences to affect their purpose in coming together – to play New Orleans jazz – but used their acquired technique as one of the means to their end. Those modern critics who condemn revivalist groups for their lack of experience and technique have never been able to level this criticism at the Bells.

They played at clubs, at concerts, went on tours, broadcast, and made their first *Ampersand*[1] records – the familiar routine. Then came the event which thrilled even the normally blasé jazz commentators. In 1947 was held in Prague, Czechoslovakia, a World Youth Festival. A Youth League in Victoria was invited to send delegates and such was its reputation by this time that Graeme Bell's Band was chosen. And the Bells, much to the Victorian Youth League's surprise, accepted! Imagine what this entailed; imagine deciding to go to the other end of the earth, having to pay the fare, having to pay your own way when you got there; no knowledge of the language; and no capital to launch the project. The Bells, by dint of a strenuous tour of New South Wales, raised enough cash to buy single tickets to Europe – no more; and decided unanimously to take the risk. Of course they had been promised all sorts of concerts and tours in various parts of Europe when they had finished their programme at the World Youth Festival; various jazz personalities had promised a great welcome for this pioneering band and it was with some justification that they set out confidently from Melbourne on 1 July 1947.

But not a soul met them off the boat at Southampton. So while they continued their trek to Prague, Mel Langdon, their manager, was left to fix up with a proper agent. The Czechoslovak Festival spelt success for Graeme – in Czechoslovakia. Audiences, with no commercialized press to form their opinions for them, were wildly enthusiastic about this new jazz music. At concerts before 5000 people, the Bells were overwhelmed by the spontaneity of

1. Available in England on Tempo and Esquire.

the welcome. But in England? Their reception was only luke-warm.

Such was the courage of their convictions that Graeme Bell and his Australian Jazz Band remained in England on the strength of only two concerts, one at the Birmingham Town Hall and one for the now defunct Hot Club of London. But this was not enough to live on and so followed much burning of midnight oil, much writer's cramp, a lot of hard work; and still they were, to quote Graeme Bell, 'scuffling hard'.

It was then that he put into practice a theory he had long cherished, the same theory which the Watters Band had clung to in their formative days – that, essentially a functional music, jazz had arisen from dancing and that therefore it should be played for dancing. Graeme holed out in one. He singled out the paramount reason why since the hectic days of Storyville and the Lincoln Gardens jazz had never stirred from its comatose state – it was because it had never fulfilled the purpose for which it had been nurtured. Just as the charm of a Devonshire regatta would be lost if held one year in the West India Docks, the spirit of jazz had run to seed on the platform of the 'rhythm clubs' and on the floors of sophisticated night clubs.

The Leicester Square Jazz Club was formed and in a few short weeks the resident Graeme Bell Band was News. They left this country in a blaze of glory, with many recording sessions to their credit and with a Farewell Concert dedicated to them, in July 1948, just a year after setting out into the unknown, with no return ticket, nothing but their firm belief in their own brand of jazz.

In addition to the *Ampersand* Australian records already mentioned, Graeme Bell has recorded many titles in Czechoslovakia, France, and England; those made here are excellent examples of the exuberant spirit of the band, the following being representative:

Oh Peter!/Jackass Blues Tempo A.8
Was Leicester Square?/Free Man's Blues Tempo A.9
South/Shimme-Sha-Wabble Esquire 10-007
Yama Yama Blues/Big Chief Battle Axe Esquire 10-008

Some representative examples of his Czechoslovakian recordings are given below, and special attention should be paid to Pixie Robert's clarinet work in *Sister Kate* and *Fidgety Feet*. Ade Monsbourgh, too, should be heard in one of his best trombone solos of that period: *Czechoslovak Journey*.

Panama Rag/Riverside Blues Supraphon C.23172
Fidgety Feet/Czechoslovak Journey Supraphon C.23173
Dallas Blues/Sister Kate Supraphon C.23174

In November 1950 Graeme Bell returned to England, where he was booked for a whole year of club and concert appearances. He received a very different welcome in 1950 from the 1947 version, and justified it by providing even better jazz. The new band had a slightly changed personnel – and great promise. Their initial concert at the Winter Garden Theatre in December 1950 carried on the Wilcox Organization's tradition of presenting the best in jazz music, and the band's tour of Great Britain during 1951 was in the nature of a triumphal procession: especially when contrasted with their previous visit. Their most recent work on record should certainly be heard, and is listed below. For sheer drive, infectious gaiety and beat, and for the incredibly sympathetic singing of our own English Neva Raphaello, *Cakewalking Babies* is highly recommended.

Black and White Rag/High Society Parlophone R.3390
When The Saints Go Marching Home/Muskrat Ramble Parlophone R.3396
Cakewalking Babies/Goanna March Parlophone R.3445

*

By the time that Graeme Bell went back to Australia in the summer of 1948, George Webb's Dixielanders had broken up, and HUMPHREY LYTTELTON (*born 1921*) had risen rapidly to the forefront to lead his own band, composed mainly of Webb stalwarts. Taking over from Graeme at the Leicester Square Club and later at the newly-formed London Jazz Club it was soon obvious that Lyttelton's Band was to be a potent force in English jazz. With WALLY FAWKES (*born 1920*) providing a vibrant clarinet part behind Humphrey's driving cornet, two real jazzmen were playing jazz which could be heard and danced to by anyone with the price of admission to the Club in Oxford Street, in the heart of London. It is with no false patriotic feeling that this writer places Lyttelton and Fawkes among the great jazzmen of this generation. Whilst Graeme Bell's Australian Band exemplified perfection in relaxation and collective improvisation, Lyttelton and Fawkes added something more – inspired individuality. Without in any way suggesting a direct comparison, it was what Armstrong and Dodds gave to jazz with the formation of Louis's Hot Five.

Humphrey Lyttelton gained his jazz knowledge from gramophone records; it might be more correct to say Armstrong records. In this he shares the experience of the majority of English enthusiasts (the fact that many of the early Oliver and Armstrong Hot Five records have been available on English Brunswick and Parlophone while they were for years unobtainable in the U.S.A. may be a reason for the present high standard of jazz appreciation here). To the instinct for getting to the root of the matter on record Humphrey added a musical ability of rare distinction. Bearing in mind a background of Eton and the Grenadier Guards (a far cry from the Mahogany Hall and the Onward Band), Lyttelton's sympathy with the jazz idiom has been masterly. Posterity will decide whether he is to be listed among the jazz greats; certain it is that he has done something more than to copy Oliver and Armstrong; he has used the old structure; but he has built into it much new material. He has employed the traditional instrumentation and played many of the traditional tunes; but into them he has infused a nameless quality; not purity in the archaic nor in the orthodox European sense; but purity in the sense of perfection in tone, technique, and orchestral balance; discipline in attack; an inspired feeling for collective improvisation; all these things merged into a whole to produce the sort of music King Oliver might have played had he been alive to-day.

Humphrey has always perceived that the European approach cannot be applied to jazz, not even in the practising of scales; like Louis Armstrong, he 'warms up' by improvising elaborate arpeggios with plenty of 'blue' notes and jazz inflexions. In jazz there is no room for compromise with text-book exercises. Recognizing that only the great jazzmen of New Orleans can expect to produce classic jazz within a lifetime, his attitude to jazz is basically one of humility. Wally Fawkes says: 'The most encouraging thing about this band to me is that it can return to the rehearsal room after a frenzied ovation somewhere or other, and Humph will put us all back on a refresher course of the fundamentals of ensemble playing – just in case we were thinking more about self-expression than band-expression.' The resultant first-rate jazz can be heard on any of his records, notably the following selected couplings:

Get Out Of Here/Sunday Morning   Tempo A.19
Melancholy/The Thin Red Line   London Jazz 1
Cake Walkin' Babies/If You See Me Comin'   London Jazz 2
Weary Blues/Working Man Blues   London Jazz 3

Maple Leaf Rag/Memphis Blues   Parlophone R.3257
Froggie Moore/Ice Cream   Parlophone R.3292
Hop Frog/Snake Rag   Parlophone R.3286
Careless Love Blues/Come On and Stomp, Stomp, Stomp Parlophone R.3274
Chattanooga Stomp/Dallas Blues   Parlophone R.3322
Trouble in Hand/Panama Rag   Parlophone R.3346
Gatemouth/Trog's Blues   Parlophone R.3379
Down Home Rag/Tom Cat Blues   Parlophone R.3413.
Apex Blues/One Man Went To Blow   Parlophone R.3436

The *Apex Blues* features Wally Fawkes on bass clarinet, and Lyttelton on clarinet, a beautifully integrated performance of the old Jimmy Noone number. The reverse is one of those trick effects, where, by a series of re-recordings, Lyttelton himself plays trumpet, clarinet, piano, and washboard. An amusing demonstration of his versatility, but not to be rated as a masterpiece of jazz.

At the time of writing, George Webb and the Christie brothers have left the band, and its reorganization is a matter for future consideration, when it has settled down into its stride.

*

Lyttelton is the star of the English firmament. But there are others who, if lacking something of Humphrey's greatness, have made a definite contribution to the English Jazz Renaissance. In the North a co-operative group, 'The Yorkshire Jazz Band', encouraged by Graeme Bell, who suggested their name, played music which stemmed more from Bunk Johnson than from Armstrong or Oliver; Bob Barclay played a tuba and they preferred a banjo to a guitar. With Dickie Hawdon playing an imaginative lead trumpet the Y.J.B. made a name for themselves in a very short time. As Humphrey's route had been marked for him by Graeme Bell, so the lads from Yorkshire came on the scene just when traditional jazz music was beginning to meet with more general approval and the Wilcox Brothers were filling the London Jazz Club to overflowing every week. The Yorkshire Jazz Band overcame the prejudice that provincial bands were not up to London standard; they met with instant approval among the Lyttelton fans – and the denizens of the basement at number One Hundred, Oxford Street, are no mean invigilators. Temperamentally the Y.J.B. have experienced many crises, but many of their records are still available on Tempo.

There have been other jazz groups, both from London and the

provinces; Mick Gill from Nottingham, Roy Cooper from Derby, Ray Foxley from Birmingham, Reg Rigden, Chris Barber, Len Beadle, Mike Daniels, the Christie Brothers Stompers from London, the Saints Jazz Band from Manchester . . . a full list would fill this page.[1] Two bands, however, deserve special mention before bringing the narrative of the English jazz revival to a close.

'The Crane River Jazz Band' hails from the western outskirts of London where they have managed to play uncompromising New Orleans jazz in a suburban area where there was no natural ready-made audience of enthusiasts. Gradually they converted the sceptics and, in easy stages, they moved nearer to London's West End, where they became resident at their club in Great Newport Street. Never a group of technicians, they approached the music from a fundamental viewpoint; for the first year of their existence they were rough and raucous, but gradually settled down to a relaxed and confident style that owed its inspiration mainly to Bunk Johnson. They claim the distinction of being the first jazz band in England to be televised, though it is regrettable that the TV producers laid a little too much stress on the novelty-comedy angle.

The other band is that of MICK MULLIGAN (*born 1928*), who acquired his enthusiasm for jazz by collecting records with Bob Dawbarn at the Merchant Taylors' School; a mutual enthusiasm which continues to the present day, Bob supplying the tailgate trombone behind Mick's driving trumpet lead. The astonishing fact about Mulligan's active jazz career is that within two years of learning the rudiments of his instrument his prestige was such that he was able to take his band on a successful tour to jazz-conscious Amsterdam. Now numbered among the best in England, the Magnolia Jazz Band (named after one of King Oliver's early bands) still lacks the finish of Lyttelton; Mick himself, always willing to learn (especially from Armstrong records), has yet to develop the capacity for variation of ideas; but the band, steeped in New Orleans tradition, plays with an overwhelming zeal which must be very close to the tradition of Mahogany Hall and the Lincoln Gardens. If further evidence of this claim is required the

1. In a nation-wide amateur contest not less than forty-five bands took part. Most of the bands mentioned can be heard on record, but if difficulty is encountered when trying to obtain them, helpful advice will be given by the Jazz Records Retailers Association, at 23, Thomas Street, London, SE18.

record of *Candy Lips/Savoy Blues* (Tempo AA.66) should be
sufficient to convince the listener, the shortcomings in technique
being offset by the infectious drive and stimulating rhythm
section.

*

Reference must be made at this point to an event unique in the
annals of jazz. On 14 July 1950, the National Federation of Jazz
Organizations staged a Traditional Jazz Concert at the Royal
Festival Hall, at which, thanks to the good offices of the Federa-
tion's President, the Marquis of Donegall, H.R.H. Princess
Elizabeth was present as guest of honour.

Despite nervousness on the part of some of the bands – a very
natural nervousness – some good jazz was heard, especially from
the Saints' Jazz Band. Others were not up to their usual standard,
and reference to the recordings which were actually made in the
Hall during the performance will show this. For the purposes of
convenience, a list of those issued is given in full:

HUMPHREY LYTTELTON
    It Makes My Love Come Down/Blues For An Unknown Gypsy
    Parlophone R.3424
JOE DANIELS
    Barnyard Blues/Wolverine Blues   Parlophone R.3425
GRAEME BELL
    Bull Ant Blues
FREDDY RANDALL   } Parlophone R.3426
    Big Butter and Egg Man
THE SAINTS JAZZ BAND
    I Want a Girl Just Like the Girl
CRANE RIVER BAND   } Parlophone R.3427
    I'm Travelling

The occasion was a spectacular one for jazz, and the N.F.J.O.
deserves great credit for sponsoring such an event. PETER
TANNER, writing in *Jazz Journal*, summed up admirably when he
wrote:

Jazz music has come a long way during the past fifty years and it is
certain that few of its pioneers could have foreseen that one day it
would be presented with all the dignity of an opera first night in the
presence of Royalty. The patronage of Her Royal Highness Princess
Elizabeth was not only a triumph for jazz music in this country and
for those most interested in its well being and promotion, but also for
those interested in jazz everywhere. In America, especially, every jazz
musician may justly feel proud; proud that American folk music, and

standing of its aims and potentialities from the Swiss conductor, Ernest Ansermet.[1]

The first thing that strikes one about the Southern Syncopated Orchestra is the astonishing perfection, the superb taste, and the fervour of its playing. . . . It is only in the field of harmony that the Negro hasn't yet created his own distinct means of expression. . . . But, in general, harmony is perhaps a musical element which appears in a scheme of musical evolution only at a stage which the Negro art has not yet attained.

Again, when writing of Sidney Bechet's clarinet solos with that same orchestra:

. . . they gave the idea of a style, and their form was gripping, abrupt, harsh, with a brusque and pitiless ending like that of Bach's second *Brandenburg Concerto*.

Prophetic words! Brave words, too, for those musically conventional days.

Carl Engel, too, Chief of the Music Division of the Library of Congress from 1921 to 1935, had this to say with reference to those who held jazz to be an atrocity:

To a great many minds the word 'jazz' implies frivolous or obscene deportment. Let me ask what the word 'sarabande' suggests to you? I have no doubt that to most of you it will mean everything that is diametrically opposed to 'jazzing'. When you hear mention of a 'sarabande', you think of Bach's, of Handel's slow and stately airs. . . . Yet the sarabande, when it was first danced in Spain, about 1588, was probably far more shocking to behold than is the most shocking jazz to-day.[2]

One has only to compare the violent outcry at the beginning of the nineteenth century when the waltz was introduced to the 'polite society' of America and England with the angry opposition to jazz in the first quarter of the twentieth century, to realize that the oft-quoted words about the repetition of history are indeed true. The waltz was described in an encyclopaedia dated about 1805 as a riotous German dance of modern invention, and the article proceeds:

The verb *waltzen*, whence this word is derived, implies to roll, wallow, welter, tumble down, or roll in the dirt or mire. What analogy there may be between these acceptations and the dance, we pretend not to say; but having seen it performed by a select party of foreigners, we could not help reflecting how uneasy an English mother would be to

1. *On a Negro Orchestra, Revue Romande*. October 1919. Translated by Walter E. Schaap for *Jazz Hot*, November–December 1938.
2. *Jazz, Atlantic*. August 1922.

see her daughter so familiarly treated, and still more to witness the obliging manner in which the freedom is returned by the females.[1]

Although these last two quotations seem to have led us from the path, they do show that the opprobrium in which jazz was held was but a natural reaction against any new form of dance music – and jazz, it must never be forgotten, has its roots firmly embedded in the dance, however much we may like to listen to it as a purely mental and emotional experience.

Dvořák was probably one of the first composers of note to make use of Negro melodies in his work – an influence which dated from his stay in America from 1892 to 1895, when he was head of the National Conservatory of Music in New York. Themes in the 'New World' symphony[2] are suggestive of this, and the dubiously nicknamed 'Nigger Quartet'[3] contains syncopated rhythm which hints at some of the characteristics of early ragtime. The insistent rhythm in the first part of the *Lento* movement invites comparison with the relentless beat of a Work Song, while the gay rhythms of the third movement and the repetition of little phrases in the fourth point to folk music origins.

It must be remembered, however, that Dvořák, himself of peasant stock, drew largely upon his own Bohemian folk music, and care must be taken not to read into the quartet something which is not there. It is true that he was interested in Negro melodies, and even counselled the basing of a native American music on them, but the fact that he ascribed the third movement of the quartet to a bird's song he heard at his retreat in Iowa shows the danger of seeking too much proof of Negro influences.

Probably the first composer to make use of ragtime (as distinct from Negro melodies) was Debussy, and the influence which made itself felt in his *Golliwog's Cake-Walk* (1908) (Decca F.7495 (William Murdoch), HMV B.9508 (Mayfair Orchestra conducted by Walter Goehr)), and *Minstrels* (1910) (HMV DA.1280 (Yehudi Menuhin)) is obviously that of Negro minstrelsy rather than the ragtime which developed out of it. Incidentally, it is interesting to note that he composed a Rhapsody for saxophone and orchestra in 1903, thus anticipating the jazz use of the instrument by some years.

1. *The Oxford Companion to Music*. Percy A. Scholes.
2. *From the New World* Symphony. Galliera's Philharmonia Orch., Columbia DX 1399–1403.
3. *String Quartet in F Major*. The Griller String Quartet. Decca AK.2080–2081–2082.

Stravinsky seems to have been next in the field, and in 1918 composed *Ragtime for Eleven Solo Instruments* (Columbia LX.382 (deleted)) and *The Soldier's Story*, but this time the influence is *post* ragtime, and, in his own words, was chiefly limited to published jazz, if such a contradiction in terms may be allowed. He says:

At my request, a whole pile of this music was sent to me, enchanting me by its truly popular appeal, its freshness, and the novel rhythm which so distinctly revealed its Negro origin. These impressions suggested the idea of creating a composite portrait of this new dance music, giving the creation the importance of a concert piece, as, in the past, the composers of their periods had done for the minuet, the waltz and the mazurka. [1]

Viennese born Ernst Křenek made much use of jazz rhythms and colourful jazz patterns in the music of the opera *Jonny Spielt Auf* (Johnny Strikes Up), which was first performed at Leipzig in 1927. This was written while he was under the influence of the *Gebrauchsmusik* movement of the early twenties, which maintained that all art should be conceived and made intelligible to the general public by utilizing everyday subjects as a medium of expression. Hindemith and Kurt Weill were also associated with the school, and although it is difficult to trace jazz influence in Hindemith's works, his attitude to musical orthodoxy is well known, and, in his textbook on the groundwork of composition he shows a perhaps not unwitting sympathy for jazz when he says: 'No chord can be regarded as ungrammatical if its use seems essential to the composer' and 'The semitone can be varied considerably according to its place in the scale, and the artist's aesthetic instinct finds the true answer in each particular case.'

Krenek now, however, blushes for the indiscretions of youth when he writes: [2] 'Many composers who worried over the salvation or re-establishment of tonality have resorted to jazz as a method of regeneration. For a time I was one of them.'

Kurt Weill together with the poet Brecht created the German version of *The Beggar's Opera* [3] – *Drei Groschen Oper:* a procedure which brought this ironic comment from Percy A. Scholes: [4]

It (jazz) even began also to be taken seriously by a certain number of composers, and its rhythmic, harmonic, and orchestral elements crept

1. *An Autobiography.* Simon & Schuster. 1936.
2. *Music Here and Now.* New York. 1939.
3. *Ballad of The Comfortable Life* from this was issued on Polydor Z.4172.
4. *The Oxford Companion to Music.*

into suites and other orchestral compositions, as also into operas. One or two operas that (supposedly) had previously lacked sufficient ginger were re-flavoured: *The Beggar's Opera*, after struggling through thousands of performances over a period of exactly two centuries, at last had life put into it by Kurt Weill, and Sullivan turned in his grave with pleasurable excitement at finding his *Mikado*, fresh from the hands of another German musician, at length made genuinely acceptable to the public (Berlin 1927).

The note of irony there is obviously directed at the interference with a 'classic' opera, rather than towards the use of the jazz idiom itself. A later composition – an opera entitled: *The Rise and Fall of the City Mahagonny*, although received by a Leipzig audience in 1929 with marked disapproval,[1] was described in the *New York Times* of 30 April 1930 by a critic as 'transitory period opera, perhaps a halting place in the day's march towards the goal – opera of the future for the masses.'

Writing in 1934, Constant Lambert expressed great admiration for Weill, placing him as the most successful and important of the Central European composers who had experimented with the jazz idiom. Of his later composition *The Seven Deadly Sins*, Lambert says:[2]

The Seven Deadly Sins marks as great an improvement on *Mahagonny* as *Mahagonny* did on the *Drei Groschen Oper*. . . . As presented with *décor* by Neher and choreography by Balanchine, *The Seven Deadly Sins* is the most important work in ballet form since *Les Noces* and *Parade*. In spite of its superficial air of bustle the music is remarkable for its extraordinary weariness, a neurasthenic fatigue, which, though sterile in a way, reaches in the finale a certain grandeur.

It is, however, in respect of the jazz element in Milhaud's *La Création du Monde* that Lambert really lets himself go. He cites the composition as a most remarkable example of the compromise possible between popular idiom and sophisticated construction. His analysis is too valuable to be missed:[3]

Darius Milhaud in *La Création du Monde* represents the primeval incantations of the gods Nzamé, Mébère and Nkwa by a three-part fugato over a percussion accompaniment. The rhythm and inflections of the fugue subject are clearly derived from jazz arabesques, yet, at the

---

1. The performance was abandoned owing to a barrage of rotten eggs. Since these are hardly a normal concert-going requisite for the well-dressed man or woman, the missiles must have been taken in on the strength of a preconceived verdict.
2. *Music Ho!* Constant Lambert, 1934. Pelican 195, Penguin Books, 1948.
3. *Ibid*.

same time, the subject is an admirable one from any save the most crusty academic view. Crudely and naïvely analysed, the percussion background provides the necessary barbaric atmosphere, the jazz inflections of the tune suggest a stylized Negro speech, the counterpoint provides the element of mingled and growing effort, while from the objective point of view the passage, theatrical atmosphere apart, is an excellent and logical 'arrangement of notes'. Had Milhaud used a Negro folk song for this scene, he might have obtained the requisite dark atmosphere, but he would have been unable to add to this the constructional plasticity allowed by the jazz idiom he has chosen. . . . That two works so strikingly different in outlook and texture as *The Seven Deadly Sins* and *La Création du Monde* should both draw their inspiration from the jazz idiom is sufficient answer to those who imagine that this idiom must inevitably produce a flat, monotonous, and restricted style.

It is unfortunate that Milhaud did not continue his experiments in the use of jazz, for he could then have more adequately refuted Ernest Newman's dictum that jazz being (in the compositional sense, apart from orchestration) merely a bundle of tricks, the composer who tries to develop jazz is on the horns of a dilemma; if he makes use of the tricks he fetters his individuality, and if he does not he ceases to write jazz.

Obviously Newman uses the word 'jazz' in its widest sense, for 'jazz composition' is really a contradiction in terms – real jazz being essentially improvisational in character; the actual musician or small group of musicians *creating* the music from a theme mutually agreed upon. Thus, although the words 'jazz composer' and 'jazz composition' have been used in this book, they relate to those who have written down or sketched out a theme upon which jazz musicians can extemporize.

That Křenek recognized the contribution which jazz has made in its insistence upon the value of extemporization may be seen from his statement in 1939: 'Jazz . . . has revived the art of improvisation to an extent unknown by serious musicians since the days of the *super librum cantare*, the contrapuntal extemporization of the fifteenth century.'[1]

This improvised counterpoint – or interweaving of different strands of melody to form an effective pattern of music – has become such a natural thing in jazz that it is not generally realized that it is a comparatively new exploration in popular dance music. It is an art which was not used in the dance music of, say, the waltz and polka.

1. *Music Here and Now*. New York. 1939.

The underlying beat of jazz, the four-in-a-bar pulse, has been described by critics as being monotonous to the point of imbecility. They have obviously not listened carefully to the irregular cross-rhythms which create a 'beat within a beat'; they cannot see the wood for the trees.

The American composer Aaron Copland has long been sufficiently interested in jazz to write on the subject at various times since 1927, when he advocated the use of jazz by modern composers, but in 1941 he had apparently been side-tracked by the swing era when he wrote:

From the composer's viewpoint, jazz has only two expressions: either it was the well-known 'Blues' mood, or the wild, abandoned, almost hysterical and grotesque mood so dear to the youth of all ages. These two moods encompass the whole gamut of jazz emotion.[1]

It is obvious that Copland is obsessed with the 'mood' character of jazz and would-be jazz, and his own *Four Piano Blues*[2] – 1, 'Freely Poetic'; 2, 'Soft and Languid'; 3, 'Muted and Drugged'; 4, 'With Bounce' – although showing intriguing mathematical pattern shot with flashes of syncopation, are examples of mood music tinged with jazz memories.

Hardly within the scope of this chapter, mention must be made, however, of the 'Symphonic Jazz' attempts by George Gershwin and Ferdie Grofé, which resulted in the creation of *Rhapsody in Blue*. The popularity of this piece of synthetic jazz might be compared with the success of the *Warsaw Concerto:* both pieces are easy to listen to, they titillate the senses and give an impression that much is being said, musically speaking.

Rhapsody in Blue falls between two stools – it appeals neither to the jazz enthusiast nor to the lover of classical music – 'classical' being used in its widest sense – and other 'symphonic syncopations' have the same drawback. Lambert has expressed their failings most succinctly by saying that 'the shadow of *Rhapsody in Blue* hangs over most of them and they remain the hybrid child of a hybrid. A rather knowing and unpleasant child, too, ashamed of its parents and boasting of its French lessons.'[3]

Constant Lambert himself is to be congratulated on being the first English composer to accept jazz with an open mind, and, in so doing, give it the seal of tolerance if not respectability, thus

1. *Our New Music*. Aaron Copland. New York. 1941.
2. *Four Piano Blues*. Aaron Copland. Decca K.2372.
3. *Music Ho!* Pelican 195, Penguin Books. 1948.

helping towards its consideration by other notable musicians. He admits that it was his admiration for the artistry of Florence Mills in the *Blackbirds* show which served as an inspiration for his *Elegiac Blues*.

His setting of Sacheverell Sitwell's poem *Rio Grande* for piano solo, chorus, alto solo, and an orchestra of brass, strings and percussion is a composition which has stood the test of repeated performances since 1929. In this,[1] apart from the rhythms which are quite obviously of jazz origin, he subtly combines those two characteristic elements of Negro music: a yearning nostalgia and a sudden explosive boisterousness.

The last movement of his Piano Concerto, too, shows intricate rhythmical patterns which hint at his exploration of the jazz world.

If Lambert was the first English composer to use jazz forms in his music, John Ireland was the first to recognize the valuable contribution jazz had to offer in the way of instrumental colouring. He has said, in fact, that his contact with jazz has always been completely involuntary, but at the time that he was writing his *Piano Concerto*[2] in 1930, he happened to meet Jack Payne, who showed him the effect of different kinds of trumpet mutes then used in dance music. At that time the trumpet mute used in symphonic music was the old-fashioned pear-shaped brass one. Ireland at once observed that the fibre mute produced an effect which he wanted, and specified it for his concerto, and it has since become used to a large extent. He relates[3] that for this he was taken to task by one or two music critics, who accused him on this account of coquetting with the jazz world – regardless of the fact that there is no trace of jazz or syncopation in the music of the concerto!

William Walton's *Façade* suite, which contains *Foxtrot*[4] and *Popular Song*,[5] has often been quoted as an example of the influence which jazz has exerted on contemporary composers. But these were deliberate parodies, as indeed is the music of the whole suite, and must be considered as an amusingly rude thumbing of the nose. The opening four-four time of *Portsmouth*

1. *Rio Grande*. Hallé Orchestra, cond. Lambert. Columbia L.2373–4.
2. *Concerto in E flat Major*. Eileen Joyce and Hallé Orchestra. Columbia DX.8178–8180.
3. Letter to the author.
4. *Facade*, Decca K.991⎱ HMV C.2887, London Philharmonic.
5. *Facade*, Decca K.992⎰ Orchestra, cond. William Walton.

Point,[1] together with the rhythmic patterns developed, deserve more attention as having a jazz basis.

Other contemporary composers admit the value of jazz in its own right, but have failed to make use of it in their work. Alan Bush, for instance, has a wide and knowledgeable grasp of the subject, and distinguishes between real jazz and its commercial exploitation when he says:

The improvisational expressive jazz style is a genuine folk-music of an oppressed people, and as such it has a cultural value, as has all folk-music, whether of an oppressed or of a free people (such as the developing folk-music of the autonomous republics of the U.S.S.R.). I do not think, however, that it has any features which are likely to prove of significance in the general development of present-day music, its influence having been that of an exotic spice to composers of countries other than the country of its origin. Just as the French Impressionists were influenced by their discovery of Asiatic and Arabian music at the beginning of the present century, so much the same has happened to some European and American composers with Negro folk-music.[2]

Antony Hopkins has been much more affected by the jazz element in other composers' works – a process in which it has been absorbed and then transmuted by him: thus going through two processes. His own view is that although there is no stricter academic mind than that of the jazz writer[3] who thinks in very limited harmonic circles, with very little real modulation, the greatest contribution jazz can make to straight music is one of *mood*. He considers that its most valuable quality is its great vitality and directness; the 'straight-from-the-shoulder' attack without any introspection or over-intellectualization.

Michael Tippett's oratorio *A Child of our Time* must not be overlooked, for, despite its construction in the classic tradition, he makes use of Negro Spirituals in place of the chorals, closing the first part with *Steal Away*, introducing *Nobody Knows the Trouble I Seen*, *Go Down, Moses*, and *O by and by* to the second, with *Deep River* as a fitting conclusion to the whole oratorio. His instructions in the introduction to the score are that these are to be slightly 'swung'. He readily admits the influence upon his music of all Negro Spirituals, particularly *Shadrack* and *Steal Away*, and pays great tribute to Mitchell's Christian Singers[4] for their skilful use of quarter tones.

1. *Portsmouth Point*, BBC Symphony Orchestra, cond. Adrian Boult. HMV DA 1540.
2. Letter to the author.   3. Note the emphasis on 'writer'.
4. No recordings available in this country.

In his own work he has substituted pure for the 'barber-shop' harmonies of jazz, and although his own view is that jazz influence on any composer is more technical than emotional, he expressed[1] admiration for the great Blues singer Bessie Smith, especially for the dexterous use of four notes with which she achieved immense effect in her rendering of *Cold in Hand Blues* (Parlophone R.2344). Possibly the fluent vitality and supple rhythms of Tippett's *Concerto for Double String Orchestra*[2] may have derived in part from the suspended rhythms of jazz.

There is no tangible evidence of jazz influence in the works of Alan Rawsthorne, but, like Antony Hopkins, he is of the opinion that in the Blues the Negro has made no little contribution to music.

This attention to the Blues on the part of many of the contemporary composers indicates its value, and may have had a subconscious effect to a greater extent than they have realized.

Chopin, Johann Strauss, Tchaikovsky, Brahms, and Richard Strauss were not ashamed to employ the waltz, the polonaise, and the mazurka as a medium for their music, nor did Mozart and Haydn think the minuet beneath their dignity; these dances were based on the folk-music of their day.

It rests with a contemporary composer, or someone of the future, to develop a work which will be satisfactorily based on jazz.

1. In a discussion with the author.
2. Orchestra cond. by Walter Goehr. Schott & Sons. 6559–64.

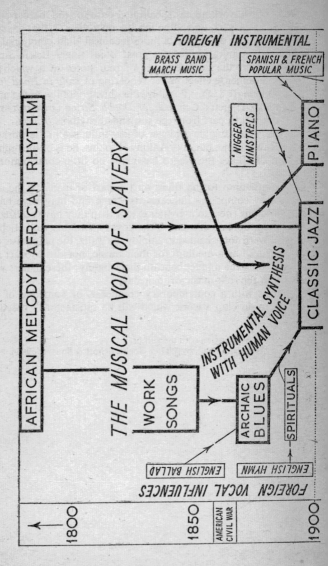

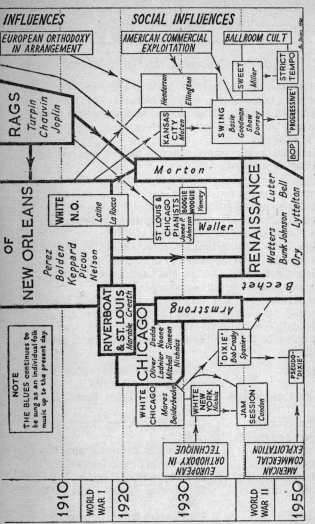

Chart illustrating origins and development of Jazz

Note on Records Cited in the Text

IT is fortunate that the invention and rapid success of the gramophone was a contemporary with the blossoming of jazz – indeed, it might well be that without this means of preserving the music of the early days, the historical development of jazz would have been lost for ever.

It is for that reason that records play such an important part in the course of the book.

Emphasis, however, must be laid on the fact that the many records cited in the text are only *representative*, and have been selected to serve as a guide for the reader. In some cases they are not necessarily the best, but have been mentioned because of their availability in this country at the time of writing.

Those issued by the E.M.I. Group, i.e. HMV, Parlophone, Columbia and MGM, and those by the Decca-Brunswick Group, i.e. Decca, Brunswick, London, and Capitol, are obtainable from most record dealers or can be ordered by them.

The smaller recording companies, whose labels have been mentioned, have dealers in different parts of the country, but if any difficulty is experienced in obtaining their records, an address list is appended which will facilitate matters for those anxious to hear them.

ESQUIRE	76 Bedford Court Mansions, Bedford Avenue, London, WC1.
JAZZ COLLECTOR	100 Charing Cross Road, London, WC2.
JAZZ PARADE KING JAZZ	100 Charing Cross Road, London, WC2.
JAZZ MAN	28a Finchley Road, London, NW8.
LONDON JAZZ	84 Newman Street, London, W1.
MELODISC	48 Woburn Place, London, WC1.
SUPRAPHON	52 Charing Cross Road, London, WC2.
TEMPO	28a Finchley Road, London, NW8.
VOGUE	100 Charing Cross Road, London, WC2.

For those readers who would like to have a condensed recorded history of jazz in their collection, The Tempo Record Society issued five double-sided ten inch records in the autumn of 1951, in which the author narrates the story of jazz music and illustrates his points by musical excerpts from recorded performances and by the use of Mick Mulligan's Band with George Melly.

These are issued on TEMPO S.1–S.5 (or automatic couplings A.S.1–A.S.5) and consist of:

S.1 Introduction: Origins
     Early Social Influences
S.2 Spirituals: Work Songs: Blues
     Ragtime: Spasm Bands
S.3 Brass Bands: Analysis of Jazz Band
     The Nature of Jazz
S.4 Exodus From New Orleans:
     Advent of Swing
S.5 Digression
     Jazz – A Folk Music

Bibliography

BOOKS

W. E. Allen: *Slave Songs of the United States*. 1867

Louis Armstrong: *Swing That Music*. Longmans, Green. 1936

Rudi Blesh: *This is Jazz*. Jazz Music Books. 1943; *Shining Trumpets*. Cassell. 1949

Ernest Borneman: *A Critic Looks at Jazz*. Jazz Music Books. 1946

Arna Boutemps and Jack Conroy: *They Seek a City*

Donald Brook: *Composers' Gallery*. Rockliff. 1946

Condon and Sugrue: *We Called it Music*. Peter Davies. 1948

Aaron Copland: *Our New Music*. New York. 1941

Nancy Cunard: *Negro. An Encyclopaedia*

John R. T. Davies: *The Music of Thomas 'Fats' Waller*. J.J. Publications. 1950

Charles Delaunay: *New Hot Discography*. Criterion. 1948

Robert Goffin: *Jazz from Congo to Metropolitan*. Doubleday Doran. 1944; *Aux Frontières du Jazz*. Sagittaire. 1932

Rev. William Goodell: *The American Slave Code*. 1853

A. L. Bacharach (ed.): *British Music of Our Time*. Pelican A156, Penguin Books. 1946

Wilder Hobson: *American Jazz Music*. J. M. Dent. 1941

Langston Hughes: *Florida Road Workers*
C. L. R. James: *The Black Jacobins*. London. 1938
James Weldon Johnson: *God's Trombones*. Viking Press, N.Y. 1927;
  Along This Way. Penguin Books. 1941
Max Jones: *Folk*. Jazz Music Books. 1945
Ernst Křenek: *Music Here and Now*. 1939
Constant Lambert: *Music Ho!* Pelican A195, Penguin Books. 1948
Iain Lang: *Jazz in Perspective*. Hutchinson. 1947
Alan Lomax: *Mr Jelly Roll*. Duell, Sloane & Pearce. 1950
Albert McCarthy: *The PL Yearbook of Jazz*. Nicholson & Watson.
  1946
R. W. S. Mendl: *The Appeal of Jazz*. Philip Allan. 1927
Mezzrow and Wolfe: *Really The Blues*. Musicians Press. 1946
Paul Edward Miller and Ralph Venables: *Esquire's Jazz Book*. Peter
  Davies. 1947.
Hugues Panassié: *Hot Jazz*. Cassell. 1936
Frederick Ramsay, Jr, and C. E. Smith: *Jazzmen*. Harcourt Brace. 1939
Percy A. Scholes: *The Oxford Companion to Music*. O.U.P. 1941
Igor Stravinsky: *An Autobiography*. Simon & Schuster. 1936
Clement Wood: *Anthology of Negro Songs*. Haldeman-Julius. 1924

PERIODICALS

*Downbeat, Jazz Appreciation Society, Jazz Atlantic, Jazz Music, Jazz
Journal, Jazz Notes, Jazz Photo Album, Jazz Record, Melody Maker
Modern Music Quarterly, Playback, Record Changer, Revue Romande,
Sound, William Morris Soc. Bulletin.*